THE BIGGEST PARTY ON THE PLANET

Other Works by the Author

M.C. Baldwin and the Mar Vista Petrified Orchestra (CDBaby.com)

Diamonds in the Rough: a Screenplay (Kindle)

THE BIGGEST PARTY ON THE PLANET

An American at the World Cup

by

Mark C. Baldwin

Edited by Leslie Goodman-Malamuth

To Hannia, Natalia, Jack, Loretta,

and the biggest soccer fan of them all,

Keiko.

Contents

INTRODUCTION

An American at the World Cup is a little like a Mormon visiting the wineries of Bordeaux. No matter how knowledgeable he is, no matter how much he enjoys himself, no matter how acutely he appreciates the finest the world has to offer, he will still seem suspect to the connoisseur, and be reviled and regarded as an infidel by his brethren at home.

And there it is. As I made arrangements to visit the most competitive sporting event in the world, I knew that I'd be watched with condescending amusement by the soccer spectators of the world. I'd be called a kook and worse by the mainstream sports fans of Yankee-ville, though I'd be hoisting our national colors and chanting "U...S...A..." at the top of my lungs in a fiercely hostile environment.

I couldn't defend my journey to the Cup by citing expertise on the subject (though I've studied the game), or the supremacy of my country's team (though I think we're pretty good). I would not, like many insecure Americans, pick some perennial favorite like Brazil or the UK[1] to support and prattle on about them to show that I knew something of *the beautiful game*. All that validated my intended sojourn in Korea was a profound love of soccer, and a deep appreciation of those who practice it well--- especially those from my native shores. Also, I have always nurtured healthy passions for travel and excessive drink. Soccer provides endless opportunities to indulge in both.

But enough of my own reasons and petty self-justifications for inflicting my overbearing presence on the poor unsuspecting citizens of Korea. Why compound the offense by inflicting my overbearing presence on poor, unsuspecting readers? Why should anyone care to read about my trip to the World Cup? Very simple. A six-foot four-inch, 220 lb. red-haired, red-bearded Gringo soccer fan in South Korea can't help but be

---

[1] These are the guys who go out of their way to refer to Soccer as "Football," cleats as "boots" fields as "pitches." If they hae lived in England, they have an excuse.

entertaining. Even the non-soccer fan will grasp that fact immediately. Try though I might to slide nonchalantly through the crowds and appreciate the spectacle in demure and unobtrusive contemplation, I was bound to fail. And fail in spades. It's like a train wreck --- you can't look away.

I am a walking billboard for the USA, like it or not. I am a peanut-butter-eating, Nike-wearing, right-hand-side-of-the-road-driving American, and there's no hiding it. I knew I was destined to be confronted by Anti-Americans of all nationalities, to be talked down to by soccer cognoscenti like a 4-year old, and mostly, I could rest assured that I'd be regarded by the native populace as a freak of nature, which, of course, I am.

Additionally, if the U.S. team were to flame out like it did in '98, you'd get to hear me kvetch and moan and whine and make excuses. That's always more fun than positive stuff.

Oh, I almost forgot, my plan in 2002 was to stay with Korean families who didn't speak a whole lot of English. That alone should be entertainment enough.

THE BIGGEST PARTY ON THE PLANET

An American at the World Cup

2002 - PREPARATIONS

Preparing for the 2002 World Cup was simple. First, learn Korean. I had a few days off before I left. It was a cinch. I bought the obligatory phrasebook and CDs. "Where is the Embassy?" *Tesaguani odiyeyo.* "Give me coffee, please." *Kopi chuseyo.* "I've got a live lobster in my shorts." *Seng padatkkajae issayo een sogot.* I was quickly mastering all the basic words and phrases I needed to get along. I've always maintained that it's much better to be able make a fool of yourself in the native language of the country you're visiting, and I was well on my way.

The truth is, I took some Korean classes at the Los Angeles Korean Cultural Center. The classes, taught by a Hungarian woman (don't ask), were a weekly affair. They were filled with second- and third-generation Koreans bent on getting in touch with their roots, though I suspected some were there just to get goulash recipes. There were a few Anglos (I guess I'm an Anglo/Celto, if you look at people this way), who were just interested in learning a new language, or who were married to someone of Korean heritage and wanted to communicate with their in-laws. Communicating with in-laws is a dangerous pursuit in my book, but I knew better than to set them straight. The class also included an older American couple going to the World Cup: Art Kempf, a big, grey-bearded bear of an actor, who coincidentally had appeared in a student film a friend of mine made at UCLA some ten years earlier. I had bumped into him, and his significant other, Joy, at Galaxy games and international soccer matches at the L.A. Coliseum. I re-introduced myself, and we fell into conversations about the Gold Cup (the Continental Championship was then under way), and the relative merits of DaMarcus Beasely vs. Eddie Lewis on the left wing.

After a few weeks of study, I learned that Korean was a "highly-declined" language. At first I thought this meant it was only spoken in a fully extended Barcalounger. I then realized it meant that there are a bunch of little endings on words that change depending on whether the word is a subject, predicate, direct object, and so forth. I'd never studied any Latin, except for a brief obsession with Christina Aguilera, but had heard from one of my paid informants that Latin is also highly-declined, so it's not enough just to memorize a word. You also have to know half a gazillion different forms of it in order to recognize it in a crowd. Or a sentence. Great.

Also, there was a whole new alphabet to learn. If you take a drive down Western Avenue in Los Angeles, you'll get a good dose of Korean signs, known to non-Koreans as "chicken scratches" or "gobbledegook." Paramedics have complained that if they don't get some friggin' English signs in this neighborhood, the next time someone calls 911, they may end up at a karaoke bar instead of the hospital.

But I say, let them use a bunch of funny little lines and circles on their signs. It was a great chance for me to practice, and I've always enjoyed confusing paramedics.

Luckily, Korean is phonetic, unlike Chinese, so there aren't a million pictographs to learn. There is a finite set of vowels and consonants. Korean uses a very clever and practical writing system, called *Hangul*.

At the point where working for a living forced me to cease attending classes,[2] I was able to read and "sound out" Korean. I was extremely proud to be able to pronounce virtually all Korean words I came across. Now if I only understood what they meant. I guess they planned to cover that in the classes I missed.

Next, I had to find accommodations on the Korean peninsula. Not content to stay in a conventional tourist hotel, I sought out something more culturally stimulating, more grassroots, more at one with the essence of Korea. In a word, I sought accommodations that were cheap.

I found, thanks to a snappy brochure provided by FIFA,[3] that Korea has had a "homestay" system since the 1988 Seoul Olympics. For a

---

[2] In fact, I was sent on assignment to Prague, where I had to learn a smattering of another "highly declined" language, Czech. Could life conspire to confuse me any more? Na schledanou.

[3] FIFA is an acronym for *Fédération Internationale de Football Association*, the governing body of international soccer, based in Zürich, Switzerland.

nominal fee, a foreigner could stay with a Korean family. The objective, of course was to promote cultural exchange, and to provide low-cost accommodations for skinflints like me. I went to the "Komestay" (read: Korean Homestay) website, registered, and came up with a family in Suwon, a suburb of Seoul. Suwon was the venue of the first U.S. game vs. Portugal and also Costa Rica vs. Brazil, another first-round match I wanted to see. It was close enough to Seoul (about 60 kilometers) that I would be able to visit the big city via subway, and it was also close enough to Incheon to allow easy airport access and subway access to the Costa Rica vs. Turkey game on June 9. The train station in Suwon turned out to be a major transportation hub as well, so making the city my base of operations made perfect sense. I could arrive, go to U.S. game 1, spend a couple of days de-jet-lagging, visit Seoul, go to CR vs. Turkey, then zip off via train for Daegu for U.S. vs. Korea. The homestay thing was a form of Russian (or Korean) roulette. You might get some wonderful mensch family who instantly loves you, or...

Gyosu Kum was to be my host in Suwon. We e-mailed back and forth several times, and learned a little about each other. He was an engineer for electronics giant Samsung. Gyosu had a fair amount of English at his disposal, though I could tell by his e-mails that the language thing was a work in progress. There were a few parts of speech missing, but I could definitely get the sense of what he was saying. His English was miles ahead of my Korean, however, so I'll keep the snide remarks to a minimum--just the absolutely necessary snide remarks will be retained.

Gyosu e-mailed me a few photos of his family, which included his wife, Mija, his son Un Ho, age eleven, and his daughter, Jiwon, age nine. They are the very picture of a "duty-now-plan-for-the-future," 1950s-style family that we Americans stereotypically associate with Asian culture. I was scheduled to stay with them for the bulk of my two and a half weeks in Korea, and I could only hope that they wouldn't get thoroughly sick of my presence too quickly.

The second family was in Daegu, where I'd only be for two days. Soohee Chung emailed me back in impeccable English. She and her husband had both lived in the States while attending graduate school, so I was relatively certain that at the very least I'd be able to make myself understood. They emailed me a picture of their beautiful one-year-old daughter, Minji.

It looked like I had lucked out with both families.

Another part of preparation concerned my wife, Hannia. We'd been married for more than twenty years, and had traveled quite a bit together: through every nook and cranny of California, Oregon, and Arizona, as well as parts of Mexico, Japan, Hong Kong, Canada, Italy, and Germany. Hannia hails from Costa Rica, a true soccer culture. She grew up yelling at her brothers and father to change the damn channel and watch something other than *fútbol*, and then she had the remarkably bad luck to hook up with one of the few gringos who would insist on watching as much soccer as humanly possible. Or more. While the rest of her family members are *Liga Deportiva Alajuelense* supporters, Hannia's naturally contentious character led her to support the opposition, *Saprissa*. This gave her years of pleasure taunting her father and brothers when *la Liga* lost to the *morados*. Though she wouldn't readily admit it, Hannia actually enjoys soccer, though I'm sure my level of obsession grates at times. We have been L.A. Galaxy season ticket holders since 1997, and have also attended games in Canada, Italy, and, of course, Costa Rica.

Hannia jokingly complained about me dragging her along to Korea. She was on the phone with her brother Luís, when I overheard the following conversation:

"*¿Que me queda, tengo que ir. Con este esposo atarantado que tengo.*" ("What can I do, I'll have to go, with this lunatic of a husband.")

Hannia had to pull her ear away from the receiver a bit so the reply didn't rupture her eardrum:

"*Estás loca? ¿Te va a llevar al mundial, y te estás quejando?* ("Are you nuts? He's going to take you to the World Cup, and you're complaining?")

She was teasing him, of course, but had to backpedal a little so as not to appear too ungrateful, "*Diay, voy a cualquier parte con tal de viajar.*" ("Heck, I'll go anywhere as long as I get to travel.")

Her brothers were the most envious guys in the world at that moment. She was getting the chance to go to the equivalent of a month of Super Bowls and World Series games, with the Indy 500 and Kentucky Derby thrown in for good measure. Much to Hannia's credit, she spent the entire trip collecting memorabilia for her family, and calling at strategic moments to keep her brothers and father up to date.

Hannia was a little wary of going and staying in strangers' homes, but she was game. And, for me, and hopefully the reader, there were many advantages to taking my spouse to the Biggest Party on the Planet. Hannia is always entertaining to watch in new situations; she speaks her mind. She'll ask the pointed question that repressed Anglos will tap dance around for hours. Also, she's a trooper, although a trooper who will complain heartily. She'll go the extra mile and make everything work, but she'll let you know about the rough spots in the road, sometimes ad nauseam.

Hannia's got substantial linguistic credentials. She was the phonetics professor at *Instituto de Lengua Española* in Costa Rica, where I studied Spanish (yes, I married my teacher). She then learned English rather well in a couple of years here in California, and she's now studying Italian. Delving into the intricacies of *Hangul*, however, didn't interest her in the least. She told me she was afraid it would distract her from Italian. It was an okay excuse, but I could tell she thought I was complete insane every time I whipped out my chart of *Hangul* characters and started to recite my syllables. I can sympathize with her reluctance, but it left me as the sole Seoul partner.

MAY 31 - AN UPSETTING PRELUDE

Our plan was to arrive in Korea on June 4, in time for the first U.S. game. The World Cup, however, started on May 31, while we were still stateside.

The inaugural game was expected to be a laugher. World Champion France, whom many people were handicapping to repeat, was set to play against a first-time participant, Senegal. I had a couple of French friends on my Culver City adult league team, who, with characteristic European arrogance, sniffed at the match-up. They were more than certain that France would kill their former colonial subjects. (Somehow, Europeans always like to refer to themselves as "former colonial masters.") Phillipe, for instance, was incredulous that I hadn't planned to go to a France game. "When will you ever get the chance to see Zidane in the World Cup? Trezeguet? Henry? Petit?" I would have loved to see France play, but I'd made my decision based on limited resources and ingrained nationalism. It was to be the US of A, win, lose, or draw, along with my semi-adoptive second country, Costa Rica. Phillipe, though also a Galaxy season-ticket holder, and generally a supporter of U.S. soccer, gave me a condescending look. "Oh, Mark, you must see France play." I knew he was thinking that I'd end up horribly disappointed by my national team, and I should get some soccer thrills from a more promising squad. I explained that the U.S. would play Portugal (ranked fifth in the world), Poland (usually a solid team), and Korea, and that I'd see Costa Rica play Brazil (always a thrill), and Turkey (who've done very well at both the club and national team level in European competitions). That would be more than enough for anyone. If the U.S. happened to get into the second round, which I thought they would, I had contingency tickets for that.

Some friends and I got up at 4:30 a.m. Los Angeles-time to watch the opening ceremonies and the first game. Zidane was out with an injury, but the feeling was that they didn't need him. This would be a turkey shoot. Senegal had other ideas. Even before kickoff, I could sense that the Senegalese were phenomenal athletes. As they warmed up, they were strikingly big, fast, lanky, and very, very skilled. They had a certain look about them, too. It's more than confidence, less than swagger. Perhaps it's best described as hungry power. They had the look of a squad out to prove themselves, and they had the focus and fire of champions. They immediately gave France fits, playing more aggressively, coming up with most of the 50/50 balls, outrunning their opponents, and generating dangerous goal-scoring opportunities. The commentators were audibly shocked. They shifted from unqualified praise and awe of France to a sudden realization that most of the Senegalese played in the French League, that the French squad was aging and had become complacent. Senegal won. This ranked as one of the biggest upsets in history. It established the tone for the tournament.

This was to be a very interesting World Cup.

THE TRIP

No matter how much you love to travel, the reality of a twelve-hour flight from LAX to Incheon, South Korea is less than enchanting. Now, if you're a coal miner or a lumberjack, or if you wrestle alligators for a living, you've got to chuckle at my whining. Sitting in a padded chair, while flight attendants periodically bring you trays of food and drinks, is a vacation by comparison. Twelve hours of it, though, gets a little old, and we were PAYING for the privilege.

We flew Singapore Air. This was strictly a price consideration, since their excursion fare was lower than any other. Everyone I spoke to said enviously, "Ahhh, Singapore, they're the best." As we got on the plane, I began to think they were right. First, the flight attendants were the cutest I'd ever seen, slender young women in tight-fitting, though tasteful sarong-like uniforms. And they were *very* attentive. It took great concentration after years of training as a husband to not gawk any more than absolutely necessary.

Luckily, we'd garnered bulkhead seats. There's no luggage compartment overhead, and a bit more legroom, so being six-foot-four is less of a liability. I could actually stand up in the middle of the flight if I was so inclined, and stretch out my frame. We slid in next to a big cowboy of a guy in his late fifties or early sixties, accompanied by a Korean woman who appeared maybe ten or fifteen years younger. I pegged him immediately for retired military. When we reached cruising altitude, I whipped out the video monitor, to see what the in-flight entertainment might be. The screen was attached to a long, jointed metal arm that swung out from under the seat, and it took a little dexterity and know-how to deploy. I noticed that the Cowboy's wife was watching me fiddle with the apparatus. She looked down at her own screen and started to tug at it, but to no avail. She tried and tried, but couldn't figure it out. I offered some help and broke the ice. They were both happy to become video-enabled.

"It's as tight in here as a C130," the Cowboy offered.

"Tighter," I confirmed, as if I knew what a C130, that famously huge military transport plane, actually looks like on the inside.

"We're headed to visit her mother," the Cowboy explained. "Only been back once in the last fifteen years, and she's getting up there."

"Maybe this last time I see her. She sick," his wife chimed in.

He was retired Army, currently living in Colorado Springs. And formerly stationed in Korea. I'd guessed correctly.

"I'm going for the World Cup," I happily proclaimed. He stared at me blankly.

I sensed the need for more detail, and continued, "The soccer World Cup."

"Oh, yeah, jeez, World Cup, World Cup. They holding that in Korea?" He appeared genuinely surprised. I wondered that he could have missed the news. Sure, the soccer coverage in the U.S. is abysmal, and Colorado Springs ranks as one of the less soccer-friendly venues in America, but they'd been reporting bits and pieces about the World Cup for months in the mainstream media. You'd have thought that the Cowboy's ears might have pricked up at the mention of the world's largest sporting event setting up its pup tents and porta-potties in his former backyard. But you'd have been wrong.

He waxed eloquent about his years south of the DMZ. "Used to be a hell of a place, but they wrecked it. They always wreck 'em."

My impression was that Korea was in rotten shape following Japanese occupation, World War II, and war with the Commies, and only within the last twenty years or so has it experienced a degree of prosperity, but, hey, I'll bite. "How do you think they've wrecked it?" I ventured.

"Used to be cheap. 'Specially the coastal towns. You could get a fish dinner, damn good fish dinner, for twenty-five cents. I used to get fly fishing equipment for a song. 'Course, you know the right places, you can get flies and reels and stuff pretty cheap still, I'm gonna load up while I'm here. But when I lived here… hey, I got tailored suits, hand-made shoes, damn fine suits and shoes, I'm telling you, tailor-fitted shirts, the works, for nothin'. Then the word got out. They wrecked it."

So we've all got our realities. I was going to a different place than he was. I was going to a place of huge trading companies and electronics firms, and a sense of climbing on the world stage to host a bazillion international visitors at the biggest party on the planet. He was going back to a place where he spent his twenties in hog heaven, where his military paycheck went farther than it had any right to, where he could order up a snappy new outfit, a sumptuous fish dinner, and chug down Hite beer until he lost focus and passed out. The Cowboy was returning to the place where he fell in love with a Korean girl and flung himself headlong into the matrimonial snare. He seemed happy and healthy, a big, handsome, swaggering, John Wayne-style retiree, fly fishing in Colorado with his Korean-bought equipment. And me? Happy to march after my own red, white, and blue contingent on the Korean peninsula, to cheer on my own American boys as they engaged the troops of foreign nations.

ARRIVAL

Incheon International Airport was brand, spanking new. It was probably the nicest airport we'd ever seen, in an upscale shopping-mall sort of way. It was all marble floors and high ceilings and Kentucky Fried Chicken and Burger King, interlaced with every convenience known to the modern traveler.

We stopped, rented ourselves a cell phone--at a very reasonable price, I might add--and proceeded to the express bus curb. We were looking for the Suwon bus, headed to the Castle Hotel, where Gyosu was to pick us up. Piece of cake, we thought. The bus was of Korean manufacture, big, comfortable, air-conditioned, much better than a Greyhound or Continental Trailways, and it only had a couple of other people on board. The other guys also turned out to be U.S. soccer fans, there for the World Cup. We compared notes on accommodations, and the homestay option intrigued them. They'd done okay for themselves, too. They were in nice mid-range hotels, paying $70 to $100 a night, but of course, we were spending a fraction of that. One guy was from the San Francisco Bay Area, and the other was from New Jersey. I asked if he was a Metrostars fan. "Oh, I have trouble getting into MLS [the U.S. soccer league]. I watch English Premiere League and Italian Serie A."

I launched into my usual spiel, "Well, I figure you've got to support what you've got if it's going to get any better. I'm sure that when the Italian League started there were lots of people who refused to support it because they felt it was inferior to British soccer. If everyone had done that, the Italians wouldn't have one of the best leagues in the world like they do now." The guy kind of nodded his head. I'd probably struck a chord, though I doubted he'd change his tune overnight. But I'd done my job as a one-man promotional squad for U.S. soccer. I could relax for awhile.

The passage through Seoul was a bit anticlimactic. It is a huge, modern metropolis of some ten million souls. If you were blindfolded, and flown surreptitiously to the Korean capital, you might think you were in the middle of Chicago or Toronto, except that there are a hell of a lot more Koreans. Also much of Seoul is new and very modern in look and feel. Largely destroyed during the Korean War, few stately old buildings remain in the city. The freeway we took through town was a huge, multilane affair. Luckily, there was a bus lane, so we zipped past the frustrated motorists all but parked in mid-pavement. It was a ninety-minute drive and cost about ten dollars. The cowboy on the plane was wrong: "They" haven't wrecked Korea just yet.

At long last, we could see the Castle Hotel looming in the distance on a busy Suwon thoroughfare.

We hopped out on the curb. It was hot and muggy and we had to schlep our bags across a big intersection, dodging Hyundais, Daewoos, and Kias to get to the hotel, where we found no one waiting for us. It crossed my ever-paranoid mind that if no one showed up, we'd be in an interesting fix. The Castle charged upward of $180 a night, which would swiftly gobble up our homestay savings. Then I couldn't get the cell phone to work properly. I kept getting a recorded message--part in English--barking out in a harsh male voice that the number "does not exist."

Hannia was anxiously asking me what the next move was. I looked into her big, brown, jet-lagged eyes and saw impending fear that could lead to nowhere but hysteria.

I went to the hotel's main desk to get some help. The clerk, a prim young woman in a blindingly white uniform, tried Gyosu's home number. "It does not exist," she informed us.

She stared at me imploringly as if to say, "Please do not blame me that I have not adequately assisted you and fulfilled my civic duty to its fullest."

Hannia was tugging at my sleeve, "Could we stay here if we can't get hold of them?"

I was wearily computing nightly prices and currency exchange rates in my head when I remembered that I had Gyosu's cell phone number in my bag. I fumbled through the zippered compartments in my luggage until I came across my itinerary, where I'd jotted down the number. I whipped it out and handed it to the hotel clerk.

She bowed, and poked the cell number into her telephone keypad. There was a long pause as she listened into the receiver, face furrowed with all the anxiety inherent in the selfless act of customer service. Her head twitched to one side as she heard something. Her face relaxed, and she happily started blathering away in Korean. Bingo! "You go lobby. Pick you up ten minutes."

"*Ship bun?*" I replied. The look on her face was priceless, well worth the time and effort spent on Korean classes. "*Ship bun,*" she responded, "Ten minutes." This was the first of many instances in which my feeble attempts at speaking a few Korean phrases paid dividends. She dropped her formality briefly, and smiled. I sensed a bit of shock, amusement, and bonding. I was a goodwill ambassador for the most tongue-tied nation on earth, and I relished the role.

We sat in the lobby and waited. In an adjacent salon, a couple of American, or perhaps Canadian, musicians were grinding out tunes by The Carpenters on a small bandstand. Hannia and I were smirking and winking at each other about this sequined lounge-lizard couple, as they sang, "On the day that you were born the angels got together and decided to create a dream come true..." We both wondered aloud how on earth they got to Suwon, South Korea.

Before I got up the initiative to ask them, Gyosu showed up, all smiles and helpfulness.

"So they sprinkled moon dust in your hair of gold, and starlight in your eyes of blue..."

"Hello, Mark, I'm Gyosu," he led off.

"*Annyong haseyo, chong mal pan gawoyo,*" I responded. ("Hello, nice to meet you.") Gyosu chuckled. He was a cherubic guy in his late thirties, with a permanent, quite sincere smile on his face. I introduced him to Hannia, and he bowed deferentially. He tried to grab our bags and there was a brief contest to see who would be the beast of burden. I outweighed him by about a hundred pounds, so I felt it was a bit less of an ordeal for me, but he managed to latch onto Hannia's bag. Gyosu showed us out the lobby door. We made our way to a taxi, tossed our bags in the trunk, and were off.

"Are you tired?" he asked. We were, but were still running on travel adrenaline. It was about eight in the evening, local time, which meant that back home, it was around four in the morning. I was glad I wasn't driving.

The cab sliced through thick traffic, past the Suwon World Cup stadium, all lit up and festooned with the flags of the nations set to play there. Hannia perked up when she saw the Costa Rican flag flying proudly, but then growled a little when confronted with the banner of their opponent, Brazil. Finally, our taxi came to an outcropping of tall apartment buildings and we found building number 225. There are apparently no street addresses in Korea. People find their way by "*dong*" which is roughly a sector, "*gu*" or district, and neighborhood, or "*do*." There's usually a landmark involved to orient you, such as "between the Westin Chosun Hotel and the Oriental Chemical building." Building numbers are painted on the apartments in huge block numbers, visible for a mile or more.

Gyosu's building looked like most others from the outside. It was eighteen stories high, with two large apartments per floor. The buildings were spaced out nicely, with parking, greenbelts, schools, and shops in between the huge dwellings. Suwon is an upscale suburb, but I believe this pattern is pretty universal throughout Seoul and its environs.

We schlepped the bags up to the second floor, and into Gyosu's apartment, where we were immediately met by his wife, Mija, son Un Ho, and daughter Jiwon. They were thrilled to meet us. I guess they just don't know us well enough.

The first cultural adjustment was related to shoes. The Koreans don't wear them indoors. They remove their shoes at the door, and wear either house slippers or socks. I'd been prepped for this in Korean class, and from the travel guides I'd read. We visited Japan once before, where the protocol is similar, and we easily figured out the drill. Hannia has always loved this custom. At home, in part because of her beloved tile floors, she always encourages me to remove my shoes when I come home. I must admit I like the custom as well. I'm never quite as comfortable with shoes on. This custom does, unfortunately, bring to an American mind of my generation the title sequence from "The Beverly Hillbillies" ("Take your shoes off, stay a while…"), but I'll insist on chalking it up to my Oriental adventures, rather than to any possible affinity for Ozark culture.

Once they have you inside and shoeless, the immediate question most Koreans will put to you after a greeting or two is, "Have you eaten yet?" They say it harkens back to an era in the not-too-distant past when food wasn't as easy to come by, when the invading Japanese or Chinese had taken it all, or the Northern Communists had blown to smithereens the fields that produced it all. Be careful how you answer the question. We found ourselves at a table with at least ten dishes in front of us, and our culinary adventure was under way. The ubiquitous *kimchi* (fermented cabbage with chili) radiated its pungent tastiness from a bowl in front of us, as it would three times a day during our stay. Rice was served at every meal, as was shredded dried squid. I liked it, though it was a bit of an adjustment for breakfast. Hannia wouldn't touch it. There was a bowl of fish soup, and usually some kind of meat--beef, pork, or chicken--to be rolled into lettuce leaves and eaten, almost as Mexicans use tortillas.

Mija, an energetic, slender woman in her early thirties, immediately assumed the role of supermom, shoving food at us as quickly as we could put it away. I can put it away pretty fast, but she was more than up to the task.

Hannia, though fairly omnivorous, immediately balked at Korean food. She's not fond of overly spicy fare, and she wrinkled her nose at the dried squid. Rice is a staple in Costa Rica, so she was comfortable with that, but *kimchi* was beyond her spectrum of tolerance. Mija, in her role as hostess, noticed Hannia's discomfiture immediately, and proceeded to force more food on her, in case it was a matter of shyness. Hannia smiled and ate what she could, but I could tell already that the food would be a point of contention.

It became apparent immediately that Gyosu's and Mija's English was less than fluent. They had obviously studied the language, but lacked the sort of practice you get from being in an English-speaking environment. I'm sure that if either of them lived in the States for a while, they'd become proficient, but at the moment, there were enough missing particles and nouns to fill a bushel basket. And having studied a little Korean, I was impressed that anyone could bridge the gap between these two hugely different languages. Hannia and I speak Spanish, and we realize that English and Spanish have enough common ground to build the Taj Mahal, with room left over for a bowling alley. Not so English and Korean. The language barrier was greatly reduced by Un Ho, however, whose English was pretty darned good. His parents would chatter away to him in Korean. He'd sit and think a few moments, furrow his brow, adjust his glasses, then formulate a very good English sentence, and pronounce it with admirable and deliberate clarity. He was always able to get his point across, and he didn't panic when he didn't understand, or couldn't think of exactly how to phrase something. This is the mark of a good linguist.

We had brought some presents with us, which we handed out. A bottle of my favorite Chardonnay from Napa Valley, a coffee-table book of California photographs, and a couple of T-shirts for the kids, emblazoned with silkscreened "LA" logos, and accessorized with little Hollywood pins. They were a big hit.

Un Ho inquired, at his parents' behest, whether we were tired after our trip. I didn't hesitate to say that I was dead on my feet, though fearing a bizarre literal translation of this idiomatic expression, I just said that yes, I was. They showed us to a bedroom, which would be ours while in Suwon. We hit the sack and blinked out like California's power grid.

Jet lag is an odd thing. Sometimes you feel like it doesn't affect you at all, then a half hour later, you feel like your system has been pumped full of heavy narcotic syrup that hardens into chalk when it hits your brain. The flip side is that you can feel excessively tired at bedtime, but then a half-hour later, you're wide awake, laying there staring at the ceiling, wondering what those acoustic tiles are really made of.

I lay there reflecting on the room. It was obviously Un Ho's, perhaps fifteen by twenty feet, and boasting a piano and a computer. A Samsung computer, of course. This kid's pretty well off. But he was also making the most of it. He was taking piano lessons, *Tae Kwon Do* lessons, he was going to start soccer classes, and was apparently studying at a very advanced level of math. He stayed after in school for math and science tutoring, was teaching himself English, and his parents had garnered an actual, unretouched pair of foreigners for him to practice his language skills on. The kid was going places.

Taking the entire apartment into account, the family was in pretty good shape, too. There was another, virtually identical room for Jiwon, and a master bedroom for the folks, which was larger. The place had an ample living room, attached to the kitchen, then a corridor on each side, one of which served as a laundry room, and the other as a patio and clothes-drying area. These guys were very much the sort of modern urban dwellers you'd find in any major metropolis in the world. I had many Americans--and some Japanese--tell me Korea was a third-world country as I was planning my trip. I had news for them.

There was a hint of 'Fifties America in Korea. People like my parents, raised in during the Depression and World War II, embraced middle-class, hard-working conformity with a vengeance during that decade. The Koreans went through much, much more than we did, and they can't seem to relax, either. Gyosu left the condo at six a.m., took the company bus into Seoul and didn't come back until seven or eight at night. He hung out with his family until bedtime at midnight or so. Mija was a stay-at-home mom, but she was riding herd on the kids every minute to make sure they didn't shirk their responsibilities. She also taught English classes to neighbors in the afternoon. I could identify the strains of my own background here, and I admire them. But at that moment, I just wanted to sleep. So I did, though I'm certain my habitual and thunderous snoring kept Hannia from following suit.

JUNE 5 – GAME DAY #1

I wasn't sure how long we'd slept, and the sun seemed to be up at five a.m., but I got up anyway to figure out the bathing situation. I ducked out my door, padded past the kitchen and dining room, and turned left into the bathroom. I immediately noticed a couple of novelties. First, there was a step down into the bathroom. The floor was entirely tiled, and there was a drain in the middle of it. The bathtub, at the far end, had no curtain or enclosure. The shower head—the hand-held kind--was attached to the end of a flex hose. There were water droplets everywhere, a bunch of rubber thongs in a row by the door, and no electrical plugs or switches inside the bathroom. Obviously, showering in Korea was a bit different than we were used to. Water goes everywhere. We'd showered in Italian *pensiones* where there was a shower curtain and no tub, but this was our first experience with the opposite.

Next, I looked around for bath towels, but all I saw were hand towels on a small rack. I went back to our room and conferred with Hannia, in case she'd spotted some towels somewhere, or maybe had had the conversation with our hosts. Hannia, who is always acutely aware of towel etiquette (heaven forbid someone else use her towel at home!), was equally perplexed.

When I asked Mija about towels, she said, "Oh, in cabinet." I figured I'd missed something, and, in fact, I had. I returned to the bathroom and found the mirrored cabinet, which I was pretty sure I'd opened before in my search for absorbency. When I looked inside, there were more towels, all right. At least ten hand towels. I looked around a little more, but then came to the inevitable conclusion that these were the towels she intended us to use.

I climbed into the tub, squatted down, and showered myself, taking great care not to spray water all over--remember, no shower curtain. I successfully kept water from spraying all over the floor, and felt like I'd even more successfully dislocated two knee joints and many vertebrae. Once done, I eyed the hand towel I'd removed from the cabinet. Then I looked at my soaking-wet 6' 4" frame in the mirror. "It might take five or six of these to get the job done," I thought, but I'd try it with one, which was an exercise in futility. I ended up using three towels.

I returned to our room, and Hannia asked how it went. I explained the ground rules for the bathroom, and she stared at me without comprehending.

"What do you mean, no shower curtain? There must be a shower curtain. You just missed it. Don't tell me you sprayed water all over their bathroom." I explained that I'd examined the entire room and that, no, there was no shower curtain, and that there was water all over the bathroom before I ever entered, but that I--wonderfully trained husband that I am--in no way had altered the general wetness of the bathroom. She asked if I'd found towels, and I explained. "You dried yourself with a hand towel?" She looked me up and down. She thought I'd either lost it or was putting her on, which, I must admit, would have been fun.

Hannia ventured into the bathroom. When she emerged, her brow was furrowed and she gave me a knowing look. Behind closed doors in the bedroom, we compared notes. She had also done the "squat and spray" routine, and used a couple of hand towels. She had also looked high and low for a socket to plug in her hair dryer. There was none. "If the bathroom is one big tub, don't go connecting any electrical appliances in there. There are no outlets for a reason," I warned her.

Once clean and dry--well, sort of dry--we sat down to a hearty breakfast of *kimchi*, rice, and dried shredded squid. In addition, Mija served a sort of onion omelette, and a few other very spicy vegetables. I enjoyed this stuff, but I was being fed way more than I usually eat. Mija was proffering dish after dish, and was doing her level best to make sure we ate our fill. I hoped the lack of carbohydrates and dairy products would keep the food from finding a way to weigh me down, but I was stuffed. Hannia looked desperate. There was no way she could face fish and fermented cabbage at seven a.m. While she maintained a diplomatic air and thanked her hosts for the food, her very expressive face betrayed her anxiety. She ate a bunch of rice and little else. Mija kicked into overdrive, and with a look of profound concern, pushed more of the bowls toward her. "I don't usually eat a lot at breakfast," was about all Hannia could say. Mija wasn't buying this, but she relented momentarily.

Jet-lagged and droopy-eyed, we scanned the table for a caffeinated beverage. Luckily, Mija plopped two steaming cups of dark brew before us. We guzzled heartily. Unluckily, it turned out to be Sanka. It seems that among other culinary and cultural influences for which South Korea can credit the U.S. military, one of the more prevalent is the abomination known as instant coffee. It seems to have caught on and even displaced tea... an oddity in the Far East.

As I've said before, Hannia is from Costa Rica, generally recognized as one of the finest coffee-producing countries in the world. She has trouble enough with American coffee, which she refers to as "*agua teñida*" ("dyed water"). Instant coffee, which preserves and enhances all the bitterness of coffee, but allows the drinker to enjoy it undistracted by superfluous richness or flavor, is beyond any real Costa Rican's powers of imagination or endurance. As for myself, I've always loved strong, rich coffee. Even before I lived in Costa Rica, well before the dawn of the Starbucks era, my philosophy was that there was no such thing as "too strong" a cup of coffee. The faint of palate can always add hot water or milk or cream, but there's no such convenient fix for weak coffee. After living a while in Costa Rica, I have to be honest: I became a coffee snob. We also are both hopeless caffeine addicts. Battling extreme jet lag, we knew the effects would be multiplied exponentially when compounded by the rigors of caffeine deprivation.

We downed our Sanka dutifully, sharing knowing glances, non-verbally assuring each other that one of our priorities would be to find an honest-to-God cup of coffee in Suwon, come hell or dyed water.

After breakfast, we told our hosts we wanted to go out and have a look at the neighborhood. The U.S. game started at five in the afternoon, so we didn't have time to go on any great excursions. Mija assigned Un Ho as guide. They were letting him stay home from school, but were putting him to work as tour leader and translator.

Un Ho led us around the street at the base of the apartment buildings. We stumbled into something of a street fair in progress. Little tented stands with street vendors had been set up, and many of the housewives, on their way to drop kids off at school, or on their way back, dawdled in front of these little improvised shops, eyeing the household goods, clothing, toys, gewgaws, and food items. I steered Hannia carefully past the stands. Shopping is always a perilous draw for her, and I had visions of being rooted to the same place while the U.S. was kicking off against Portugal some eight hours later.

Un Ho took us past his school, which was about a block away. The school's closeness to home was very convenient, and it looked like all but the very smallest kids made the trek alone on foot. I was impressed by how safe it seemed for kids to be out alone at all hours. We never felt security was an issue, either in the metropolis of Seoul, or in the provincial capitols of Daegu or Jeonju.

The kids started school a little on the late side, by our standards, beginning at eight a.m. and staying until three p.m. Un Ho's sister, a few years younger, got out at 1:30 p.m. Un Ho told us he was looking forward to progressing to middle school. Once there, the fun really begins. They start at a quarter to eight in the morning, and don't get home until somewhere around ten p.m., when they have to contend with homework and whatever Mom and Dad make them do to keep the household running smoothly. Some of this time is spent in after school study groups and private classes and tutoring, but you could see them in their uniforms hopping off the bus and strolling home in groups as late as eleven p.m. From middle school on, most kids only get about five hours of sleep a night. Un Ho was proud of the fact that Koreans study hard. He was obviously up to the task, but I couldn't help but feel he was a little apprehensive about what awaited him.

The school building was a five-story, rectangular affair that lacked the vague look of institutional architecture we're so accustomed to in U.S. school buildings or in the former Eastern Bloc. Out front was a dirt soccer field, ringed by swing sets and monkey bars. The field was filled with kids playing a dusty, but spirited, game of soccer. On the periphery of the field was a wire mesh cage in which were partitioned rabbits, quail, and chickens. It was clearly some kind of animal husbandry project for the students.

On the way back to the apartment, we passed a group of really tiny school kids--probably kindergarteners--being herded onto a bus. At the risk of sounding condescending or patronizing, I'll say that they were the most adorable group of little brats I've ever seen in my life. A few very serious teacher types were all but tossing them into the bus. The tots were decked out in royal-blue, lederhosen-style uniforms with bright-yellow T-shirts. Every kid had an identical bright red-and-yellow backpack, which made them look like a miniaturized paramilitary group, on their way to overthrow a Korean Toys'R'Us, or Baskin-Robbins, or something. With the chaotic earnestness of five-year-olds everywhere, they made you want to go into the sort of cheek-pinching, head-patting, child-hugging frenzy championed by Italian grandmothers. We successfully fought off the impulse and proceeded home.

As we rounded the corner by the apartment building, I spotted a small bakery wedged between shops. I told Un Ho I wanted to go inside for a moment. I entered, and stood behind a patron who was receiving a bag of small cookie-like things. My eyes scanned the room. Pastries and cakes and doughnut-like confections, some of which looked familiar and some of which did not. At last my eyes came to rest on that most gleaming of monuments to Western civilization: the cappuccino machine. I'm sure that a huge smile gripped my bearded face. I gestured to Hannia, who shared the caffeine junkie's strung-out smile. I greeted the shopkeeper in Korean, and asked for some coffee, pointing to the cappuccino machine. The baker, a tall, gangly man with huge spectacles, smiled and asked, in passable English, if we were staying nearby. We informed him that, yes, we were staying in the apartment building across the street and that we'd be in Suwon for most of the World Cup. We'd love a couple of cappuccinos. The smile on his face clouded. "Just a moment." He went behind a counter and opened some cabinets. He rummaged around intently pulling our boxes and dishes and tools of his trade. Un Ho popped his head in impatiently. "My mother will worry we are gone so long." I assured him it would just be a moment, we'd get a cappuccino and head back promptly.

The baker's face finally brightened. He'd located the object of his search, and removed it from the cupboard. Then his expression sank once more. He held up a large glass receptacle with a coffee scoop inside. At the bottom of the jar, three lonely coffee beans rattled around.

"I'm afraid we are out of coffee beans." Hannia and I, our hopes dashed, stared back in disbelief. The baker, sensing our dissatisfaction, pointed at a table to his left.

"We have instant." Our eyes swung to the table, where an open jar of Sanka yawned at us next to an electric hot-water pot.

"No, thank you," was about all I could say.

"When will you have more beans?" Hannia chimed in at last. I was thankful that her synapses were firing well enough to formulate such a constructive question.

"Tomorrow morning," the baker responded, eager to please his new potential customers. We assured him we'd return the following morning. We smiled and thanked him, and wandered off with Un Ho.

Back at the apartment, Mija informed us that she'd escort us to Suwon Stadium via the #2 bus. They had a car, and she would have driven, but the traffic was gonzo-crazy with all the World Cup folks in town, and it would be much simpler to leave the driving to the pros. I had to dissuade her from picking us up after the game. I was pretty sure we could hop back on a #2 bus afterwards, and there was no point making her go search us out in a crowd of thousands. Mija argued at length, but at last we prevailed. We'd been to Hong Kong, Tokyo, Mexico City, Vancouver, Rome, Florence, Frankfurt, and New York, and had managed to creatively lose ourselves with enough verve, panache, and native curiosity to stumble home safe, sound, and thoroughly entertained. Mija looked very worried but politely relented. "You call you if you have problems." "Yes, we'll call." We wrote down more information than the SEC had on Martha Stewart in order to be able to navigate back to the apartment. As a last ditch effort, I knew that any cab driver given the address could return us to the proper "*dong*," "*ku*," and "*do*."

USA vs. Portugal

The U.S. started off with what was seen as our toughest game. Portugal was ranked fifth in the world, and many soccer cognoscenti were touting the Iberians as real contenders to go all the way. They boasted a stellar line-up, including Luís Figo from Real Madrid, voted world footballer of the year in 2001. Other standouts included Rui Costa (whom we'd seen play for Fiorentina in Italy), Nuno Gomez, who had a great run in Euro 2000, Concecaio, Jao Pinto, Pauleta, Beto, and many more. They have been referred to as the "Golden Generation," the best team Portugal has ever fielded. Most played in the big European leagues in Spain, Italy, Germany, and England. This was a damned good squad.

The U.S., on the other hand, was the universal butt of jokes and scorn. We had flamed out ignominiously in France in 1998. It would take us forever to live that down even if we had a history of wonderful soccer. We don't. Most newspapers were handicapping the group like this: Portugal would kill everyone (probably 5-0 vs. the U.S.), Poland would do respectably, Korea would hopefully put on a good show, being the host nation, and the U.S. would again prove it shouldn't be allowed past the bouncer and into the club.

My own take was a little different. I had faith that the U.S. squad was much better than most people thought, but that didn't necessarily mean we couldn't have a disastrous tournament. I figured we might tie Portugal, beat Poland and Korea, and sneak into the second round. We had just beaten Korea in the Gold Cup in Los Angeles, but we had lost to them in a friendly in Korea just prior to that. Despite having a talented squad, the possibility existed that we could be as snakebit as in '98 and get eliminated. I really felt that the '98 squad was also quite talented.

I had steeled myself to the possibility of the worst, but was hoping--deluded dreamer that I was, and am--for the best.

As the #2 bus chugged along, a few Portugal fans, sporting maroon jerseys, climbed on and tossed their 600 *won* into the fare box.

They scanned the crowd, and spotted me in my U.S. jersey and cap. They smiled. It was a smug, condescending European sort of smile, tinged with a hint of pity. They were going to kick our sorry asses. Poor, pathetic Americans! I nodded and smiled. This was supposed to be fun, remember. They smiled back, a little embarrassed, I thought, to be caught thinking what they were thinking.

At the stadium, we hopped off the bus, waved good-bye to Mija and Un Ho, and plowed into the crowd. It was a throbbing miasma of humanity. The Koreans had organized support groups for both teams, and there were dancing, singing, gyrating bunches of Koreans sporting jerseys from both countries. Americans and Portuguese roamed the sidewalk, carrying flags, banners, placards, and chanting "USA, USA, USA," or "POR-TU-GAL, POR-TU-GAL," respectively. There was a group of Americans being interviewed by Univision, the Spanish-language network from the United States. We gravitated toward the video camera to watch and listen as the correspondent whipped up the crowd, getting them to chant, "*Olé, olé, olé*, USA, USA, USA."

As he was finishing up, I noticed that his press credentials identified him as Costa Rican. I pointed this out to Hannia, and she instantly displayed the sort of exuberance anyone in a faraway land feels when he or she finds a compatriot. She attacked him with the usual qualifying chatter about what part of Costa Rica he was from, where he was based--Miami--and where he was staying. I asked him how he thought the *Ticos*4 would do, and he was hopeful. They were in the same group as Brazil, but had already put away China 2-0 and could probably get a good result against Turkey. I ask him what he thought the U.S.'s chances were against Portugal. He smirked, but diplomatically responded with the typical Costa Rican shrug and, "*¿Quien sabe?*" ("Who knows?").

We put our heads down and shoved our way into the stadium. The security was formidable. They searched fanny packs, camera cases, backpacks, purses, everything. They made us walk through a metal detector, and then individually used handheld detectors on each spectator.

---

4 "*Tico*" is a slang term for Costa Rican. It derives from a linguistic quirk. While the proper way to form the diminutive in Spanish is to add "ito" or "ita", Costa Ricans will frequently add "ico" or "ica" instead. Thus if you're being asked to wait a brief moment, "*un momentito*" becomes "*un momentico*." The term "*Tico*" refers to a Costa Rican, or more broadly as anything from Costa Rica.

Considering the events of the previous year, we were more than glad to see them going a bit overboard. I was also disappointed that the cute Korean girl among them didn't insist on a strip search, and didn't even seem interested in patting me down.

The air crackled with enthusiasm. Win, lose, or draw, life can't be bad if you're halfway around the globe at a World Cup game. People scrambled around, waving banners, chanting, cheering, taking pictures with fans sporting decorations from both sides of the fence. This is the world's biggest bash--and you're invited.

When we reached our seats, we discovered that we were sitting with Sam's Army--the U.S. supporters' group. They follow the team around the world, trying to make them feel like someone's on their side. We've been with Sam's Army before, and it's always a boisterous experience. We knew they'd watch the entire game standing. They have worked out songs and chants for any and all occasions, and are dedicated to making their presence felt. Among them were a few guys in Elvis costumes, and the guy who has shaved his head in the pattern of a soccer ball, and dyed the remaining patches of hair red, white, and blue. We were in the end zone, right behind the goal that the U.S. was to attack in the first half.

The U.S. team took the field to warm up, and the festivities began. The goalkeepers came out first, and Sam's Army started the chants, "Frie--del, Frie--del," "Ka-sey Kel-ler" followed by a five-clap, and some more nondescript yelling to Tony Meola, of WC '94 fame. We were turning a few heads with all the noise.

Then the Portuguese team hit the field. The rest of the stadium came to life, and you'd think it was the Super Bowl back home. Waves of white noise drowned us out, though Sam's Army kept up a strong, pulsating stream of its own.

The Koreans were, for the most part, cheering for the Portuguese. In addition to Portuguese star-worship, the Koreans figured that Portugal would be one of the two teams to advance from this group to the next round, so they wanted the U.S. and Poland to be crushed as badly as possible, increasing their own chances. Plus, there was the lingering annoyance with the U.S. Olympic short-track speed skater Apolo Ohno, who'd so recently beaten Korean favorites, but more about that later.

The ceremonial flavor of the match was impressive. The teams paraded onto the field with Korean schoolchildren as escorts. The flags of the two countries were carried out, and our national anthems played. I grew up in the '60s and '70s during a period of great disillusionment with government. Grappling with the Vietnam and Nixon eras, it was hard not to questioning blind patriotism and the symbols of nationalism. Since then, I've discovered that there's something about the international character of soccer that makes you instantly respond in a very deep and sincere way to the trappings of your native country. Thousands of miles from home, outnumbered by the opposition, shoulder to shoulder with compatriots, and preparing to duke it out on the field with a foreign squad, the red, white, and blue suddenly seems to make sense as a rallying symbol.

The referee finally blew his whistle. The ball was kicked off, we were all standing, electrified beyond belief. OUR WORLD CUP HAD BEGUN!

The Portuguese team started by controlling the ball and outrunning the U.S. The U.S. didn't look bad, but they were obviously starting conservatively, and feeling out the Portuguese.

Suddenly, in the third minute, Earnie Stewart put a beautiful corner kick directly on Brian McBride's head. McBride hammered the ball at the Portuguese goalkeeper, who managed to parry it out of the goalmouth. The ball dropped in front of an onrushing John O'Brien. The Playa del Rey native slammed the rebound into the back of the net, and amazingly, the U.S. was ahead. Sam's Army went absolutely bananas. The huge pro-Portugal contingent, comprising some ninety-seven percent of the fans, went resoundingly silent.

The Portuguese team shook it off and started attacking. What was one goal? They had guys that could light up the nets all day, especially against a soccer neophyte like the U.S. They started working their magic, spinning the ball around, making crisp short passes, working it up field. The U.S., contrary to expectation, did a good job of dispossessing the fabled golden generation, and counterattacking. They put a few more shots on goal, and generally looked pretty damned good. Around minute 29, Landon Donovan scooped up a rebound on the right wing, and tried to thread in a cross to McBride, who was open at the top of the box. The man coming out to mark Donovan, however, deflected the ball. It spun high and back toward the keeper, who was caught off-guard by the redirection. The ball found its way into the Portuguese net. Donovan shrugged as if to say, "I'll take it." The Portuguese team stood in shock, just staring at each other. They were down 2-0 to the biggest nobody in the kingdom of soccer. This just couldn't be happening.

A few minutes later, Minnesota native Tony Sanneh brought the ball up the right wing, made a beautiful, pinpoint cross and Brian McBride sent one of his trademark diving headers into the goal. Three unanswered goals. Euphoria reigned. Sam's Army chanted on. The rest of the stadium remained as still as a morgue.

Of course, the Portuguese turned on the heat. They stuck one in before the end of the half, and the crowd exploded with thunderous cheers.

When half time gave a moment to contemplate, none of us could believe that we were up 3-1. Hannia and I looked into each other's eyes. We looked and felt thoroughly intoxicated.

In the second half, hapless Jeff Agoos put in an own goal, meaning that Portugal was one goal from a tie.

Still, attack as they might, the Portuguese couldn't quite push the U.S. around. Tony Sanneh, Eddie Pope, and Agoos were monstrously tough in the back, and the midfielders supported like crazy. Figo and Rui Costa flailed away, showing character and ability, but the Yanks were a match for them, and then some. This ranked not as a flukey upset, but as a stellar performance by the U.S., who met the challenge of a world-class opponent with laudable tactics and technique. When the final whistle blew, the U.S. team was ecstatic. They'd done the unthinkable. The Portuguese slunk out with their tails between their legs. The Sam's Army section burst into delirious cheering and applause.

Outside the stadium, the party was in full swing. Groups of U.S. supporters danced in delirium, chanting "*Ole, ole, ole*, USA! USA!" for the myriad television cameramen from around the globe. Hordes of Koreans stopped red, white, and blue-clad fans, myself included, and insisted on taking pictures with us. Hyundia Motors had a stage show going with dancing girls and techno-pop. Conga lines sprang up spontaneously. In one single game, the U.S. had wiped out the nightmare of '98. Win, lose, or draw from here on out, this was their defining moment.

When we hit home on the #2 bus, Gyosu and family all greeted us at the door.

"Congratulations on your victory," they all chimed, bowing and smiling. They offered us watermelon and *soju*, a rice wine, something like Japanese *sake*.

They were surprised and concerned that we'd taken so long to come home, so I had to allay their fears. "Big celebration," I told them. They nodded and smiled. They understood. On the television behind them, the news summaries endlessly repeated highlights in incomprehensible Korean.

Our government sponsored supporters section, USA vs. Portugal, Suwon Stadium.

A Red, White and Blue dance party weekend.

Mija and Un Ho watch the festivities.

Elvis has entered the building. Actually, a few of him.

Traditional Korean procession.

Celebrating the win over Portugal. Stars, stripes and cheese.

Golden State girl and a fellow celebrant.

Signing the big ball.   Our hood in Suwon.

JUNE 6TH - BACK TO TOURISM

The next game we had tickets for was Costa Rica vs. Turkey, three days away. Gyosu and family had offered to take us to see a few sights in Seoul and Suwon in the meantime, and that suited us fine. It's always good to have a guide, and this was even better, a whole family of them.

Gyosu explained over breakfast that he wanted to take us to the famous traditional Korean village in Suwon. Hannia watched the bowls of rice, *kimchi*, and shredded squid plop down in front of her. Her all-too-expressive face was unmistakably in panic mode. I watched Mija watch Hannia. Mija's pained expression told me that she wanted very badly for Hannia to be happy and well-fed. I whispered to Hannia that if she kept wrinkling her nose like that every time food appeared, Mija was going to have no recourse but to feed her hamburgers. "Ha, ha, very funny," she replied, stuffing her mouth with rice, hoping to prove she was eating her fill.

It was Korea's Memorial Day, so Gyosu was off work. We piled into the car and made our way to the village. We didn't know what to expect, but when we arrived, saw that this was obviously a big deal. The parking lot was as huge as a theme park's. Gyosu ignored the parking attendants, who waved and screamed and jumped up and down, and drove right up to the front to drop us off with his family.

We went up to the ticket window, and I insisted on paying for everyone, scandalizing Mija. I stood my ground, and stood in line. While trying to decipher the ticket sign over the booth, written in both Korean and English, I was tackled from behind by Gyosu, who pushed me out of line. He took my place, and Mija blocked my path so that I couldn't get back in line to pay. So be it. I can take a hint, however subtle. When someone ejects me bodily from a line, I'll bow out gracefully.

As we entered, Hannia remarked that almost the entire crowd was Korean. Since it's a tourist spot, I figured it would be full of foreign visitors, but it seems to be a big destination for Koreans getting in touch with their roots. And since it was Memorial Day, the Koreans were out in force.

One of the first places we stopped was a photo stand. Here, for a small fee, they'll dress you up in a traditional Korean *Hanbok,* an elaborate get-up with leggings, a robe, and the trademark wide-brimmed black hat, and take your picture. Gyosu and Mija felt this was a "must" for Hannia and I.

The attendants led us to different sides of the wardrobe tent, and went about dressing us. My shoes went off first, leggings slid up my enormous calves. After three or four tries, they came up with boots that almost fit my size-thirteen feet, a robe slipped around me, and a hat plopped over my brow. I looked up, and noticed that a crowd of fifty or sixty Koreans had gathered. They found this process wildly entertaining, snapped pictures like mad, laughed, and pointed. Hannia emerged from behind a screen, similarly transformed. The crowd was entranced. She did not look comical, carrying herself stylishly and with a sense of ceremonial seriousness that befit the occasion. The photographer, a middle-aged man in wire-rimmed spectacles, clapped his hands together to quiet the crowd. I put my arm around my bride, and assumed a pompous pose, provoking a ripple of giggles in the crowd. The photographer snapped his picture and bowed. The crowd applauded riotously. We bowed, drinking in the pandemonium.

The traditional village was well worth the effort. It's akin to a Korean Williamsburg, a functional 17th- or 18th-century town. Some of the buildings are actual restored houses, others are replicas. Much of the fun comes from seeing what kind of kitchens, bathrooms, work, and study areas Koreans inhabited then. It's always a marvel to see first-hand just how much physical labor was necessary before the advent of electricity and internal-combustion engines. Imagine housekeeping and farming at a time when water had to be carried by hand, wood chopped endlessly by hand, and goats, pigs, and chickens kept fed—with no provisions for man or beast delivered by truck. It's helpful to be reminded, now and then, what a bunch of lazy whiners we've become.

When we stopped for refreshments, Gyosu and Mija treated us to a rice-based drink. Hannia looked suspiciously at the brownish liquid. When I tasted it, I reported that it was very good, reminding me of *horchata,* a rice-based beverage from Latin America, though this was brown in color, rather than the milky-white we knew. Hannia took a tentative sip. The eyes of Gyosu's family were upon her, knowing that she was less than adventurous when it came to food. A smile spread across her face, and our hosts smiled happily in return. Good and cold, the drink revived us from the midday heat and humidity.

Un Ho and Jiwon were having a blast running around, looking at all the animals, and playing some of the village games they had set out in a square. There was a teeter-totter, and a set of tall, slender buckets into which you were supposed to throw arrows from a distance of ten feet. I was never able to sink one, giving up after fifty attempts or so.

The buildings made me wonder how the occupants coped throughout the Korean winters, which are famously severe, without insulation or central heating. Imagine working outdoors, all winter long, while living in single-story, wood-frame houses, raised three or four feet from the ground. Calling these Korean forebears "hardy" would be like dismissing Muhammed Ali as merely a "good" boxer.

As we walked from exhibit to exhibit, our little group spread out a bit. Hannia and Mija sauntered along together, Un Ho and Jiwon led the way, at a distance, while Gyosu and I strolled together down a tree-lined path, conversing as best we could in English.

A young woman of perhaps twenty-five approached us, questioning Gyosu in Korean. I had the feeling she was asking about me, and my suspicions were more or less confirmed when I caught, among the incomprehensible Korean phrases, the word "homestay." Gyosu looked proud as he spoke, as this was clearly a cool thing to do, perhaps akin to hosting an exchange student. The young lady continued to quiz him, while obviously sizing me up. Balding, middle-aged, and extremely married, I harbor no illusions of resembling a "babe magnet," but I had the distinct impression that she wondered, "Hey, where can I get my hands on one of those?"

From having lived abroad, I've learned that some women are just fascinated with Americans, no matter what the description. Heck, even back home, we see people who only date "exotic" foreigners, or harbor obsessions with people of a certain race or nationality. Gyosu was starting to look a little embarrassed. I felt he was trying to extricate himself unsuccessfully from the conversation. Soon, she grabbed me by the arm and said, in very rudimentary English, "You come visit my city. I show you my city." In her hand, she held a tourist brochure with the name of her town, as well as pictures of some temple or other. Thinking that she must work with the local Chamber of Commerce or something, and was just promoting her town as a tourist destination, I thanked her. I said that since her town was on the way back from Daegu, perhaps I'd get the chance to visit. "You come to my house, here is phone number," she said, jotting it down on the brochure.

Instantly, Hannia appeared at my side. "What's your phone number?" the Korean girl continued, pointing at the cell phone hanging around my neck. Hannia gave her a look that would drop a charging rhino and grabbed me by the arm, a clear indication of proprietorship. The young lady ignored her completely.

I fumbled and stumbled, pulled out a pen and wrote my cell phone number on the corner of the brochure, and tore it off for the girl. I said, "Maybe my wife and I can visit your town." I was sure she didin't understand a word, staring at me all doe-eyed and smiling. "Yes, you visit" she insisted, before rejoining a group of giggling young women who had been watching the proceedings with interest.

Hannia immediately demanded of Gyosu, "What was that about? What did she want?" Gyosu, visibly embarrassed, hemmed and hawed, and succeeded in making the young woman's inquiries seem much less innocent than they probably had been.

"She wants you to visit her town," Gyosu responded, a little fearful of Hannia's demeanor. Anyone who has experienced the wrath of a jealous Latin woman knows that her response was not unfounded.

"Is that all?" Hannia continued suspiciously.

"Yes, she is just proud of her town," Gyosu replied, knowing full well how lame this sounded.

Fortunately, our next distraction was provided by a spirited and lively display of drumming and acrobatics, performed in thick, traditional Korean garb despite the ninety-degree heat and near-hundred-percent humidity. This act was followed by a tightrope-walker, a man perhaps in his fifties, whose constant banter kept the Korean-speaking crowd rolling with laughter, between his amazing stunts. He maintained perfect control as he walked, jumped, and ran back and forth on the rope. When he appeared to slip and fall, he hooked his leg over the rope and swung himself back upright. He'd follow this stunt with an obviously wry remark that left the Koreans in stitches.

This performer made me reflect on the luck of the draw. Had he been born into an English-speaking culture, his comedic career might have followed an entirely different path. Though he definitely held an audience's attention, but his language is spoken by forty million people—rather a lot, actually, but a fraction of the English-speaking world. You have to think about show biz as a very narrow cultural phenomenon, no matter what universal elements it contains. The idioms and references he employed to keep his spectators laughing were meaningless to someone like me, but he mesmerized the rest of the audience. So many high-profile U.S. entertainers whom we consider brilliant, had they been born into a smaller culture, might have never gotten beyond the level of this guy. Not that this was a bad gig. He'd found a pretty good niche, apparently, bouncing up and down on a rope, doing flips, feigning an imminent fall, joking about it, vacillating between peril and comedy.

Think of how many comedians started out as magicians, or musicians, or emcees, before they established themselves exclusively as comedians. This guy's one of them, a brother in arms. For all I know, he's another Will Rogers, or George Carlin, or Jerry Seinfeld. But he'll never be able to play the Strip in Vegas, or even a Holiday Inn near you. You have to wonder if English-speaking performers realize how lucky they are to have such a vast potential audience, despite the vagaries of show business.

JUNE 7 - APPEARING AT THE PALACE

The next day, Friday, we had thought we'd go into Seoul to get to know the big city, but Gyosu told us that on Saturday he'd take us to the Palace, in downtown Seoul. Not Caesar's Palace, but *Hungson Tae Won Gun*'s. Mija wanted us to go observe Un Ho's soccer class, so we felt a little obligated. And, what the heck, it'd be interesting.

On Saturday, Mija took us to meet Gyosu after work--he works every Saturday--in the *Insa-Dong* district, which is lined with art galleries and shops that sell traditional Korean artifacts. One gallery had *papier-maché* sculptures of Korean life, mostly traditional themes, with two-foot-high figures wearing *Hanboks*. Hannia pointed out one scene to me that featured a young girl farting. She was bent over, face puckered, with cotton balls representing the puffs of gas. The other figures were holding their noses and grimacing, and their hair and clothing blown back, as though by a mighty wind. It was a very funny, irreverent depiction, nestled among much more serious art. Westerners typically view Asians as buttoned-down—more than we are, at least--but here was an example of Korean humor shining through in a universally accessible way.

Gyosu arrived, and we made our way to the palace, where the ceremonial changing of the guard was under way. This was an ornate procession with ritualized greetings, and a drummer (always present in Korean pageantry, as far as I can tell). According to the English narration broadcast through a public-address system, the intricate methods of identification and confirmation when changing guards assured the departing guards that their replacements were legitimate.

The Palace offered a good glimpse into Korea's history. The last resident, Emperor Yung-hui, was deposed in 1910, when the Japanese began their official occupation of the Korean Peninsula. So it's not all that long ago that the court was full of politicians, generals, and fools catering to the whims of Korea's Choson Dynasty.

The palace structures embodied an old-style, ornate Korean architecture, with painted wooden façades and eaves, tile roofs, and gargoyle-like dragons and other sculpted creatures on the peaks. We joined a Korean tour group, but Gyosu and Un Ho helped translate, and there were enough signs in English for Hannia and I to learn about this elaborate forbidden city of sorts, now surrounded by the very modern metropolis of Seoul.

What I came away with was the universality of a country's need for history. While we Americans flock to Washington, D.C, Philadelphia, or Virginia to stroll through our founding fathers' homes, offices, and memorials, the Koreans come to the Palace to feel their connection to a long history. Despite the fact that this palace was off-limits to most of their ancestors, today a visit allows all Koreans to feel their connection to their history and culture. However few Americans are direct descendants of Revolutionary War veterans, or of those who drafted or debated clauses of the Constitution, most Americans either visit such historic landmarks as Monticello or Mount Vernon, or learn about them in school or on our own. Similarly, the Koreans visiting the Palace shuffle around reverently, feeling patriotic about the ornate and elaborate buildings in which decisions of state and war were handed down. And Koreans can brag of a hell of a lot more history here than on the East Coast of the United States—five thousand years of it.

The Koreans may have been manhandled by the Japanese and Chinese over the centuries, and may be misunderstood by much of the modern world, but they've shown an impressive durability, maintaining a distinct history and language alive in the face of extremely virulent cultural imperialism. While we Americans can be rightfully proud of the democracy we've forged, Koreans can be equally proud of just keeping their asses intact.

We ended the day at Itaewon, the fabled shopping district of Seoul. There you can buy any major clothing manufacturer's line at a fraction of the price. Don't look too closely, or you'll realize that some of the merchandise consists of knock-offs, but most of it is good quality and available at surprisingly low prices. Leather goods are well made, and a bargain, as are jewelry and luggage. The trick of the experienced shopper is to arrive early, buy a "grow bag"--a multi-zippered, expandable piece of luggage on rollers--and during the shopping frenzy, fill up the bag as each zipper lets out a new bulge to be filled with trinkets.

We bumped into a couple of Costa Ricans, sporting team colors. Roberto, in his mid-forties, and his eleven-year-old son, Jaime, were excited by Costa Rica's win over China, and looked forward to tangling with Turkey, who had become a force in European soccer in the years immediately preceding the World Cup. Roberto and Jaime were amazed by the variety of merchandise at all prices--a *Tico's* dream. And you can bargain. A few tourists in Turkish jerseys bopped past, and both Turks and *Ticos* good-naturedly taunted each other with their flags and jerseys. These teams vied for the group's second slot, knowing with impending certainty that Brazil would occupy the first position.

The Costa Ricans told us they'd rented an apartment together with a large group of fellow travelers. They'd purchased small appliances and brought their own food, in order to keep prices low and palates happy for the month or so they planned to spend in South Korea. They planned to leave their kitchenware behind when they flew out. Hannia longingly asked if they were eating *gallo pinto*. "Of course," Roberto responded, "and *platanos maduros,* and *palmito,* and we even brought a couple of jars of *pejivalles*." I had to forcibly restrain Hannia from following them home. Dried squid, *kimchi*, and caffeine deprivation had turned her into a zombie who would mindlessly trail the scent of Costa Rican cuisine anywhere it might lead.

We turned out attention to shopping--one thing that will excite Hannia's interest even more than *platanos maduros*. She had wanted a leather jacket, and we needed an extra piece of carry-on luggage for our train trips. Mija waded in on our behalf, spewing out a stream of shopping-wise Korean that bludgeoned shopkeepers into submission. A force to be reckoned with, there was no way that Mija would allow her guests to leave Korea without feeling like they'd gotten fabulous deals. That's exactly how we felt.

JUNE 9 – GAME DAY #2

Our hosts were a little apprehensive about turning us loose on the Seoul subway system alone, but I assured them that we had successfully navigated public transportation all over the world, in other, equally perplexing languages, and actually kind of enjoy it. Gyosu bought us a subway map, and helped me plot out transfer points. It was fairly direct, just two transfers, very logical and comprehensible. It is particularly gratifying for an Angeleno to use a mass transit system that actually works.

I was able to buy tickets in Suwon easily, by walking up to a ticket window and saying, "Incheon." The attendant pointed to the proper fare. So far, so good. We hiked up the stairs to the train platform. A train came almost immediately, and I double-checked the name of the line on the front panel above the driver. We got on board, amidst the throng of rush-hour passengers. We were going into town, against traffic, so we weren't pressed in like sardines--yet. The trains were modern, well-maintained, and air-conditioned. As the train headed out from Suwon, the head of the line, we started picking up more passengers, and the air-conditioning had more body heat to contend with. It was a muggy summer day, and I could feel the warmth of humanity overcoming the chilling effects of technology. I gave my seat up to an tiny older woman, probably in her late seventies, bent over with what appeared to be osteoporosis. A lot of the older people in Korea are very small and stooped, evidence of the rough life and short rations before, during, and after decades of war. Once I was standing, I noticed that I couldn't see the names of the stops out the window, which always makes me nervous. I told Hannia what to watch for, and she appeared a little panicked, hoping that a sign in English would be readily apparent now that the responsibility was on her shoulders. Inside the train, however, I spotted a screen, which read out the name of the next stop, alternately in Korean characters, Chinese, and English. On some but not all of the trains, a pleasant woman's voice also reads the stop name aloud in each of the three languages. This train was audio-enabled, letting Hannia off the hook a little.

The transfers went smoothly, and we were at the stadium in a little over an hour. This ride cost us just about a dollar each, for a substantial ride of forty or fifty kilometers.

COSTA RICA VS. TURKEY

The stadium was huge. It was destined to be a multipurpose sports complex after the World Cup, so it had a large track around the field. This generally distances the audience a bit from the game, but as we had "nosebleed seats," it didn't make much difference to us. We were sitting on the sidelines, way up in the rafters. This provided a delightful opportunity to study the construction of the ceiling joists, but a less immediate view of the athletic proceedings. I looked longingly down at the cheap seats: right behind the goal. Still, watching soccer from high above can be interesting. It reveals the formations and passing patterns. You can really judge how the teams are playing strategically. We have, however, become spoiled. Our seats at L.A. Galaxy games are so close to the field that we can see every little expression on the face of every player, though we lack the panoramic perspective.

There were not many Costa Ricans in our section. A few Koreans decked out in CR jerseys, yes, but no legit *Ticos* close by. I scanned the audience, and spotted some Costa Rica jerseys a section away. I went to the railing to get their attention. They smiled when they spotted my jersey, but my overall appearance must have made them wonder. There are a few redheads living in Costa Rica, particularly in the towns of Grecia and Tilarán, but in general, they were certain to peg me for a gringo.

"E maje, que tanate de Ticos!" ("Hey, man, what a ton of *Ticos!*") I said, pointing to the big contingency of flag-waving Costa Ricans on the far side, close to the field. The expressions "*maje*" and "*tanate*" are about as authentically Costa Rican as you can get, and the guys blinked hard at me. Finally, an African-American guy in a *Tico* jersey spotted us, and came over to shake hands. His name was Robert, and since he'd only decided to come to the tournament at the last minute, he couldn't get a ticket near his family and friends. Robert was ecstatic to find some compatriots.

We got our own impromptu cheering section together, and were soon joined by a small group of Americans, who wanted to support their brothers from CONCACAF, our regional soccer federation. The rest of the stadium decidedly seemed to favor the Turks. One American in our group theorized that since Turkey was an ally of the South Koreans during the war with the North, they've maintained cultural and economic ties since, including their preference in soccer teams.

One foreboding note was sounded in the opening ceremonies. Each of the participating countries performed a dance. The *Ticos* chose a favorite, *"Punto Guanacasteco,"* in which shy *ticas* are courted by village boys, set to lively marimba music--a quaint, pleasant little dance from a happy town in a simpler time. When the Turks did their dance, it was an all-male saber dance, performed to pounding martial music. We hoped the game didn't reflect these polarities.

Robert vocalized what a lot of us were thinking, "Can you imagine the security these spectators from Turkey had to go through to get here, post-9/11?" Hannia and I looked at each other, remembering the X-raying and the careful scrutiny our bags received upon boarding our flight in Los Angeles. Coming from the Middle East had to be a nightmare. Still, the place was packed with Turks, eager to see their team on the world stage.

The game was on and lively. The *Ticos* showed wonderful technique and flair, but the Turks were playing very hard, pressuring and forcing errors. The *Ticos* seemed in control most of the game, generating opportunity after opportunity, but failing to score. In qualifying, the *Ticos* finished first in CONCACAF, beating Mexico in Mexico City, a first in World Cup Qualifying. I feared that they had peaked in that game, however. Their veteran striker, Hernan Medford, now used as a super-sub, had been instrumental in the win over Mexico. He was subsequently injured, and, though he was on the bench that day, ready for action, he was thought to be less than a hundred percent ready to play. In the second half, Medford came charging in, prompting a big cheer from the *Tico* contingent. He handled the ball well, but when a midfielder popped one down the wing for Medford to run onto, I immediately saw a problem. His formerly blazing speed was barely smoldering. The Turk defender easily beat him to the ball. What would have presented a dangerous scoring threat a couple of months ago was now snuffed out casually.

The *Ticos* brought in a young kid, Winston Parks, who played for Udinese in Italy. He's an exceptionally talented forward, and I remembered seeing him play for Costa Rica's under-twenty squad. He immediately made things happen, crossing up the defense, and opening space with his speed and trickery. Finally, he put in the lone Costa Rican goal. When Turkey tied it up, however, the Costa Ricans flailed away, generating opportunity after opportunity, but not paying them off. In many instances, they were within shooting range but continued to be too cute, passing the ball around the goalmouth, or taking the extra dribble and getting caught. A couple of Argentinean guys sitting near me had been cheering Costa Rica on, as fellow Latins, but now they just hid their heads in their hands. *"¡Hay que tirar!"*, they shouted. ("You have to shoot!") Parks had a bad moment at the very end where he got an easy ball with an open net in front of him, and he skied the kick. He had it within his grasp, and lost it. I couldn't fault him too much, however. The kid was only twenty, and he had scored their only goal. Give him four years, and he'll be REALLY dangerous.

Robert was horribly disappointed at the outcome of the game. Hannia was screaming at the top of her lungs. All the *Ticos* realized that this was their opportunity to advance. Now they had to play Brazil. We all had a sneaking suspicion Costa Rica would not beat Brazil.

Outside of the stadium, the *Ticos* made the best of it. Even though they'd blown the opportunity, they were having fun, dancing, laughing, and chanting. A Costa Rican newsman from Channel 7 interviewed me. "Well, gee, this was a drag, but I guess we'll just have to clobber Brazil,"I remarked. The irony was not lost, even in Spanish. When my comments were broadcast in Costa Rica, my in-laws later told me their jaws nearly shattered on the floor. There they were, watching the post-match round-up on Hatillo 3, and their big, red-haired mug of a son-in-law came up on their screens. Just call me the "global village idiot"—everybody's favorite gringo in Korea.

We flowed back with the crowd to the subway station, bid adieu to Robert, and retraced our steps back to Suwon. We watched the thick concentration of Costa Rican and Turk jerseys in the subway cars thin out as the pert female voice ticked off each subway stop with mechanical precision in Korean, Chinese, and English.

Back at Gyosu's, we were consoled about Costa Rica's plight. The Kum family had dutifully watched the game on television, and they concurred that Costa Rica had played very well. Mija gave us the requisite watermelon slices as a late-night dessert, and Gyosu served glasses of *soju*. We toasted the Costa Rican team, and I felt the sweet elixir slide through my tired muscles, allowing me to embrace the exhaustion I'd successfully ignored until then. We toddled off to bed.

Toilet balloon.   At the Hwaseong Fortress.

Tico for a day, Incheon.

Pre-game ceremonies, Costa Rica vs. Turkey.

Incheon Stadium at night.

June 10th - Travel to Daegu, Game Day #3

Over breakfast, Gyosu told us that he had very made reservations for us to go to our next destination, Daegu. It's only three hours away, but since we were traveling on game day, with the game involving South Korea, it would have been very dicey to just show up and try to buy train tickets on the spot. Hannia glanced over the breakfast offerings on the table before serving herself rice. Then came the moment I'd warned her about. Mija opened the oven and pulled out a plate of hamburgers—not on a bun, just four patties on a plate. "Here, maybe you like better," said Mija. I had to avoid Hannia's eyes, because I knew I'd break out laughing if I looked at her. Though she was touched by the thoughtfulness of the offer, it was so wonderfully absurd that Hannia almost laughed herself. She found herself accepting, and eating the patties. We knew all too well that around the world, everyone assumes that Americans eat hamburgers at every meal. We couldn't disillusion them. Hannia actually enjoyed the change of pace.

Mija insisted on packing a lunch for us, but we declined, saying that she was already doing too much work on our behalf.

Gyosu and his family accompanied us to the train station to make sure we had our tickets. He had reserved them at a discount by using his train pass, but the cardholder was required to purchase the tickets.

The train station was part of the same subway station we used to get to Incheon. Tickets in hand, we hit the boarding gate, slightly south of the entrance to the subway trains. The intercity boarding area was orderly, though I had my usual apprehensions about whether we were in the right line. Luckily, the train number and name, Saemaeul Express, were easy to decipher, and when I asked a Korean man in line with us, he confirmed with a nod that we were in good shape.

When we boarded, we were impressed by the comfort, speed, and efficient air-conditioning of the trains. It was much more relaxing than driving the same distance would have been, and the train trip allowed us to take in the scenery and hoist some Hite beer. A vendor hawked dried squid up and down the aisle. I passed on that. Another thing Koreans like as a snack food is hot dogs. I don't mean a cooked hot dog in a bun with mustard, I mean just a hot dog, cold, right out of the plastic wrapper. The Korean gentleman who had told me I was in the right line was sitting nearby, and he insisted that I share the rest of his hot dogs, with five or six remaining in the bag. I tried to decline graciously, but he insisted with such an appealing smile that I really couldn't insult him by refusing. I replied with the requisite, *"Kamsamnida"* as I took the tubesteak. I haven't eaten an uncooked hot dog--actually, all hot dogs are pre-cooked, but you know what I mean--since I was a kid, but, when in Rome... Not bad, really. Not something I'd go out of my way to procure, but really, not bad.

Hot dogs and hamburgers, the all-American repast... I asked Hannia how she'd enjoyed her breakfast burgers. Her nose wrinkled involuntarily. "They tasted like they were fried in fish oil," she confided. So much for my trooper wife.

The countryside was very interesting. I'd heard it said that Korea looks much like southern California, and that's not a bad assessment, though I've never seen many rice paddies on the road from San Clemente to Del Mar. There are, after all, forty million Koreans to feed, three times a day, so they've got a heck of a lot of little grains to grow. Other than that, the hillsides do have that kind of dry, craggy, oak-and-scrub-filled look that you become accustomed to in SoCal. It's more humid, but the temperature is about the same. This was the first time I'd been out of the urban sprawl of greater Seoul/Suwon/Incheon, and the atmosphere was very different, more tranquil. By the time we reached Daegu, I was feeling well rested, pleasantly filled with hot dogs and beer.

In Daegu, we were met at the train station by our second homestay family, the Chungs. Soohee was the point person, a married woman in her early forties, with a year-old daughter, Minji. Soohee had lived in the States as a child, returning later to attend graduate school, so she not only spoke perfect English, but she was familiar with potential points of cultural and culinary friction between East and West. Her husband also had gone to grad school in the U.S., and had a good knowledge of English, but he was very shy about speaking. He let his fluent wife do the talking.

"Have you eaten yet?" began Soohee.

The Chungs immediately took us to Pizza Hut, for some authentic Korean pepperoni pizza and Coca-Cola.

Soohee was the president of a biotech firm, and her husband was a professor of political policy at the local university. She was originally from Seoul, but had decided that a move to the more rural Daegu would be good not only for her career--the surrounding agriculture is the focus of her firm—but also for their personal lives. The Chungs wanted to buy a house, an unattainable prospect in Seoul or other large cities. Though Daegu itself is a pretty big city, its location in the heart of the countryside offers the advantage of lower real estate prices on the periphery of town.

They owned a condominium--many apartments in Korea, it seems, are purchased rather than rented. They took us to their thirteenth-floor home, which was roomy and newly renovated. The living room and kitchen were very large, and nicely appointed. The kitchen had beautiful, new, blond wood cabinets, and tile countertops. We removed our shoes as we entered, just like everywhere in Korea, but there were some Western touches. While the bathroom was built with a step down and a drain in the floor, the bathtub had a shower curtain, and since there were also electrical outlets inside the bathroom, we suspected that the floors stayed drier than at our last homestay. When I discovered Soohee's full-sized bath towels, it became obvious that she'd been corrupted by her stints in Georgia and Pennsylvania.

The game would begin in only a couple of hours, so we quickly stowed our bags. I donned my Galaxy jersey, and got briefed on transportation. The stadium was very close to Soohee's apartment. In fact, if it weren't for the apartment building across the street, you could have seen it out the window. A free shuttle bus ran in a big loop through town, and the Chungs escorted us to the bus stop, just a hundred yards or so from the apartment. Within fifteen minutes, we stepped out of the bus into a sea of red shirts, all emblazoned with "Be the Reds!" We were playing the host nation, and it seemed that the entire population had shown up for the game.

USA VS. SOUTH KOREA

Our seats were once again located in the end zone with Sam's Army. We were so incredibly outnumbered that I felt I was watching a U.S. vs. Mexico match at the L.A. Coliseum, minus the vicious anti-American epithets and flying beer. The Koreans, so quiet in the other matches I've attended, were amped up for this one, leading a nonstop chant of "*Dae Han Min Guk*," or "Republic of South Korea."

There was also an air of revenge to this game. The Koreans were still smarting from the "Apolo Ohno affair" at the Winter Olympics. We Americans who remember Ohno's short-track speed-skating exploits also recall that he fell in one of his races, placing second, only to have the first-place skater disqualified by the judges for having knocked him down. What Americans forget is that the guy who was DQ'd was Korean. No way that Koreans would forget that detail, especially given Korea's powerhouse standing in the sport. They saw Ohno's ranking as a flagrant example of the Americans' desire to win at all costs, and that if we don't win outright, we rig it so we do.

Hannia had raised this question with Soohee, who had tried to downplay it, saying, "Yes, Koreans remember that, but it's no big deal." I only saw a replay on ESPN, but I seemed to remember some contact, though it struck me as incidental. Not knowing the fine points of judging short-track speed skating, I had never formed a concrete opinion, and I wasn't keen to voice one at that juncture. I then asked if she thought that the contact between the skaters warranted the judge's ruling. She reacted viscerally, "He didn't even touch him, it was more like a gesture toward him."

Soohee conceded that the Koreans were still pretty irked about the whole thing. In fact, the expression, "to Ohno," has worked its way into the Korean lexicon, meaning to pretend to be a big shot and a winner without actually earning it.

Sam's Army started its chants, and I heard a disturbing one: "We hate *kimchi*, we hate *kimchi!*" I have a distinct policy against making personal remarks, especially when surrounded by 60,000 screaming Koreans. I contemplated a move to a different section. Once the chants became more positive, more pro-U.S. in nature, rather than anti-Korean, I relaxed. Then I heard a guy behind me talking about his four years living in Korea, punctuated with the loud statement, "I don't think people realize what a political powder keg this game is."

I imagined headlines the following day: "Red-haired American fan immolated by angry Korean mob," or perhaps, "60,000 Korean fans single out American supporter." As I've said before, in appearance, I do stand out as a stereotypical American.

Luckily, the Koreans concentrated on cheering on their own team heartily, and that's an understatement. Any little success--winning a 50/50 ball, dribbling around a defender, making a half-hearted shot on goal--got the sort of cheers usually reserved for liberating armies and rock stars. And the Koreans played wonderfully. The U.S. scored at minute 24. A beautiful long ball by John O'Brien split the defense and landed in front of Cowboy Clint Mathis, sporting his new Mohawk 'do. Mathis brought the ball down masterfully at a full gallop, two defenders nipping at his heels, and hammered it home. This temporarily silenced the red-shirted crowd. Sam's Army chugged along, chanting "USA! USA! USA!" A few minutes later, the Korean crowd got back into it, *"Dae Han Min Guk"* shook the nice, new rafters of Daegu stadium. They don't give up, and neither did the team. The Koreans picked themselves up, and started hammering away at the U.S. defense.

The most phenomenal play of the game can be credited to U.S. goalkeeper Brad Friedel. At minute 39, with the U.S. still up 1-0, the World's Most Snake-bit Defender, Jeff Agoos, egregiously fouled Korean striker, Hwang Sun-Hong, in the penalty box. The referee rightfully awarded a penalty kick. It looked like the Koreans were going to tie it up. The Sea of Red began to pulsate and throb and scream. The kicker, Lee Eul Yong, approached the penalty spot, a scant twelve yards from the goalmouth. Friedel, hung out to dry, but plucky, extended his arms to show his imposing wingspan. The kicker paused and scanned the goalmouth. He regarded Friedel, a six-foot-three, shaven-headed condor of a man, glaring back. Lee struck the ball. Friedel dove and smothered it. Keepers seldom stop penalty kicks, but Friedel came up HUGE.

Finally, at minute 78 the Koreans got one in. Lee Eul-Yong served a free kick from midfield into the penalty area, and Ahn Jung-Hwan rose up to flick a header into the right-side netting. Ahn headed for the sidelines to do a little celebration dance, and broke into a pantomime of--you guessed it--a speed skater. The crowd went wild.

Without intending to, the U.S. had done the most diplomatic thing possible, by tying the host nation. While I wished they'd won--we'd pretty much have been assured a spot in the second round--it made my exit from the stadium much less tense. In fact, the atmosphere was extremely festive. There were the usual dancing, chanting crowds, Koreans who insisted on having their pictures taken with me and with other red, white, and blue-clad Yanks.

Back at the apartment, the Chungs had been watching the game on television, with the rest of Korea keeping them company. They were fairly content with the tie, and thrilled with Ahn's "speed-skating" goal celebration, but this result set up an odd dynamic. Portugal had thrashed Poland, and now seemed poised to regain dominance in the group by beating Korea. The U.S. was favored to beat Poland, so it was ostensibly a contest between the U.S. and Korea for second place, and advancement to round two.

The Chungs' beautiful year-old daughter, Minji, was very precocious and verbal, and Hannia, who is wonderful with children, immediately became her best friend: reading to her, playing little games, asking her questions, and walking around the apartment with her. Minji, however, had more than a little trouble warming up to me. She would be talking away with her mom and dad and Hannia, and then I'd say something and she'd come to a dead halt, watching me warily and trying to inch away. My own daughter is all grown up—she was twenty-two at that time--but I'd always related well to little girls. Except Minji, who had other ideas. Once or twice her parents tried to hand her to me, but she wouldn't let go of their arms, her eyes locking onto mine with a stare of extreme panic.

To Minji, I must have looked like some beast from a distant planet--huge, red-haired, blue-eyed, and pasty-skinned. At one point, she was flipping pages in a children's book, and I started to read the Korean script aloud. The book was very simple, with just one word per page, like apple, or banana, or ox, illustrated with a large picture. But the fact that I was sounding the words out and pronouncing them in Korean both fascinated and alarmed Minji. She turned each page slowly, keeping an eye on my reaction. For a moment, she almost seemed to drop her guard, but she caught herself, stopped smiling, and again eyed me warily.

Over dinner--traditional Korean fare--we asked Soohee's advice on interesting places to visit the following day. She suggested several possibilities in Daegu proper, but she advised that best of all would be a trip to Gyeonju, one of the most historically rich cities in Korea.

JUNE 11 - TO GYEONJU

A distance of a hundred kilometers, Gyeonju was an easy trip by express bus. These buses go virtually everywhere in Korea, and in some ways are more convenient than trains, cheaper and more direct.

Soohee dropped us off in the morning by the university, where we paid about $10 apiece for the express bus. The trip took about ninety minutes, and took us deep into the rice-growing countryside. Everywhere we looked, neat little water-filled paddy rows extended out toward the horizon. Graceful white cranes flew and walked among the bright-green fields, their long legs immersed past the knees (if you call them "knees" on a bird) as they picked their way through the water, seeking grain and bugs and whatever other goodies a rice paddy has to offer.

Gyeonju, a city of some 300,000 inhabitants, plays host to the crowds of tourists who come to visit the tombs and temples marking the seat of the former Silla Empire (57 B.C. - 935 A.D.). Gyeonju's genuine antiquities are always a draw for the Bermuda-shorts-and-snapshots set.

A tourist-information kiosk was located just fifty yards from the bus station. We arrived there along with three twentysomethings from the States, one of whom was of Korean descent. They planned to book a hotel room—we were returning to Daegu that night--stow their gear, and rent bicycles to see the sites. One visitor had come from the Bay Area, and the other two were from Pennsylvania. I'm not sure how they got hooked up together, except that Brian, the Korean-American, had been to Gyeonju before and was serving as guide. I got a map and some directions from the very proper, slender, young tourism information clerk, and also quizzed Brian about where I should go. Tumuli Park was a short hike, also close to the observatory, which in turn was close to the Museum. Bulguksa temple was accessible from the Museum via city bus, and a must-see. The Americans and I parted company as they sought accommodations.

Though Gyeonju is known as "the museum without walls," most of the stuff we looked at had, in fact, walls around it. These walls forced us to pay a few thousand *won* to gain entry. We found Tumuli Park easily enough, and strolled among the huge, grass-covered mounds that our brochures assured us were the tombs of kings and princes and high muckety-mucks of old. On such a hot and muggy day, after the walk through town, we took a refreshing break to dally amongst the greenery. In the rear of the park we happened onto the Flying Horse Tomb (*Cheonmachong*), named after a work of art found within depicting... a flying horse. This tomb had been excavated, with an opening left for hapless tourists like us to enter. Inside are replicas of the artifacts discovered there, dating back to one heck of a long time ago. There were gems and clothing and all the sorts of things that evidently are indispensable in the afterlife. An entrepreneur with a stand outside offered the opportunity to dress up in a *Hanbok* in order to have your picture taken. Since we already had done so, we declined.

Pressing on southward, we came across the Cheomseongdae Observatory, paid a few *won*, and entered the grounds to observe the observatory. It's an interesting old pile of stones, 362 of them to be precise, which supposedly is the number of days in the year calculated using the lunar calendar. A wrinkled, old Korean guide insisted on telling me all about the observatory, in a dialect of English completely unfamiliar to us. He chattered away, obviously proud of his linguistic abilities, while Hannia and I gritted our teeth, smiling and nodding as if we understood him, which we, unfortunately, did not. After the tirade was over, we bowed and thanked the gentleman, and he cornered another group of Westerners to give his speech anew. Hannia, who, of course, is not a native English speaker, whispered, "Is it just me? I didn't understand a word he said." I assured her that she had company on that score. The one piece of information I managed to decipher was that the observatory's twelve sides or facets correspond with the months of the year.

In front of the observatory, a young Westerner was being mobbed by a group of several dozen schoolgirls who demanded his autograph, wanted their pictures taken with him, and generally made themselves a flirtatious nuisance. Was he a rock star? A famous actor? No, he was just a Westerner. While in Seoul, or Suwon, or even in downtown Daegu, there was a fair amount of exposure to foreigners, and a more cosmopolitan atmosphere, there in Gyeonju, we were a tremendous novelty, as I was about to find out.

We headed farther south to the Gyeonju National Museum, a large complex of several buildings, and a pavilion housing the divine bell of King Seongdeok, a large bronze contraption with a suspended log with which to ring it. As I entered, I noticed that the courtyard around the bell was filled with eight or ten groups school kids, each group containing thirty to forty students, and most between the ages of nine and twelve. Suddenly, they rushed me, shouting "Hi!" and "Where are you from?" like a flock of boisterous magpies. I responded in Korean, "*Annyong Haseyo*." The cliché of "jaws dropping open" was no exaggeration. They also gasped audibly. Some applauded.

A group of kids pushed a young woman forward, and stopped her in front of me. She was covering her mouth and giggling.

"They want me to talk to you in English. I am their English teacher," she offered between giggles, turning red with embarrassment. Her accent was very, very thick, but she got the words out fine.

"What do you want to talk about?" I asked.

"I hope you have a very happy trip in Korea."

"I've enjoyed myself so far."

The kids exploded in laughter. The young woman scrambled back into the safety of the crowd.

The kids continued to mob me for my autograph, and some went so far as to run their hands along my arm, to feel the hair on it. Just as with tiny Minji, I must have looked like some kind of big, hairy, blue-eyed beast to them.

The museum had the requisite collection of impressive old stuff, jewels and coins and implements and clothing from different historical periods, but I was much more interested in how the modern-day Koreans took it all in, reverently strolling from exhibit to exhibit in stoic contemplation.

When we exited the buildings, the large groups of kids had all vanished. A few visitors remained by the snack bar, in front of which was a big World Cup display, fashioned out of plywood, showing figures from the Korean national team. A hole was cut through the front of the display, so that people could try to kick a soccer ball through it. Some kids were pounding a ball at the opening, and then some workmen came by to try their hand (or feet) at it. Finally, I no longer could resist the temptation. I got out in the dusty heat, and tried to blast a few balls through. Though it took me a few tries, I ended up doing better than I had done at the Korean village with the "arrow toss." Whenever I threaded one through the opening, the of the remaining kids cheered loudly. So I made exaggerated bows to show my appreciation for my adoring public.

From the museum, we traveled by city bus to the Bulguksa Temple. It was lay even farther into the endless expanse of symmetrical green rows of rice paddies than the museum.

Something of an oasis on the hillside, the Temple offered relief from the heat in the form of a lush, tree-lined path that rose and fell over the hills that inclined upward toward the main entrance. It was bit of a hike, past vendors selling soft drinks, as well as dried creatures from the deep that we were afraid to ask about. We were very warm by the time we reached the temple itself.

Inside the temple grounds were even more lush, filled with trees, ponds, and ornate buildings dating from the Silla Empire. A sign at the entrance announced that UNESCO has designated this temple as one of the most important cultural sites in the world. It's probably hard for Americans--I know it is, for this one--to think in terms of thousands of years, or to conceptualize what it was when tribes first started banding into kingdoms and empires, but it was relatively easy for anyone who entered the temple grounds to grasp that the Silla Empire was a pretty big deal on the Korean peninsula. These buildings helped transport us back in time, and make us realize just how sophisticated life was one hell of a long time ago, in a corner of the globe we know precious little about.

Once again, we were subjected to passing groups of schoolchildren, though these were a little older, perhaps of high-school age. They were all determined to wave and say, "Hi," and again they recoiled with shock and delight when I responded in Korean.

This set of temples dwarfed the palace we had visited in Seoul, and was much prettier. It had an odd, contemplative quality that stopped visitors in their tracks. Groups of tourists found themselves immobile, staring at the outcroppings of trees and rocks and water and buildings. It took a conscious effort to move on from building to building.

We took a different bus back to town, and this one was much more "down home," more rickety, and definitely shabbier. Instead of the Western and Korean tourists who had ridden on the express bus from the museum, armed with cameras and water-bottle-filled backpacks, this bus was entirely filled with Korean locals, many of them older. They all regarded us with curiosity, and most of them looked like they'd probably just knocked off work on the farm to head into town for shopping, or heaven-knows-what. This bus took a much more circuitous route, zigzagging through the rice paddies, and stopping every few hundred yards to pick up a guy carrying a large potted plant, or a woman with a bushel basket of cabbages.

This was where I wished I really could have spoken Korean. None of these folks spoke English, and I'm sure they would have been very interesting to talk to. The lined faces of the elderly passengers, and their diminutive, stooped frames spoke volumes about lives of hard labor and difficult times, which I couldn't approach with words. The visual tableau, however, will stick with me.

These rural Koreans had that weathered, tanned look shared by farmers across the globe. Their clothing was much more rugged and pragmatic than stylish. Unlike the schoolkids, these adults paid minimal attention to us. They each gave us a brief once-over as we plunked into our seats, but soon resumed their calm assessment of the passing scenery as we rode. The woman across from me was particularly interesting. She could have been in her seventies, dressed like a Russian peasant in baggy layers of well-weathered, but clean, clothing. A white scarf hid her hair, framing her lined face and calm eyes with reflected afternoon sun. She made eye contact, smiled, and then her gaze politely swerved out the window, to observe the passing rice paddies, which I suspect she'd observed thousands of times before. The sun was reaching a low, afternoon angle, and the green of the countryside glowed with a particular magic-hour luminosity.

The city bus took us to the intercity bus, which returned us in front of the university in Daegu in the late afternoon. The primary advantage offered by institutions of higher learning, of course, is the proliferation of coffee houses around universities. We found one with a cappuccino machine. The place was a western-style, air-conditioned, glass-walled coffee shop, filled with young people who were spending a ridiculous amount of money to sit over a coffee and pastry while staring into the eyes of their significant other, or to chatter away with a group of friends. The dress code ranged from U.S.-logo T-shirts to coats and ties.

The contrast between this café and the bus we took from Bulguksa to Gyeonju could not have been sharper.

After sufficient recaffeination, we returned to our adoptive home.

The Chungs' apartment was a very welcome sight after all day on the road, and they were eager to hear how our trip had been. Over dinner, I described the school kids at the museum. Soohee was embarrassed at their behavior, especially by the students who wanted to touch the hair on my arms.

"I'm sure I'm a very odd beast to them," I said. "I understand entirely. There was nothing malicious about it, they showed legitimate curiosity and wonderment."

Soohee talked about her own experiences growing up in both cultures. She wanted her daughter, Minji, to grow up exposed to a little bit of everything, as Soohee had been herself. As a native of Seoul, she said that her participation in the homestay program was partially motivated by the relative lack of exposure to Westerners in Daegu.

She confided that she and her husband were a bit off the Korean norm. Since they both had wanted to have professions, they postponed having children, despite enormous pressure from friends and families to start their family earlier. However, due to their years of doctoral studies, after which they established themselves in their professions, they had felt the need to wait. Fortunately, they employed a nanny whom they both trusted implicitly, and who adored Minji. Things seemed to have worked out very well for this gracious couple.

Soohee took us downtown, and we discovered that Daegu, though a smaller city than Seoul, had a vibrant, modern downtown. We wandered around the shops, and the street vendors' stands. Everything was available, from the slightest World Cup trinket to designer clothing of every imaginable brand and design. We stopped for a snack in a restaurant, and Hannia and Minji had a wonderful time playing with a little girl in the next booth.

As they took us to the train station the next day, we lamented that we couldn't have spent more time with the Chungs. They were such nice, intelligent, engaging people, I told them that I hoped they'd come to visit us in the States. Minji never quite warmed up to me, but I'll bet that in time she'd shed her fear of red-haired foreign devils. At least, she and Hannia had hit it off famously, and Minji smiled and waved at Hannia as we packed the bags out the front door, pausing cautiously when I caught her gaze and waved.

The train ride back to Suwon gave us a chance to rest up and think about the Costa Rica vs. Brazil match the following day. Whenever your team plays Brazil, it is a mixed blessing. You're testing yourself against the best team in the world, you get to see the brightest stars, but you also may well get pummeled. There's really no shame in getting pummeled by Brazil: It has happened to the best of them, but it can also be no fun whatsoever.

As I watched the rice paddies flash by out the train window, my cell phone rang. I answered and heard the voice of the young woman from the traditional Korean village in Suwon who had so politely asked us to visit her town.

"Who is that?" Hannia asked. She could tell by my expression who it was. I covered the receiver.

"It's the girl from the village in Suwon," I whispered. Then I uncovered the phone and dove in.

"Hi, it's kind of hard to hear in the train. How are you?"

"I am fine. Are you going to come visit?"

Hannia glared at me as I formulated my response.

"You know, my wife and I are very busy, and it turns out we have to travel to Jeonju sooner than we thought. So, no, I don't think we'll be able to visit your town."

There was a long pause. "You not come visit?"

"No, I don't think WE can."

"Can we be friends? I write to you."

"Sure," I replied. Hannia's gaze sharpened.

"What is your address?"

I gave her the address, fully expecting Hannia to hit me over the head with some large, weighty object.

"Okay, I've got to go now, good-bye."

"Good-bye."

I clicked off the phone. Hannia stared at me.

"What was that about?" she demanded.

"I've got a new pen pal," I said.

"What?"

"She said she was going to write to me."

"She'd better not."

"I'm sure she's totally harmless," I said peremptorily, not believing it for a moment. Hannia watched me very closely for a very long time as the train sped its way back to Suwon.

When we got back to the Kum apartment, Gyosu was very happy that the U.S. and Korea had tied. It made life--and foreign relations--much simpler. He told us that he wanted to take us to the Hwaseong Fortress the next day before the game.

Playing the home team in Daegu.

The hometown fans converge. *Dae Han Min Guk.*

Imagine a sea of red shirts. They are the Reds. We are outnumbered.

L: Hannia in front of the Cheomseongdae observatory.
R: Bulguksa temple, Gyeonju.

Mark with his fans in front of Gyeonju National Museum.

JUNE 13ᵀᴴ – GAME DAY #4

Hwaseong Fortress is the central fixture of Suwon. It is an old walled city, but not as old as some Korean landmarks. The fortress was built between 1776 and 1800, though the style could easily be mistaken for the same time period as the Bulguksa Temple, or the Palace in Seoul.

We set out early, finding a lot of festivities going on at the fortress. There was a soccer game for children, at which they could shoot a ball at a moving target and win a prize. I'm sure that this must be a newly devised activity in this baseball culture. There was also another of the ubiquitous "dress up in traditional clothing" stands, and Mija again insisted that I get dressed up. Though the activity was less of a surprise to us than at the Korean folk village, I'm sure Mija would have continued to insist that I participate as many times as I had the opportunity.

We walked the length of the fortress walls, which the brochures say are 5.7 kilometers long. It's kind of a miniature Wall of China. The wall enclosed quite a bit of real estate, and you could see where in the days of cannon and muskets, it would have provided some much needed security in this country, so frequently beset by foreign invaders.

A very large balloon in the shape of a soccer ball, banner trailing, caught my attention (see photo). The banner read "TOILET." I had to investigate. I'd read online about the campaign to create beautiful Western-style public bathrooms for the World Cup, and so I just had to see for myself. When I pointed this out to Hannia, she assured me that I was lunatic of the highest order But, then, we all need reassurance from time to time.

The bathroom was, in fact, quite modern and beautiful. But don't take my word for it. The back of the Suwon guide map boasts the following proclamation:

"Suwon to the world! For the future!

"Suwon is leading the toilet culture" (which sounds like some sort of petri dish experiment)

Inside the map, readers will find a paean to Suwon's toilet culture. Excuse me while I quote at length:

"Suwon's Beautiful Toilet

"In Suwon's beautiful toilet many modern features have been included, such as beautiful landscapes decorating the walls, reading desks supplied with newspapers and magazines, lighting gives a soft but bright atmosphere, music that makes one feel comfortable and easy, and air purifiers freshen the air.

"The above is the result of our 'Campaign to Beautify our Toilet' which has been functioning since 1997 with the purpose of making Suwon the city with the most beautiful toilet. Within the toilet facilities you will find bidets, disposable toilet seat covers, etiquette bells, automatic sensors to detect when something is in use, baby seat and booth, ladies' rooms for freshening up, etc., as well as other amenities. Comfortable facilities and updated sanitary equipment have been installed.

"… In addition, at one time every month there is a contest to choose the best toilet shop and badges are put in the toilet of the shop that wins."

Following are photos of sixteen toilet facilities, with descriptions and awards. I'll quote from the Banditbuli Toilet,

"The name was chosen because of the numerous fireflies that inhabit the unspoiled Gwangyo Mountain. The theme for this toilet complex is the harmonious union of nature and mankind. Won the Grand Prize at the first beautiful toilet inspection."

Now aside from the natural attraction of toilet humor, and customary "slightly warped" English phraseology, which provide no end of mirth and merriment, these quotes reveal much about modern Korea.

Koreans perceived--and rightly so—that the style and condition of sanitary facilities presents one of the major reservations that Western tourists had about visiting their country. When I told a co-worker I was going to Korea, she related her son's experience on a business assignment in Korea, where his toilet consisted of "a hole in the floor and a hose." Any Westerner that has dealt with an Asian-style "squat toilet" knows the meaning of frustration and discomfort. However, these traditional facilities were said to have given the Japanese wrestling team an edge in the 1988 Seoul Olympics. Some observers felt that the customary squatting strengthened the Japanese team's thigh muscles beyond those of mere Westerners.

The Koreans launched a widespread campaign to improve both the perception and the reality of Korean sanitary facilities. While both the effort and its verbiage are admittedly over the top, a campaign like this illustrates the determination and communal spirit the Koreans can summon up. It makes one wonder how long it will take Korea to become the dominant force in Asia. Today the toilets, tomorrow the world!

COSTA RICA VS. BRAZIL

Our favorite #2 bus took us to our favorite stadium, Suwon, to see my second-favorite team play what is perhaps the world's favorite team.

Gyosu and family tagged along, just to see the festivities. There were plenty of Brazilian supporters swarming the stadium, and the Samba beat fused with Korean drums to create the sort of outrageous cacophony available only at the World Cup, or in a multicultural lunatic asylum.

The *Ticos* just needed a tie to advance, but against Brazil in the World Cup, this was a tall order. By virtue of wins against Turkey and China, Brazil had already advanced to the second round, but anyone who knows anything about soccer will tell you that no one is ever complacent about World Cup games. The Brazilians, who had struggled mightily in qualifying, and who were therefore the object of scorn and hostility from their domestic press and fans, wanted to light up the nets to erase all doubts about their abilities. They fielded a squad including many bench players, but a very strong squad, nonetheless. Additionally, Ronaldo and Rivaldo were starting, and they were very much in contention to lead the tournament in goal scoring. They had to relish the opportunity to beat up on tiny Costa Rica and pad their statistics. They both trailed Bode, of Germany, who had gained the lead spot in Germany's lopsided thrashing of Saudi Arabia.

Costa Rica had a very good team, but Brazil was and is on another level. Remember that Brazil's population is about 200 million, whereas Costa Rica's is around four million: A talent pool versus a talent puddle.

Hannia was trembling with anticipation. She was scared that her team would be embarrassed by Brazil. I assured her that she could relax, nobody could hold it against the *Ticos* if they lost to the biggest power in the game.

I have fond memories of the U.S. national team beating Brazil 1-0 at the LA Coliseum in 1998, but I had my doubts about a repeat of those heroics. Alex Guimaraes, the Costa Rican coach (ironically, he's a naturalized Brazilian), had proclaimed that his team would not sit back and "pack the box" (i.e., play defensively, seeking a 0-0 tie). He insisted that his team would play attractive, attacking soccer to the end.

They didn't disappoint. They held the Brazilians admirably for a while, created many opportunities of their own, and showed their flair. But the *Cariocas* were too much for them. Ronaldo hit the net twice, and the final score was 5-2. Sticking two goals in against Brazil was no mean feat though, and, while the *Ticos* went out in the first round, they could hold their heads high. One big positive was a young defender named Gilberto Martinez. I had watched him carefully through qualifying-- remember that the U.S. is in the same confederation as Costa Rica--and I felt he might be the best defender in the region. In this game he had to go head to head with Ronaldo and Rivaldo, and guess what? He stopped them cold, nearly every time. His contract supposedly had been picked up by a team in the Italian league (Brescia), and I fully expected this kid to have a great career in Europe. I really think that if another star defender and captain, Reynaldo Parks, hadn't been injured and replaced by Mauricio Wright, who's very good, but not stellar, the *Ticos* might have at least stanched the bleeding.

The Costa Ricans celebrated after the game with no hint of rancor or disappointment. They were very happy to be in the Big Show. They probably should have beaten Turkey, in which case they'd have qualified for the second round, but they'd had a good run. The *Ticos* love to celebrate and were dancing and drinking and chanting seemingly forever.

Hannia was sad at her native country's departure from the tournament, but had the consolation that her adoptive country was still in it, and still in it in a big way.

A NIGHT OUT

Gyosu and Mija decided to take us out. They suggested a karaoke bar. Hannia winced. She doesn't like to sing... at least not out loud, and in front of adults. I'm not much of a singer myself, but I thought it might just prove to be a hoot.

In the evening, Un Ho and Jiwon went into action. They were unusually animated as they put away their homework and scrambled into Jiwon's room to get dressed. Jiwon allowed her mother to fuss and fiddle with her hair and clothing almost without complaint. The kids obviously lived for this stuff.

The six of us left en masse, a squad of revelers, raucously careening down the stairs to let loose our high spirits on the unsuspecting city of Suwon. Gyosu guided us across through the calm residential streets, through the evening flocks of suburbanites, past the tranquil shops and sidewalk cafés. On the way, Un Ho and Jiwon waved and called out to friends they passed. They were out for fun and wanted everyone to know it. We paraded over the pedestrian bridge to the other side of the ten-lane main drag, and into the entrance to one of the large buildings on the west side of the street.

I hadn't paid much attention to the buildings, at least above ground level. We'd searched for coffee, food items, and postage among the street-level establishments, but had ignored what to L.A. sensibilities seemed like office buildings above. We squeezed into an elevator and spilled out onto the fifth floor into a restaurant and karaoke bar. As we entered, I saw that down the hall were other restaurants, shops, and video game parlors. Unlike many establishments in Los Angeles in which average people can inflict their below-average vocal talents on large groups of innocent bystanders, this was a more intimate affair. Each group of four to twelve people got their own room and could sing in relative anonymity. The old saying, "You only hurt the ones you love," seemed quite appropriate.

Our family singing chamber was wood-paneled, with a varnished wood table in front of a karaoke machine with a large video monitor. Gyosu ordered a couple of beers for us--perfomance lubricant--and the wives and kids got soft drinks. Soon the drinks appeared, with some french fries as appetizers.

The kids leapt into the bench seats and wrestled each other for the song menu. Before Hannia and I knew what was going on, they had the karaoke machine spitting out tunes with subtitles. Un Ho had first honors, and he launched into a spirited rendition of some Korean pop tune whose title I know not.

Un Ho, usually so reserved and thoughtful, astounded me with his exuberance and stylishness. As he finished the first chorus, and launched into the middle sixteen, the subtitles switched from Korean characters to English words in Roman script. Un Ho literally didn't miss a beat, and cranked out the English-language portion of the ditty with verve and panache. His accent in English was interestingly American--just like so many of the British when they sing. He was rocking and rolling and gesturing and acting, just like the performers in music videos. Jiwon was also swaying in time to the music, her usual put-upon nine-year-old demeanor magically gone.

Jiwon got her turn, and to a hip-hop beat she launched into a rap song in English and Korean. Then, in the middle of it, I noticed Chinese characters pop up on the screen. Not missing a beat, Jiwon rapped the rap in whatever language it was in... Chinese, I assume. Then the song switched back to Korean, and she followed suit.

Gyosu took the microphone and launched into a wonderful version of "My Way" that at once inspired and amused me. His Korean accent somehow improved on the campy Sinatra-esque proclamation of self-assertion. He built the song nicely to a crescendo of emotion and sound, always with a little smile that fell somewhere between sincerity and irony. Though his voice was not professional, his demeanor throughout was oddly self-assured--not what you would expect from a Samsung engineer with thick glasses and a pocket protector.

Mija sang a poignant ballad in Korean, though in a very Western idiom. She likewise showed self-confidence far beyond that which I've seen generally displayed in the states at karaoke gatherings. It seems that karaoke was a frequent entertainment for this family.

Hannia passed, despite much good-natured urging from her hosts. Jiwon especially wanted Hannia to sing and have a good time, and was a bit disappointed that she refused so adamantly. Hannia clung to my side to as if to hide behind me.

Then, of course, all eyes turned toward me. I had been rifling through the songbook, frantically searching out something easy. I'm always a little surprised by how many pop tunes I don't recognize, or at least don't remember well enough to be able to replicate in their entirety. I always can remember the hook line, but get a little lost around the middle sixteen bars. I picked the Beatles' "Yesterday," partly because I've played it on the piano for many years. I wouldn't be thrown for a loop by some strange chord change or coda I didn't remember. I launched into the melancholy tune with as much feeling and enthusiasm as I could muster, but, as frequently happens, it was in a key that didn't suit my voice. (Of course, the key that truly suits my voice may not exist in this or any other universe.) I believe that most karaoke machines can transpose songs into different keys, but I wasn't about to stop and fiddle with my accompaniment. Most pop songs are sung in a higher register than I'm comfortable with, and as I reached the "why she had to go…" run up the scale, I could feel my throat seize up, my eyes water, and my voice crack. I limped through the rest of the tune and hit the approximation of a final note. I felt I'd done an abysmal job of it, but my hosts seemed very pleased. Everyone cheered and clapped that I had so expertly butchered this classic song. I knew deep down that somewhere on the planet Paul McCartney had been gritting his teeth and holding his breath for the past three minutes, and was now calling his lawyer.

I quite gladly handed the microphone back to Un Ho who leapt at the opportunity to dial in a new song.

Scratching and popping sounds spewed forth, and the strains of a popular rap song filled the air. Un Ho started rapping and riffing in Korean. He was doing all the requisite rap moves, throwing signs and posturing like an aggressive gangster. Hannia and I looked at each other, wondering that we'd come thousands of miles, to the opposite side of the globe, to be serenaded by someone who might as well have been one of Compton's finest.

Then Jiwon joined in the chorus, and the two little, well-behaved, studious Korean kids were acting just like your average American suburban delinquent wanna-bees. I couldn't help but wonder what the Korean words for "bitch," "ho," and "motherf-----," were. I was sure I was hearing them, but when I looked over at Gyosu and Mija, they were smiling and clapping their hands in time to the music, like it was some sort of warped Andy Williams Family Christmas Special, featuring the Osmonds, Ludacris, and Chan Ho Park.

I raised my beer glass and drank a long, hearty draft.

June 14 - to Daejon, Game Day #5

We were off for yet another train ride, this time from Suwon to Daejon. We were getting the hang of getting around. Almost without thinking we grabbed the 2-1 bus to the terminal, then the very comfortable express train to Daejon.

Once in Daejon, the adventure began. I had made an online reservation at the Utopia Hotel, which is near the stadium, but that's about all I knew. The tourist information kiosk at the train station was very helpful. The clerk there called the hotel for me, and told me which bus to take and the landmarks involved. They don't speak English at the Utopia. We were told to get off at the Riviera Hotel (pronounced "Ree-pee-eh-ra Ho-te-ru"). The girl at the kiosk pointed out the general vicinity on a map, and we were off. We got on a crowded bus, and I asked, "Riviera Hotel?" The driver nodded affirmatively, but with the typical Korean reserve that made me wonder if he had really understood. The bus was crowded, so I had to stand. As on my first subway ride, when I stand I can't really see out the window, to look for landmarks or identifiable cross-streets. Hannia had a better view, but was less well-versed in Korean writing. We were forced to rely on the kindness of strangers.

It was a long ride, crossing a couple of rivers and many busy intersections until we came upon the district in which the hotel and the stadium were to be found. I squatted occasionally to peek out the window, and managed to spot signs that indicated, "Yuseong-gu," the district the hotel was in. Finally, the driver turned to me and said, "Ree-pee-eh-ra," so I knew we had to get off.

The girl at the tourist information kiosk had told us that the Yuseong Hotel was behind the Riviera, and the Utopia was behind that. We wandered up the street a bit, and found the Yuseong Hotel. On the front of the hotel was a banner that read," Welcome U.S. National Team." We felt at home. But the directions became problematic. There didn't seem to be an efficient way to get to the back of the hotel. It was ringed by other businesses, and there was no clear route or street to take. I stopped a young woman on the street, clad in the official FIFA helper's jacket we had seen at other venues. Her English was marginal, but probably good enough to get the job done. I managed to give her the name and number of the hotel, and she called them on her cell phone. She insisted on leading me to Utopia, the best offer I'd had in weeks, and one I felt that very few people could deliver on. We threaded our way through a parking lot behind the Yuseong, and onto a dirt and gravel road, which spilled into a large parking lot in the back. There we encountered a woman in her fifties, obviously the proprietress of the hotel, insanely happy to see us. "Utopia, Utopia" she chimed in enthusiastically. The FIFA woman made her exit, as I thanked her, and the Utopian woman lead us into her establishment, in which English is unknown. There was a brief mix-up about payment. I'm used to showing a credit card to identify myself, and to confirm what was promised on the Internet. When I gave her my credit card, however, she thought I wanted to pay that instant. Finally, she called the outfit that had handled the Internet bookings. They ironed things out in a jiffy, and we got a room key.

The hotel was smallish, seven floors high, with eight rooms to a floor. It was very Korean, and I'm sure few Westerners had been here. As we walked down the hallway to the room, I noticed red lights on the ceiling above me. I hoped that the cultural significance was different than in the U.S. I was right, thank God, but I was a little disturbed to see what look like escort-service ads on the matchbooks and Kleenex dispensers in the room. I had a feeling that it was fairly standard practice for traveling businessmen to avail themselves of those services while on the road, though that's pure speculation. The room was wonderfully clean, very nicely appointed with dark wood paneling, a large television, air conditioning, and a refrigerator. The bathroom was a hybrid of Korean and Western styles. Though the tub had a shower curtain, I don't think anyone had ever used it. The floor was recessed, tiled, with a drain, and there were no electrical outlets. Towels were hand-sized.

We showered, I donned my USA jersey, and we started the trek to the stadium. As we passed the Yuseong Hotel, we noticed a crowd gathering. Members of Sam's Army, decked out in every kind of red, white, and blue accessory imaginable--and some that defied imagination-- were filling up the parking lot, where a big bus with a FIFA placard idled. There was a contingent of twenty or thirty Korean police officers in formation to create a corral from the hotel exit to the parking lot.

The chants began, first to the tune of the '70s classic, "Funky Town":

"Oh won't you take me to... the second round..."

As the chants went on and on, I noticed people in the crowd looking up at a sixth-floor window, where I spotted a smiling Josh Wolff, as well as the dreadlocks of Pablo Mastroeni. Armed with a video camera, Mastroeni was taping the crowd. Clearly, Wolff was enjoying himself—typically, the U.S. players aren't used to being treated as celebrities.

Finally the bus, empty but for the driver, crept into position at the end of the chute of Korean police. Trainers, coaches, and players started to trickle out of the hotel and onto the bus. The crowd went bananas, chanting the names of each player as he appeared. The players were extremely amused by this. It was a little unusual, not entirely new, but the novelty hadn't worn off.

One woman in the crowd held up a placard with the message, "Happy Birthday, Cobi." Tony Meola, star goalkeeper from '94, spotted it, laughed, and turned to winger Cobi Jones, who was already on the bus. "Birthday?" he mimed. Cobi chuckled and nodded. Though I couldn't hear them, the players on the bus were obviously teasing him about being the birthday boy. Cobi raised a video camera and filmed the thoughtful fan and her placard. That woman, of course, was my wife.

Cobi's birthday is actually June 16, but this was as close as Hannia could get to a game day.

The bus pulled out, and the crowd gave its last hearty yells of, "USA! USA! USA!"

The throng of red, white, and lue fans started moving toward the main thoroughfare to the stadium, three or four kilometers away. We hopped on a city bus and followed the flow.

USA VS. POLAND

Daejon stadium was crawling with fans, as buses deposited load after load of spectators at the curb. The masses funneled into a pedestrian bridge, and streamed across the street to the beautiful new stadium.

The stadium was my second-favorite, after Suwon. It was also "soccer-specific" so we were really close to the action. Once again, we were seated in the end zone, directly behind the left goal post. We were right beside a big Sam's Army contingent, and the bulk of the Polish fans were to my right along the sideline. I noticed a big group of young Korean men to my immediate right, and found out a little later that they were from the Korean air force academy, which is based in Daejon.

This game was pivotal for the U.S. With a win and a tie under their belts, a win against Poland would clinch the first spot in the group, and a tie would clinch the second spot. Either way, the Yanks would go through to the second round. Korea was to play Portugal simultaneously, and everyone expected Portugal to prevail. Portugal looked back in form when they played Poland, beating them 4-0. The U.S. was now expected to beat Poland, which had lost two matches, and was already mathematically eliminated.

The U.S. team seemed very loose, both from what we'd seen by the team bus, and from their workout on the field prior to the game. They were smiling, joking, having a good time.

Then the game started. Two minutes in, Poland scored a goal. Whoops. The U.S. roared back with a goal by twenty-year-old phenomenon Landon Donovan, but wait, the ref nullified it, claiming Donovan pushed the defender. (I've watched the tape of this over and over, and I really think Donovan and the U.S. got boned here.) Then the Poles scored a second goal at minute 5. This is a nightmare. It suddenly felt like 1998 all over again. The win over Portugal would be regarded as a fluke, and the U.S. would trudge home, ignominiously eliminated once again.

To add insult to injury, the freakin' Koreans, comprising the majority of the spectators, were rooting for Poland. They thought that Portugal would beat them in the game going on simultaneously, and that their only hope of advancing was if Poland beat the U.S.

The Polish coach was quoted as saying that his team "would give our hosts, Korea, a big present in their last match." This had gotten the Korean public even more behind his squad.

Meanwhile, the Poles were giving us fits. They were now ahead, so they were playing in a defensive posture, dropping most of their men back behind the ball, but every time they mounted a counterattack, they looked extremely dangerous. Their forwards were big, fast, and skillful, and they ran marvelous diagonal patterns that allowed quick penetration and crossed-up defenders.

Jeff Agoos, a mainstay of our defense, got whacked in the calf, and went down. He got up after a bit, but was limping. A few minutes later, BANG, he got whacked again. This time, he was out for good.

The U.S. tried and tried to come back, but the Polish keeper, Radoslaw Majdan, made dazzling save after save to deny us. At minute 66, the Poles scored a third goal.

The Korean fans kept up their *Dae Han Min Guk* chant all the way through, squealing ecstatically when Poland scored. Then a funny thing happened. Many Korean fans were watching the Korea/Portugal game on little hand-held TVs. Suddenly, a cheer rippled through the crowd. A Portuguese player had been thrown out. Then another. More cheers. It was knotted at 0-0. Then Korea scored in minute 70. A huge cheer spread stadiumwide.

Suddenly, the Koreans were chanting, "USA! USA! USA!" Korea looked like it would beat Portugal and finish in first place in Group D. If they won, our game against Poland was meaningless. We'd have clinched second place.

It was an indescribably ugly way to qualify for the second round, but we'd take it. The U.S. had suffered so much bad luck in the past, it finally looked as though it might all come out in the wash. Sam's Army went ballistically happy. Then Landon Donovan scored his first goal of the tournament at minute 83.

The players came out after the game to wave to the rooting section, and we were all ecstatic to see them. The second round was our objective, and we'd made it. Then it suddenly dawned on everyone: We'd be playing Mexico. Our archrival, next-door-neighbor, CONCACAF brothers. Nothing would be sweeter than to beat them on the world's biggest stage.

The requisite dancing and chanting and carousing went on outside the stadium. You'd never have known we lost. The TV cameras caught the frenzied partying on videotape. A Univision cameraman stuck his lens in the face of a young guy, who seemed to be of Mexican descent.

"If the U.S. plays like it did tonight and Mexico plays like it did against Italy, Mexico will win," he said. And he had a point. Mexico had been on a roll. They'd shocked everyone by beating Croatia, who finished third in 1998, Ecuador, and by tying perennial contenders Italy in a game from which the *Azurri* were lucky to squeeze out one point.

The cameraman stuck his Univision logo in my face, and the reporter asked me, "Do you think the U.S. can beat Mexico in the second round?"

Without hesitation, I responded, in Spanish, "Sure. These two teams have been very even for the last two World Cups. In qualifying, we each came up with wins at home. Mexico's been playing very well, but the U.S. knows how to play them. Tonight's game was tough, but it was an anomaly. It's ironic that it will come down to the Battle of CONCACAF."

There were a lot of smirking Mexicans around me. They felt like their team had lucked out by getting an easy opponent.

On the bus back to town, perhaps twenty Poles in red costumes piled on, and sang nonstop. The highlight was a Polish rendition of "*Guantanamera*," the only word of which I understood was "*pivo*," which means "beer."

They danced up and down the central aisle of the bus, under the impassive gaze of the driver, who kept one eye riveted on them in his rear-view mirror. Their drunken joy was infectious, and the U.S. fans started to join in, certainly mangling the Polish language, but repeating the chorus with as much phonetic accuracy as possible.

JUNE 15 - THE SCRAMBLE FOR TRAINS

The next day, which we had intended to play tourist, instead was consumed with preparations for the second round. It took us a while to figure out that Jeonju was accessible from Daejon by train, but it turned out that the train left from a different station than the one at which we'd arrived. By the time I realized I could apply my ticket back to Suwon toward the trip, all the tickets had sold out. Luckily, I discovered that an intercity bus made a direct trip to Jeonju. We made our way to the intercity bus station, where they booked our tickets and helped us find accommodations.

When I first contemplated my trip, I had known that the U.S. could get into the second round, and that Jeonju was a possible venue. I had looked into accommodations on the Internet, and found the hotel where I felt I had to stay. The name alone made the sale. It was called, Dreams of Pigs Motel. I had jotted the phone number down diligently, but now that I tried calling, the phone number didn't work. I was powerfully disappointed, but had to press on. There would be no Dreams of Pigs, at least this time around.

The clerk at the tourist kiosk kindly found us a hotel near the train station in Jeonju, where we had a train trip booked back to Suwon.

Having gotten up a little late, and having spent the majority of the day making travel arrangements, we had no time left to see any of the sights, but we used the couple of hours we had left to explore Daejon. We found some cappuccino, changed money, shopped for clothes, and watched the end of the Germany vs. Paraguay match in a large appliance store, on one of their HDTV sets.

Our hosts in the appliance store kept a close eye on us as we sat on their couch. "Okay to watch?" I asked. It was a pretty slow afternoon. I wasn't in anyone's way, and there were only fifteen minutes or so left.

"Okay," replied an appliance salesman. I think he thought it would be entertaining to watch us watch the game. Thin and slightly stoop-shouldered, he had the universally harried look common to retail salesclerks. We at least provided a distraction in the middle of an otherwise boring day.

It was a tough, negatively played game, as expected. Paraguay, a small but scrappy nation, always manages to field fair-to-middlin' teams. But in recent years, they have risen above their station by virtue of their goalkeeper, José Luís Chilavert. A hulking linebacker of a guy, Chilavert is the Ty Cobb of Paraguayan soccer. He's tough as nails, maniacally aggressive, and arguably the best goalkeeper in the world, although fans of Oliver Kahn and Peter Schmeichel might differ. Aside from performing well between the pipes, Chilavert basically runs the team, screaming and yelling and directing traffic from the backfield. More impressively, he takes all their free kicks. He's a tremendous set-shot man, and has the bravura to abandon his own goal and come up field and take a free kick twenty-five yards from the opposing goal. He has scored more goals than any other goalkeeper in the history of the game.

Chilavert is also the undisputed South American bad boy. Recently, at the end of a World Cup qualifier against Brazil, mighty mite Roberto Carlos came over to Chilavert to exchange shirts and give him a pat on the back after a hard-fought contest. Chilavert, who'd apparently exchanged hard words with the Real Madrid wingback during the game, spat in Carlos' face. FIFA suspended Chilavert for the first match of the World Cup, but Paraguay managed to squeak into the second round anyway.

Paraguay's game against Germany was in some ways a replay of their game against France in '98. Against the Gallic squad, Paraguay held them scoreless for ninety minutes, hoping to force a penalty kick shoot-out, where most felt Paraguay had an advantage, with the intimidating Chilavert both shooting and goalkeeping. They lost on a golden goal in overtime, with a minute to go. Germany also had a tough time scoring off Chilavert, and it looked like he might put his team on top around the thirtieth minute, when his free kick, punched out by the other legendary goalkeeper, Oliver Kahn, landed in front of José Cardoso, whose cross found Celso Ayala alone in the box. Unfortunately, Ayala couldn't put the ball on target. Chilavert had another set piece at minute 72 that just missed--a foot too high.

In minute 88, that inevitable Teutonic lightning struck. The Germans put one away. Paraguay once again was narrowly defeated. Chilavert, already a bit over the hill in most people's minds, definitely won't be back in 2006. It was the end of an era. I snapped back to the immediate reality of the appliance store. The salesman was watching me intently. He smiled and nodded, in recognition of the end of the game, as if to ask whether I enjoyed it. I returned the nod and smile and thanked him in Korean. If I had really been able to speak Korean, I could have told him all about Chilavert and Paraguay, and the underdog story, which had reached its end, nobly, but without success. Unfortunately, all I could muster was, "*Chukku choayo,*" which basically means "good soccer." The salesman chuckled, and I'll bet he remembers this moment in the World's Biggest Party.

Once back in the hotel, I got a call from Un Ho, congratulating me on the U.S. ascension to the second round, and asking if we'd be returning to Suwon. I congratulated him on Korea's victory over Portugal, and told him of our arrangements to go to Jeonju. I could hear Mija prompting him in the background. They were doing their best to keep track of the wayward foreign devils.

We hit the sack early. The bus was scheduled to pull out at eight a.m.

Costa Rica vs. Brazil, Suwon.

Tico pride.

L: Hannia in front of her favorite bar.
R: Daejeon Stadium, Poland vs. USA.

Rallying the Elvises.

Pole position

Shellacked or Polished?

A backhanded celebration.

JUNE 17TH - LEAVING UTOPIA

As we left Utopia, the proprietress came out from behind her glass booth to wave goodbye and wish us luck.

We took a city bus to the intercity bus station, and hopped on the Jeonju Express. It was an hour and a half drive through hills and rice paddies, and a good chance to take a little nap. We both drifted in and out of consciousness as the green countryside flashed past.

In Jeonju, a clerk at the tourist information kiosk called the hotel where we'd be staying, and wrote down the address for me to hand to the cab driver.

The new hotel turned out to be very similar to the Utopia. It was close to the train station, which allowed for an easy escape. When I asked the attendant if he knew where the FIFA ticket office was, as we had to pick up our contingency tickets for the second round, he insisted on taking us there personally, though it was perhaps a mile away. I wasn't even sure he really understood what I'd asked, but I once again took a chance, and it paid off. The attendant took us to a nondescript office building, with no markings to indicate having anything to do with FIFA. We'd never have found it. On the second floor, we entered the ticket office, and the FIFA official produced the tickets for me without delay.

Once we left the ticket office, the hotel attendant showed us where we could catch a bus downtown to see a few sights. The bus let us off at the Gaeksa, which is a traditional Korean building at the center of what was once a castle. It originally had been used for ceremonies in which to pledge one's loyalty to the king—and what wacky, zany, fun-filled occasions those must have been!—and to house royal messengers and visiting governors. To the untrained eye (i.e., mine) it looks very similar to the palace in Seoul and the temple in Bulguksa, though it was built in 1471. The brightly painted woodwork under the eaves and the ornate tile roof makes the Gaeska the perfect counterpoint to the modern, boutique-filled shopping streets that surround it.

In our ongoing quest for decent coffee, we found a couple of cappuccino emporiums, as well as AHOP, or the American House of Pancakes. It turned out to be neither very American, nor much of a house of pancakes. It did highlight pancakes on the menu (I was given a menu labeled, "RUNCH"), but mostly served such familiar bar fare as Buffalo wings and Mexican food. The meal was actually pretty good, though very different from what a California boy expects.

Hannia had long since reached her limit when it came to traditional Korean food. We ate lunch at restaurant touted as a Texas barbecue, a place with wonderfully western décor, road signs from Route 66 and Texas towns, a rustic wood-paneled interior, and really, really lousy food. Not just really lousy food, but really expensive, lousy food. I was served something resembling a pork cutlet, surrounded by unrecognizable ersatz Texan side dishes. I guess since they'd spent all their money on eBay buying the furnishings, they couldn't afford a chef. We got what we deserved for seeking out authentic "Western" food in a provincial capitol, or probably anywhere in Korea, but at that point Hannia could take no more *kimchi*.

We walked south from the shopping area in search of some of the gravely named "district of culture and tradition" that we'd read about. As usual, when we stopped to ask directions, we were immediately adopted by a group of Koreans, in this case college-aged girls, who insisted on accompanying us to a cultural festival going on in the historic district. They walked us to the South Gate (or *Pongnammun*) of the formerly walled city, where a traditional musical group was warming up for a concert later in the evening.

They then took us farther south to a street fair, where all sorts of vendors had stands set up, selling traditional food, clothing, knickknacks, whosits, and whatnots. I wound my way through the street fair until I found the calligraphic art gallery, as well as a exhibition of traditional crafts. It was all the more interesting for the hustle and bustle of the street fair, which included a Korean punk rock group in full sonic attack mode. Jeonju is a happening town.

JUNE 17 - GAME DAY #6

In the morning, we went to the train station to figure out the shuttle-bus situation. It was impossible not to notice the flow of green jerseys coming out of the station. Mexican fans were arriving. They eyed my USA cap warily.

The game started a three-thirty, so an early lunch was in order. We went to one of the traditional Korean restaurants near the hotel, and ordered *Bibimbap*, which sounds like a *Ranchera* song by Selena, but is, in reality, the best-known local dish. It consists of a bowl of rice with thinly chopped vegetables mixed in, spicy sauce, and a raw egg on top.

It was very tasty. The "spicy sauce" was very, very spicy indeed, but it was one of the best meals I had in Korea. Very simple, yet tasty, and filling. Hannia, her cravings for American food held in check by the Texas barbecue's poor showing, braved the restaurant, and came away pleased, if not enamored.

We got to the station early, but found that the line for the shuttle bus was enormously long. Some U.S. supporters and I got together and decided to get a cab. As we were about to head to the taxi stand, we were approached by a Korean kid in his early twenties who managed to pronounce, "Ride to stadium? 10,000 *won*." This was roughly eight dollars, and divided four ways, it seemed preferable to standing in the hot sun for an hour or two, and possibly missing the opening minutes of the game.

We piled into his white Hyundai, and sped toward the stadium. The other guys were from Chicago and Seattle. The Chicago guy (wrapped in the city's flag) told me that they hoped Wolff and Beasely (from the Chicago Fire) would play. We commiserated about Chris Armas, Chicago's phenomenal defensive midfielder. Armas had been a major factor in getting the National Team through qualification, then, after they'd won the prize, in a meaningless friendly game against Uruguay, the last tune-up match before shipping out to the big show, his knee buckled and he went down on the turf, howling. He had torn his meniscus, an injury that would require major surgery followed by months and months of rehabilitation. Armas was pushing thirty, so this might well have been his last shot at playing in the World Cup. Major bummer.

Our driver zigged and zagged through the mounting traffic with a South Korean bravura usually reserved for fighting Northerners. He flipped on his radio, and found a pop station blaring a Korean cover of a Macy Gray song, not just sung in Korean, but sung with a voice that sounded EXACTLY like the distinctive cat-like yowl that Ms. Gray is known for. Luckily, it wasn't "The Star-Spangled Banner."

The Jeonju Stadium is north of town. If the builders had hoped to reduce the traffic snarl, in this case, it didn't. People were swarming into the stadium on every conceivable mode of transport and from every direction. Traffic cops directed us away from the bus entrance, and we landed hastily at the side of the busy thoroughfare. We popped out of the car and were engulfed in a pulsing mass of red, white, and blue, and Mexican green, and Korean red jerseys, and flags, and banners, and hats, and T-shirts, and every conceivable type of clothing. All roads led to the stadium, a gem of a "soccer-specific" facility.

MEXICO VS. USA

We pushed our way through security. They checked every bag, pouch, purse, camera, bulge, or backpack before we were allowed inside. Our seats were in the second level of the south endzone, and a large contingency of Sam's Army was to our right. Suddenly, they sprang to their feet and started out the exit en masse, someone shouting, "There's a bunch of space on the first level!" We followed.

Sam's Army filled the lower right corner of the end zone seats, next to a heavy contingency of Mexican jerseys to our left.

I surveyed the stadium. While there was a healthy concentration of Mexican fans, we had them slightly outnumbered. The enthusiasm and organization of Sam's Army far outstripped the "*si, se puede*" factions that peppered the audience. This was pure culture shock.

I've seen Mexico play the U.S. and other teams at the Los Angeles Coliseum, Pasadena's Rose Bowl, and the Oakland Coliseum. Virtually anywhere in the Southwest, U.S. fans are vastly outnumbered by their Mexican counterparts. And the rivalry is bitter.

I watched a friendly in the Coliseum in 2001. There were perhaps 60,000 Mexican fans, and about 2,000 gringos. And the Mexican fans were not shy about showing their hostility. At one point, when the U.S. scored, I instinctively jumped up and cheered. The friends I was with--veterans of Coliseum games--both clamped their hands on my shoulders and forced me back into my seat, saying, "Shut up and sit down." No sooner did my derriere touch the seat than a beer came flying through the space my head had just occupied, and struck a woman in front of me. And ironically, the woman was Mexican, out for a fun evening with her three elementary-school-age children. So much for wholesome family entertainment. Josh Wolff, the goal-scorer, purposely raised his arms victoriously to the hostile crowd, then stepped back and dodged the shower of cups and bottles and hot dogs and trash.

The Gold Cup final between the U.S. and Mexico at the Coliseum in 1998 was a legendary security nightmare. Anyone and everyone on the U.S. side, including the players ("Take an umbrella with you for that corner kick") were doused with every liquid known to humankind. It was disgusting.

Here, however, we were strong in number, and the crowd was a little different than the mob the Coliseum attracts. As the game began, the U.S. chants were drowning out the Mexicans. The Koreans, who probably comprised the majority of the crowd, sat in polite silence, except when the occasional *"Dae han min guk"* chant got going.

The Mexican team was on a roll, and they played well, pressuring from the beginning. The U.S. strategy became apparent immediately. They didn't really even try to keep possession of the ball, they just tried to interrupt whatever attack the Mexicans mounted. The Mexicans would move the ball up field with a few nifty, short passes, make a nice move and then, BOINK, some U.S. defender would poke the ball away, without much concern for getting it to a U.S. player. This happened over and over, and the Mexicans plainly became frustrated. The U.S. was out-hustling them, outwitting them strategically, and nettling their every move.

In minute eight, the U.S. countered. Claudio Reyna made a great run, crossed the ball to Josh Wolff, who made a beautiful back pass to an uncovered Brian McBride, who deftly shot it past the keeper.

Sam's Army exploded in cheers. The Mexican contingent got really quiet. To my left, however, was one obnoxious guy among the green jerseys who was constantly screaming insults at the U.S. team, and cheering for Mexico. He was cheering in English, so I wondered if it wasn't some resentful Canadian.

At around minute 27, Mexico subbed in Luís Hernandez, one of the leading all-time Mexican scorers. Hernandez played a couple of years for the L.A. Galaxy, and proved that MLS defense is a bit better than what he was used to. He had played adequately, but never performed well enough to merit his exorbitant salary, hype, and hubris. As he ran onto the field, he was met with the Sam's Army chant of, "MLS reject, MLS reject..."

The Mexican team redoubled their efforts, but the U.S. defended tenaciously, especially goalkeeper Brad Friedel, who made some spectacular saves.

The first half ended with the 1-0 score intact. I talked to one of the Elvises that were there supporting the team. Two of them were from the original group, but the third and fourth were new. Two Elvises had to go home after the first round, but they had left their "uniforms" behind for replacement Elvises to use. I felt thankful that we had not one, but four Kings on our side.

The second half was more of the same. Spirited attacks met with dogged defense. Then in minute 65, Eddie Lewis made a wonderful cross to Landon Donovan, who coolly headed the ball home. We were up by two with twenty-five minutes to go.

It was shortly after this that the Mexicans, just off their monumental game against Italy, lost their cool. They got thoroughly frustrated and started fouling the living crap out of the U.S. team. Not just little ticky-tack fouls, but really nasty, potentially dangerous fouls. Cobi Jones was the recipient of the worst of these. Any time he had the ball, he was pounced on by a couple of Mexican players, who made sure to dig their cleats into his Achilles tendon, or knocked him down and kicked him. This culminated in an egregious foul in minute 88 by defender Rafa Marquez.

Cobi went up for a header, and well after Cobi knocked the ball away, Marquez went full-force into the diminutive winger, head-butting him on the side of his noggin. Jones went down hard, clutching the upper portion of his jaw. I've seen Cobi play a lot, both for the Galaxy and for the Nats. I can say with some authority that he's not one for theatrics, and usually springs to his feet after being hacked. This time, however, he stayed on the ground for quite some time, hurt badly. Hannia sprang to her feet, outraged. You won't find a bigger Cobi fan than her, and this dangerous, malicious foul was too much. Marquez was instantly ejected.

When the final whistle blew, the Mexican team left the field immediately, not waiting to shake hands or exchange jerseys. They were what's known in my neck of the woods as "sore losers."

The U.S. team and fans were ecstatic. We had beaten a bitter rival on the biggest stage in the world, giving us bragging rights in perpetuity.

The U.S. fans streamed out of the stadium chanting, cheering, singing, taking pictures of one another, waving flags, and generally reveling in the victory. There was a giant fountain in front of the stadium, and one red, white, and blue-clad enthusiast dove in headfirst. One Korean police officer looked absolutely aghast, as if it were an act of true moral repugnance. He made a beeline for the diver and extracted him immediately, berating him the entire time in Korean, and shaking his baton at him more indignantly than threateningly.

After drinking in the exuberance of the crowd, we sought out the line for the shuttle bus. We discovered that the line was literally a mile long. A couple of other fans and I moseyed down the street looking for taxis, but they were all occupied, responding to telephone requests. We decided to walk further afield, and traipsed past a gas station to what looked like a public bus stop. We hopped onto a bus that was headed in the general direction we wanted, figuring that if it didn't take us to the center of town, or somewhere else we recognized, we'd be able to grab a cab in town to take us where we wanted to go.

After a while on the bus, I unfolded my map and tried to figure out where we were, and where we were headed. I asked a gentleman next to me, "*Yogiga odiyeyo?*" ("Where are we?") He looked quizzically at the map for a moment, and then asked in tentative English, "Where you going?"

"Gaeksa," I replied, knowing that it's on the edge of the shopping area we'd been in before, and knowing there are a few restaurants in the area, and knowing how to get back to the hotel from there.

The man took the map and studied it long and hard. "Where does this bus go?" I asked. The man either couldn't articulate an answer, or couldn't figure it out on the map to show me. "You go with me," he responded at long last. I figured his stop must be a transfer point. When he hopped off, we hopped off with him. He hailed a cab. I noticed that a friend had hopped off the bus with him. I wondered if we were being set up. Hannia and I piled into the cab, then so did my new Korean friends. I was getting a little nervous. I looked over the friend of my new friend. He was maybe forty-five, hadn't shaved in a couple of days, and sported an earring. Very strange for a Korean man his age. Hannia and I exchanged nervous looks. It was getting dark. The cab lost itself in side streets and odd short cuts. I trying to remind myself that I was twice as big as these guys, but these assurances were intruded upon by memories of my old *Tae Kwon Do* professor, a Korean gentleman who was all of five-foot-two, but could kick my ass all day. Just as I was about to get really panicky, I heard my Korean friend say "Gaeksa" to the driver. We spun out of a narrow road onto a main street, and there was Gaeksa house. Hannia and I both exhaled a deep sigh of relief. I thrust my hands into my pockets as I looked at the meter. My Korean friend said, "No, no, no, I pay." He tried to extract a few bills of his own, but I stopped him. "No, thank you," I responded, "I'll pay. You were kind enough to help me out." I felt a little odd that I'd suspected him of something fishy, and also guilty that I'd taken him out of his way. I could have easily jumped in a cab and said, "Gaeksa," myself.

We ate again at AHOP, to get a good cappuccino, but I also ordered a traditionally prepared pork cutlet. I noticed a group of green-jerseyed Mexican fans dining in the back of the restaurant, and asked them, in Spanish, as I left, "How're the enchiladas?" They laughed, and replied that while the food was good, it bore no resemblance whatsoever to Mexican food.

So, in essence, our trip was over. Here we were in Jeonju, glowing in the aftermath of what is perhaps the greatest run U.S. soccer has ever had, drinking in the sights, sounds, and, yes, drinks of an exotic foreign land. We were invited to the biggest party in the world, and partied until dawn in full regalia.

The streets of Jeonju.   Squid anyone?

Jeonju Stadium, Mexico vs. USA

A patriotic gal.

L: I can't go anywhere without being hounded by the Paparazzi.
R: Dual banners.

Our Korean Brothers.

Hannia hoists the Cup again.

JUNE 18ᵀᴴ - ALL ROADS LEAD TO SUWON

The train ride back to Suwon was a tranquil affair, which gave me ample time to reflect and relax. We wished we could stay for the quarterfinal match against Germany, but our allotted time was up, and I had to say I had no regrets. Even the nightmarish match against Poland had served a vital function as a dramatic device, providing a requisite dark and scary moment to contrast with the headiness of victory. Beating Germany would be sweet--but a tall order. Whatever happened in the quarterfinal match, I knew that we'd already acquitted ourselves nicely. I could rest assured that we'd play well against Germany.

In Suwon, the Kum family greeted us with enthusiasm. Both our teams were doing well, and their big contest against Italy was approaching.

They took us to a public square to see the game, among thousands of Koreans, who had spread blankets across the cement surface to picnic. An enormous big-screen TV had been installed in the square, for communal viewing. We arrived late, and Mija pushed her way into the middle of the crowd, trying to carve out a space for us in ground already staked out. I felt uncomfortable claim-jumping, as well as blocking the view of spectators behind me. The screen had been set up a bit too low, and a tall fellow like me was going to prevent people from seeing.

I popped up and informed Mija that I'd stand in the back and watch over the heads of others. She protested, but I was off. Hannia followed.

Standing in the back of the group, I realized something interesting. Certainly I'm much taller than the average Korean. Even back home, people complain when I sit in front of them in a movie theater. I noticed, however, that many of the younger Koreans were pretty darned tall. Here in this public square, the fact was starkly graphic. In front of me were rows of teenagers and twentysomethings. They were blocking my view. The guys were all six-footers, mostly big, burly guys. Certainly, there was some natural selection going on, with tall young guys standing in the back to help the rest of the people see. But these tall young folks weren't just a few oddballs, this was the next generation. The Koreans refer to the Japanese as "midgets"--in response, I'm sure, to being called "garlic-eaters" by the people of the Rising Sun--and I only see that trend amplifying. Korea is growing, and so are its people. The malnourished World War Two and Korean War generations are now giving way to a well-fed, well-developed younger bunch that will make their ancestors proud.

The game against Italy was pure drama. Italy, a perennial powerhouse, and perennially defensive squad--the inventors of "*catenaccio*"--were favored to snuff out the Korean offense. Their talented set of strikers, Totti, Chiesa, Viera, Del Piero, all promised a hail of bullets on the Korean goal.

Conversely, the Koreans were not going to roll over. They realized early in the tournament that they could stand up to anyone. They were playing in front of a home crowd that they desperately did not want to disappoint.

The story of the game would be bad officiating, but it should have been about a tenacious and potent Korean squad, out-matched, except in terms of spirit. There were some disputed off-side calls that the Italians felt denied them goals, but the big play was the expulsion of Francesco Totti (of AS Roma) for diving in the box. The replay showed that there was probably a foul, and hence that he should not have been sanctioned for "simulation," but I beg to differ. Much though I appreciate Italian soccer, it is characterized by a very thuggish, dive-y ethic, and WC 2002 was no exception. They were diving and fouling up a storm through the entire tournament, and if the ref got it wrong in this instance, he was most likely influenced by their behavior to date. It is a classic example of the boy who cried wolf: The Italians can't insist on perfect refereeing when they spend so much time and effort trying to subvert justice.

The game went into overtime, tied at 1-1. The Koreans prevailed in minute 117. Ahn, who had missed a penalty kick in minute five, flicked in a deep cross, and the golden goal ended things.

The crowd went wild. Newscasters later estimated that five million Koreans took to the streets in joy. It was the perfect Cinderella story. Korea had been considered one of the weakest teams, from one of the weakest confederations. Many thought Koreans wouldn't have been in the tournament if they weren't the host country. Cinderella had beaten four-time-champion Italy. Dancing in the streets is an understatement. Fireworks whizzed into the air, exploded, and smoked up the night sky. The pulsing crowd cheered and screamed, hugged, shook hands, and chanted the omnipresent, "*Dae Han Min Guk*" with joyous, religious fervor. We retreated to Gyosu's apartment for a celebratory beer or two. Gyosu's usually broad smile was doubled or trebled in width and intensity. The normally serious Un Ho was bouncing off the walls, and Mija and Jiwon were dancing in circles. Radios and TVs blared the results, and the legendary name "Hiddink," the Dutch coach of the South Korean team, was echoing from Seoul to the most remote corner of the republic.

After hiding out in the apartment for a while, Gyosu and I braved the crowds to see the celebrations in his neighborhood. We trudged to the small commercial area a few hundred yards from the apartment. It was crammed beyond full. I passed a few very old men and women as I entered the throng, all dancing and singing and screaming. When they saw me, they waved their flags at me, gesturing for the big, red-haired foreigner to join in. I used my catchphrase, "*Hanguk chukku cho ayo!*" ("Korean soccer is good!"), to their indescribable shock and delight. At the other end of the age spectrum, kids of five or six were in the middle of the street, firing off bottle rockets, and chanting and yelling and screaming. And this was an upscale, professional neighborhood. I could only imagine how rowdy it must have been in downtown Seoul. When I went back to Gyosu's apartment, I found out: News teams were reporting excitedly from the city hall area of Seoul that the pandemonium was as big as they'd ever seen. The beautiful thing, though, was the peaceful, joyous quality of the celebration. I'm sure there were some crowd-control problems somewhere, but the overall vibe was one of pure bliss. The revelry lasted all night. Even in my more demure neighborhood, I could hear the nation's joy through my window between short stints of sleep.

June 19 - The Professor

Hannia and I were done. We had followed our beloved U.S. team on its voyage to the biggest tournament in the world, and seen it prevail. We were budgeted through the first round, and had stayed through the second. The U.S. still had to play Germany in the quarterfinals, but we had to turn our attention to the trip home. I already had extended our return date once, so I needed to make the final changes official and actually get the tickets firmly in my sweaty hands before venturing to the airport.

We needed to make one last excursion into downtown Seoul.

By that point, taking a bus to the subway station was old hat. I got directions to the Singapore Airlines offices over the phone, and figured out more or less which subway stop we needed to navigate toward. When we hopped off the bus and entered Suwon station, I paused momentarily in front of one of the posted maps of the subway system for one last route confirmation. As I might have expected, I instantly had a Korean helper.

A tiny, stooped Korean man in his late seventies appeared at my side. "Where are you headed to?" he asked, in very comfortable American English.

"Singapore Airlines. It's in downtown Seoul between the Westin Chosun Hotel and the Oriental Chemical building."

"You'll want to get off at the city hall exit. Just follow me."

We already knew where we were going, but he was being very nice to help us out, and obviously wanted to chat up the foreigners. We followed.

We boarded a train and sat down with the gentleman. He was a tiny guy, short in stature, and very, very skinny. He had a little goatee and wore a beret, which gave him a quasi-beatnik sort of look. He was very curious about us.

We explained our little adventure, and he was very interested in what we thought about Korea. He wasn't very interested in soccer.

"How do you like the food?" he queried. My wife's eyes rolled. I jumped in, "I like it a lot."

"Ahh, but your wife doesn't."

"She's a little put off by the chili," I offered diplomatically.

"I ask because when I was a student in Canada, my roommate asked me about the food in Korea. I described a typical dinner, and then he asked, 'But what about breakfast?' I replied that that was what we ate for breakfast, too. Then he asked, 'What about lunch?' and of course I replied that lunch too was very similar, if not identical to the other meals.

"He though for a few minutes and finally said he didn't understand how we could eat the same thing three times a day: rice, fish, pork, and lettuce. I was twenty-two or so, and I realized it had never dawned on me before that this might be odd, to eat the same thing three times a day. Finally, I told him that at that time, after the Korean War, we were very happy to have <u>anything</u> to eat. Monotony was not an issue. Starvation and nutrition were our only concerns. My Canadian roommate still could not understand, so I changed the subject."

It turned out that this unassuming man was a professor of philosophy, had obtained his master's and Ph.D. degrees from a Canadian university, and had spent the rest of his life teaching in Korea. He was now retired. His name was Bo.

I looked at his frail little frame, and thought about the big, strapping Korean youths I'd seen all over the country.

"Yes, the kids today don't understand what we went through. But why should they? They've grown up in prosperous times," he explained.

Bo chuckled about the priorities of the youth in Korea, who now, he said, only thought of cell phones and DVD players and cool tennis shoes. But still he felt that Korea would not slide into the insidious slackerdom that plagues America. At least not yet.

"Koreans still can't relax," he told me. "Even now when things are good, the Korean feels he must keep working hard, studying hard, and saving. It is still within our memory that we came so close to total destruction. If we let our guard down, we will be overrun by the North, or the Japanese, or the Chinese. Or we'll just be poor and hungry again. It has happened too many times in our history."

This was a pretty good explanation for the tremendous industry we'd seen, the Fifties-style, "duty-now-for-the-future" attitude that Gyosu's family displayed, and the overwhelmingly long hours that Koreans seem to work and study.

Professor Bo then asked how we had been treated by the Korean people. I assured him that the reception had been wonderful, that in fact we were sometimes overwhelmed by the helpfulness. I asked him if there had been a public campaign to encourage the populace to help out the poor, dumb foreigners.

"Oh, yes," he confirmed. "It went on for months and months before the World Cup. The public was well prepared for your arrival."

I also told him the story of the kids in Kwanjiu who wanted to touch the hair on my arms, and how they regarded me as some kind of odd beast from a foreign land.

Then after looking at me long and hard, he turned to my wife and said, "Koreans would consider your eyes very beautiful. Different, but beautiful." Anyone who knows Hannia would concur. She has large, beautiful brown eyes. I started to thank him for the compliment, but he cut me off. I hadn't seen where he was going with this.

He pointed at her, then at me. "Koreans would think her eyes were beautiful, but not yours." He raised his eyebrows in an odd way. His tone was conspiratorial. I was a little taken aback by his bluntness.

"Everyone here has brown eyes. Even Japanese and Chinese have brown eyes. Blue eyes look very strange. They look wild, insane, and fierce."

I noticed that some Koreans who were sitting around us-- obviously eavesdropping, as a lot of people understand English in Seoul. They were involuntarily nodding their heads in agreement.

Professor Bo noticed the reaction, too. "That's why I asked how you were treated." He shrugged, a sort of confirmation that his curiosity was satisfied, his fears allayed.

It hadn't occurred to me, but it made sense. I frequently had Koreans staring at me with a sort of deer-in-the-headlights look.

I thought immediately of some Alaskan huskies I see in my neighborhood when out walking my dog. Unlike most dogs, whose eyes are brown or honey-colored, these huskies have light-blue eyes. Though I personally know these dogs to be very civilized and sweet animals, every time I see them, my initial reaction is that they seem vicious and wild. I'm sure my own eyes produced a similar reaction among Koreans, and perhaps elsewhere in Asia. (This could come in handy when bluffing in poker.) The fact that the kids at the museum were so fascinated by me seemed related to this phenomenon. I was indeed a bizarre-looking creature to them. I'm sure this was especially true in a provincial town.

I can only imagine what the reaction was to the very first European visitors to the Orient, in the days before MTV, U.S. feature films and slick magazines paved the way for the "foreign devils." We must have seemed scary, indeed.

The professor regaled us with stories of life in the Canada of his youth as the subway rattled on. The stops dinged, and that sweet, mechanical female voice told us in three languages which stop was coming up. Finally, when city hall pinged its way into our consciousness, Professor Bo got up, bowed, and bid us a fine, philosophical farewell. We toddled off, and he sat waving in the window of the train as it disappeared into the dark tube, his beret making him easy to distinguish in the distance until we could see no one.

"What a cute little old man," Hannia proclaimed. His cuteness struck me much less than his perspicacity.

We completed our errand, re-booking and confirming our flight for the following day. I guess I should adhere to the cliché and say it was with melancholy that we bid adieu to the fine city of Seoul. Parting is such sweet sorrow, and all that. That wouldn't have been far off the mark, really. But then again, I was getting a little tired. I was a little "templed-out" a little museum-weary, longing for a cup of home-brewed Costa Rican blend, and a hamburger that didn't taste like it was fried in fish oil.

I was ready to head back to the States.

OF FAREWELLS AND CANINES

We backtracked to Suwon, and our irrepressible hosts insisted on taking us out for a farewell beer. We were more than happy to oblige. Gyosu and family guided us to a sidewalk café not far from their condo, the same street where we'd seen the wild celebrating after the Korean victory over Italy.

It was a pleasant, cool evening, and a tranquil stretch of street. Many families were out strolling, or dining, or traipsing through the shops. We downed a few rounds with some appetizers.

Hannia, in her inimitable way, asked with palpable nervousness, "What is this?" every time a new plate appeared in front of us. Gyosu and Mija explained through Un-Ho, who paused characteristically to think before explaining. Hannia joked, "I just want to make sure it isn't dog." There was an awkward pause, and both of our hosts very emphatically told us that it wasn't. But Hannia couldn't leave it alone.

"I told my dog, Keiko, when we left, 'Keiko, I'd take you with me, but they'd eat you.'"

"No, no, no," they stumbled over each other to respond. "Koreans don't eat <u>pet</u> dogs. It's a special breed, just for eating. It's different. Koreans wouldn't eat a pet dog."

We asked what kind of dog was bred specifically for eating, but we couldn't muster enough English and dog knowledge to figure out what the anointed (and seasoned) hound was in name.

Finally, Hannia felt compelled to put it bluntly.

"Have you ever eaten dog?" she asked point blank. Mija was scandalized and shook her head, "no," as politically correctly as she could. The kids both froze in apprehensive expressions, staring at their parents for guidance. How would the folks react? Gyosu smiled his little smile, and said--much to his credit, I think--"Yes, I have. Not regularly, but a couple of times." Mija looked beside herself. I don't believe she was shocked that he'd eaten dog meat, but shocked that he had told us. I'm sure there had been much press about Westerners' aversion to eating our canine friends.

"How was it?" Hannia asked.

Gyosu paused and thought. "It was good. Very good."

"What did it taste like?"

Gyosu thought long and hard. He was earnestly searching for the description.

"It tasted like... like dog," he finally proclaimed. Oddly enough, it was a satisfactory description. Dog lovers that we are, we couldn't quite muster too much indignation. It was more akin to wonder and surprise. It's the way it is. We would change it if we could, no doubt, but we couldn't.

The conversation drifted off to many other topics, mostly relating to what we had liked best about our visit, and a most pleasing buzz set in after a few beers, aided by the coolness of the evening and the relaxed surroundings.

We toasted each other repeatedly, and with feeling. We assured each other that we were the most wonderful representatives of each other's culture that we'd ever met. We opined favorably about the future of U.S.-Korean relations.

Finally, we packed it in, made the trek to the condo, and called it a night, but only after Mija served us watermelon slices... the nightly pre-bed ritual. Gyosu would be up very early the next day and off to work, so we said our goodbyes. We were quite grateful. It's an odd thing to invite strangers into your home, and we'd certainly had an opportunity to witness Korean home life in a way that few Americans have. Gyosu is an adventurous guy to have done that. And a likable guy, too, always jovial and enthusiastic. I hope to bump into him again. It was an emotional moment.

June 20 - Departure

We said goodbye to the kids in the morning. Un Ho was probably happy to get his room back, but I knew I'd miss the little guy. He was about to start middle school, when the serious stuff begins, so this may have been his last summer of fun. I hope he remembers the big red-haired gringo fondly. Jiwon was a bit shy with us, but she also dutifully said her goodbyes. Mija took us to the airport bus stop the next morning. It was right behind the Castle Hotel, where we had first met Gyosu. As we lingered in front of a loudly idling bus, diesel smoke wafting between us, Mija stepped forward and very carefully and precisely pronounced a few phrases in English.

"We will miss you very much," she said. There was a heart-felt tremble in her voice. "Thank you for visiting."

We were more than a bit choked-up, too. She had been our den mother for weeks, and who knew if or when we'd meet again. We all said goodbye over and over, not able to say a whole lot more without Un Ho to officiate. The bus driver finally climbed on board his waiting rig, and it was time to go. We hugged our hostess.

I got out my final, "*Kamsamnida. Annyong.*" We climbed the steps. The door closed with a whoosh of hydraulic punctuation. Mija stood and waved and wiped her eyes as we eased out into the street.

The bus gave us the reverse tour of the city streets and freeways, now quite different from the bus ride in... not because Seoul and Inchon had changed, but because we knew it all much better. It wasn't the overwhelming blur of new sensations any more, but something familiar. Still foreign, but now familiar.

SOCCER DENOUEMENT: AN AMERICAN ADVENTURE

The World Cup, of course, was not over. In fact, the U.S. had made the quarterfinals. We were scheduled to play Germany, the team that had beaten us rather ignominiously in 1998. I could have perhaps stuck around for this match, but my schedule and money were at an end. We'd gotten more than enough entertainment out of the biggest party on the planet, and could watch the rest of the festivities safely from our humble little palace in Mar Vista.

When we reached Los Angeles, and de-jetlagged over a few days, we psyched up for the impending match. Germany was the odds-on favorite. They've got a history that few countries can match in World Cup competition. Considering how soundly they'd thumped us in '98, the world anticipated a thrashing.

But this was a very different U.S. team. There were some tough MLS guys on this squad, Tony Sanneh (who played in Germany at the time), Pablo Mastroeni (a real bulldog of a defensive midfielder), Landon Donovan (who'd served an apprenticeship at Bayer Leverkusen), Brian McBride (who'd been in WC '98, but had now really hit his stride), in addition to usual stalwarts like Earnie Stewart, Cobi Jones, Claudio Reyna, Eddie Pope, and Carlos Llamosa. The odds of actually beating Germany were still long, but I couldn't help but feel that we'd put on a good show that year.

As a Galaxy season-ticket holder, I was invited to go to the Staples Center, where the L.A. Lakers, Clippers, and Kings play, to watch the Germany vs. USA game in the club restaurant. Due to the time difference between the U.S. and Ulsan, Korea, the game was scheduled for four-thirty in the morning. Hannia made the wise decision to stay in bed and snooze as long as possible. I knew she'd be awake at four-thirty, like the rest of us loonies, but after the jet lag and weeks of *kimchi* and shredded-squid breakfasts, I can't exactly fault her for wanting to enjoy home comforts.

I, on the other hand, am an implacable force of nature, a spirit burning bright, a keeper of the flame, charter member of the inner sanctum, the secret society, the clandestine brotherhood, the few, the strong, the faithful. I am, in short, a masochist bent on inconveniencing myself beyond the range of human endurance. Recognizing and embracing this, the pre-dawn trek to the Staples Center seemed a minor pilgrimage next to my Korean odyssey. By nature, inclination, and conscious decision, I again became part of the World Cup underground of Los Angeles. While the rest of the city slept beneath a blanket of darkened smog, thousands of other maniacal fans traversed the quiet streets looking for the secret sports bar, or the friend's house where the game was to be served up on a glowing tube. Cars zipped through largely deserted streets, sprinkled with zombie-like, half-conscious soccer fanatics. When you came to a stoplight and saw seven or eight cars, where on a normal night there'd be none, you scanned the bumper for a Galaxy logo, a Brazil sticker, or a Man U. banner. It had been like this for a month. On that night, all roads led to the Staples Center.

I contacted Christopher Dill, the coach of my metro league team. He brought his fourteen-year-old son Gabriel, also a player. They were dubious about what the turnout would be at this ungodly hour. I was not. In 1998, the World Cup final pulled a 40 share in Los Angeles. (For an explanation of the television ratings system, ask somebody much smarter than I am—but trust me, that number is huge.) Surely we can fill a fair-to-middlin'-sized restaurant.

I picked Chris and Gabriel up in my Volkswagen, a fitting vehicle for this game in particular and for the U.S. World Cup experience in general (a German car, remember, manufactured in Mexico). They groggily piled into the People's Car, and we talked in conspiratorial whispers as befits an enterprise under the cover of wee-hour darkness.

At about four a.m. on June 21, we pulled into the Staples Center parking lot. It became immediately apparent that the event was a success.

American flags were everywhere.

Cars were swarming over the asphalt like roaches on a moldy tuna sandwich. As we swung around the corner into the lot, a tall redhead in a bathrobe and pajamas went waltzing across the street. It was none other than Alexi Lalas of the L.A. Galaxy. I told Chris to roll down his window, and yelled across my passenger, "Go Galaxy!" Lalas gave us the thumbs-up as he bounded up the sidewalk. Gabriel was incredulous. Was that the Alexi Lalas, one of the most famous and recognizable U.S. soccer stars? "Stick with me, Gabe," I said with my best mock-swagger. "You're with a true insider."

It turned out that many of the Galaxy players were at Staples, though none of them as imaginatively--or appropriately--dressed as Alexi.

The Staples bar was packed with more than four hundred fans, according to newspaper estimates the following day. We jockeyed for a table, swirling amidst the boisterous painted faces and National Team jerseys making their way through the crowded aisles between tables and bar. Reporters hovered around Galaxy players. Pete Vagenas held court, as did Sasha Victorine and, of course, the inimitable, irrepressible Lalas, showing off his Hugh Hefneresque attire and oversized personality. We finally ended up in the balcony overlooking the basketball court, three of us at a table for two.

None of us had been there before, and I'm sure we looked like hayseeds, craning our necks, taking in the architecture and ambient frenzy. It was loud and fraternal and anticipatory.

When the game came on, the cheers were deafening. Everyone in the crowd knew the roster by heart, and most knew the history from WC '98, when we were ignominiously routed by thugging Teutons. When Jens Jeremies' face came on the screen from Munsu Football Stadium, the Staples center shook with boos and rowdy epithets.

We braced ourselves for a wild ride.

The game started as anticipated. The Germans came out physically. But this time, the U.S. pushed back. The likes of Tony Sanneh, Reyna, and Donovan had played against these jokers in their domestic league, and they weren't intimidated in the least. Pablo Mastroeni, emboldened by his phenomenal play against Portugal and Mexico, gave as good as he got, or better. The Germans realized in short order that the Americans were a force to be reckoned with.

The U.S. possession and passing were impressive. They set up many scoring opportunities, and only barely missed several goals. The Germans were also dangerous, but you could sense an air of apprehension in their play. We were frustrating them, out-playing them, out-hustling them. We were hungry, fit, and skilled.

The scoreboard remained 0-0 until minute 39, when Michael Ballack managed to put his head on a Christian Ziege corner and knock one in. Ballack was Germany's top scorer in the tournament, and it was no surprise. As I have said before, there is no shame to losing to Germany in the World Cup. It has happened to some of the best teams in the world (Hungary in 1954, Holland in 1974, England in 1970 and 1990). The only thing I asked was that we not get pushed around. My wish was more than fulfilled. Our boys kept the Germans back on their heels. Then in the fiftieth minute, Greg Berhalter took a shot that beat legendary goalkeeper Oliver Kahn. Kahn managed to tip the ball into defender Torsten Frings' arm--a pretty clear hand ball. The American players raised their hands and looked to the ref, Hugh Dallas of Scotland. Amazingly, there was no whistle. It was unjust, but I couldn't help but remember John O'Brien's blatant, uncalled hand ball against Mexico. (We beat them 2-0, so it wouldn't have mattered.) Were the soccer gods evening things out, as they so often do? Chris and Gabriel and I leapt to our feet screaming "PK! PK! PK!" The Staples center erupted with indignant screams. American flags flapped aggressively. Still, there was a good vibe in the air. Maybe we could come back and beat the dreaded Hun horde.

On the whole, it was Oliver Kahn's day. He made several brilliant saves. With a lesser German keeper, the result may well have been different. Unfortunately, from my narrow nationalistic perspective, the score held up. The match ended, 1-0 Germany.

When the game was over, it was evident that the Germans felt they'd dodged a bullet. When journalistic microphones were thrust in the faces of the German players, they praised the U.S. team much more than I expected. They looked truly spent, and had less of the triumphal glow than one might expect.

As the U.S. team left the field, I detected something that surprised me even more, and left me with renewed pride and hope for my U.S. squad. It was palpable in the players' body language and expressions.

They were angry.

They didn't collapse on the field in exhaustion and despair, as so often happens at the end of a hard-fought match. They felt they should have won, and they were furious. They weren't blaming anyone or offering excuses, they were just plain pissed, clearly thinking, "Just give us another fifteen minutes, dammit, we'll kick their asses."

This team, from whom no one in the world expected anything, whom the Portuguese thought would be easy prey in game one, had played their hearts out and lost in the quarter finals to one of the all-time world powers of soccer. Instead of patting themselves on the back and consoling themselves, they were frustrated that they weren't going to the semifinals or beyond. This makes me feel that the future looks bright. This bunch has shaken the underdog, snakebit history of the U.S. soccer team, and they felt they should be right up there with the big boys.

So ended the American adventure. Of course, Germany went on to beat South Korea, and then lost to Brazil in a very exciting final, but for an American fan like me, the dream ended at the Staples Center in Los Angeles, and on the field at Munsu Football Stadium in Ulsan, South Korea. I had come full circle, and full circle I would stay. Until Germany 2006?

FINAL OBSERVATIONS

I have none. Sure, it's required for me to scratch my beard and wax philosophical about the nature of travel at this juncture. I should make all my acquaintances out to be saintly emissaries of foreign lands, engaged in a meeting of the minds with that most worthy and appreciative of human beings: me. I'm expected to blather on about the broadening experiences in other cultures, about the beauty of diversity and all that sort of claptrap. And, heck, I believe in a lot of that claptrap. My life is nothing if not a hodgepodge of multicultural experiences, and if I can't justify them here and make myself out to be a marvelous maven of multicultural magnificence, then what kind of writer do I pretend to be? But, let's face it, I went to Korea to have a fabulous time, and I did.

A soccer nut like me at the World Cup is like the proverbial porker in a puddle of putrescence. I wowed to some of the most phenomenal acrobatic displays in the most competitive sport in the world, played at its very highest level. A game I love. I traipsed halfway around the globe, with my beautiful wife in tow, and had a perfectly valid excuse to do it all. I was able to drink heavily, eat large quantities of exotic chow, meet a bunch of lovely people who treated me very well, and shared a moment of ecstatic, childlike self-indulgence. Why would I want to sully that bright and shining month of my life by resorting to self-serving pseudointellectual platitudes about the deep social resonance of it all? Well, because I'm an egotist. But in spite of that, I'll restrain myself, and stick to the fundamentals. Gyosu and his family were marvelous, and I must say, very much like you and me. Language, menu, and towel questions aside, they're trying to get along, get their kids set up nicely in life, have a few laughs, work hard, and learn a few things. I hope we fit into their plans nicely. I hope the kids got a chance to practice their English a little and observe the Foreign Devil at close range, and get their little brains ticking a little harder. I don't consider myself an ambassador from the U.S., but of course you can't help but be taken as such, no matter where you go. I couldn't have asked for better hosts. I only spent a couple of days with them, but Soohee and her family were also delightful. I hope to cross paths with them again some day. And again, they were a young professional couple like any number of young professional couples

I know here in the States, though I know more film editors and musicians than chemical engineers.

Still, if I feel privileged to have experienced Korea, it is for this reason. As time goes on, the homogenization of the world continues, and it'll be much harder to "find" Korea, or Italy, or Scotland, or Costa Rica. My biggest fear, and it is one that receives a discouraging amount of confirmation as I make my way around the globe, is that we'll end up living in one continuous strip mall, filled with GAP stores, Pizza Huts, MacDonald's, IKEAs (I sit writing this in a home office filled with their furniture), serenaded with Britney Spears-like Muzak, indistinguishable from the Pepsi commercials. It's why I steer clear of resort hotels, package tours, and theme parks whenever I can. And I can't help but feel it's a losing battle. Particularly with the dominance of the U.S. in the world today--generally a nation of xenophobes--the Americanization of the world seems well under way, and inevitable.

Instead of enslaving and oppressing the people of the world, we have the tendency to give them what they want, which may be a far crueler infliction. There's nothing necessarily wrong with that. We Americans do have a flair for making things functional with less fanaticism than the Germans, and comfortable with less drama than the Italians, for instance. And ultimately, people vote with their pocketbooks and entertainment choices. What capital of the world isn't inundated with pop music in American English? Kabul? Gee, let's move there. Are the people around the globe being forced into cultural slavery by imperialistic centurions from Vespucciland? No, they're clamoring for all the soulless garbage we can produce, and embracing it more tightly than we Americans do ourselves.

But I digress. I had the singular good fortune to experience a very Korean Korea, no matter how "ruined" the old soldier on the plane over claimed that it was. I got to run around in Korea before it submerged entirely into "Three's Company" re-run hell. And I don't know about you, but I find that interesting. I hope that when I'm in my seventies, like Professor Bo, I have the perspective on my own culture that he does. By having visited other cultures, I will have had a chance to contrast and compare. And I hope I can help some hapless tourist find the right subway stop, even if he already knows which one it is.

December 9, 2005 – The Draw

Every four years, the world stops what it is doing and hovers around a television, radio, or Ethernet connection. World Cup qualifiers have ground noisily to a halt, and everyone knows who is going to the Big Dance. But they don't yet know exactly where or with whom they will play. This could be rectified quietly and logically behind the scenes with the aid of a computer or a couple of legal pads, but that would be bad theater. Instead, the process is seen as one of the richest photo opportunities human beings are capable of fabricating. In order to fully exploit this opportunity, the host country consults its glitz specialists, finds a suitable studio, and whips its national team of set designers, lighting directors, and makeup artists into a hyperkinetic frenzy. The result is an absurdly ornate and earnestly silly pageant, featuring the famous and infamous, the genial and the obnoxious, but mostly FIFA stiffs.

It is known simply as: The Draw.

Germany 2006 was no exception to the rule of obligatory frivolity. But before they actually pulled the rabbit out of the hat, they had to build the suspense. Planes, trains, and automobiles arrived from all corners of the globe, containing all sorts of people. There was the requisite red-carpet lunacy, where everyone glad-handed everyone else. Local stars, like Germany's own Heidi Klum and Franz Beckenbauer, paraded around for no particular reason, and luminaries and dignitaries and ordinaries all appeared on camera for a brief moment to remind us that we had to wait to find out who was in which group. They filed into their studio. They taunted us with the World Cup trophy and annoying mascots: a lion named Goleo VI who wore a shirt and shoes, but no pants, and Pille the talking football, who wore no clothing whatsoever. The mascots participated in a song and dance with children (who all wore pants), and a magician put on a show including a spiked human-being-perforating box, balls of fire, and heaven knows what else.

FIFA had conveniently placed the names of each participating team in goldfish bowls on pedestals, and designated soccer stars, including our own Cobi Jones, to pull names out of each bowl and place them into eight other goldfish bowls, designated A through H.

But wait, that would have been far too simple. First, there were a number of favorites who had to be separated from one another, so that the contenders wouldn't meet in the preliminaries. This time around, the seeded teams were Germany, Brazil, Argentina, England, France, Spain, Italy, and Mexico. Out of these, only Spain and Mexico had never won the World Cup. The inclusion of Mexico was a bit disconcerting to *Yanquis* like me, considering we had qualified ahead of them in CONCACAF and that we had beaten them in the last World Cup. But such is life. I couldn't imagine FIFA naming the U.S. as a seeded team.

Another consideration was that some of the teams came from the same confederation. They'd already played each other in qualifying matches, and were probably heartily sick of one another. It was probably best to keep them apart, and mix things up a bit. So there was an elaborate scheme to separate teams from their own regional rivals, wherever possible. Since so many European teams—thirteen—had qualified, there inevitably would be a few groups containing more than one Euro squad, but they were to be separated by qualifying group.

The eight groups were to consist of a seeded team, a South American team, and a team from Africa, Asia, Oceania, or CONCACAF.

They drew out the draw as long as possible for maximum effect. The names in the goldfish bowls were written on strips of paper, sealed inside little plastic eggs, not unlike fortune cookies.

The world audience hung on every moment, every twitch and movement and revelation on stage. As each team was named to a group, sighs, nods, and harrumphs emanated from the audience, and I'm sure that entire nations breathed, sighed, and groaned in unison as their fates were meted out. The U.S. ended up in Group E, and it turned out to be a difficult one. Group E had two top European teams: Italy (three-time winner, and always a contender) and the Czech Republic (rated number-two in the world, and a close third in the last European championship). To round out our discomfiture was Ghana, known as the "Black Stars," the top qualifying team from Africa. I immediately started to refer to ours as the "Little Group of Death." Every tournament has its so-called "group of death", i.e., the group with the strongest teams. This time around, I have to think the Group of Death Award had to go to Group C, which boasted Holland, Argentina, Serbia and Montenegro, and the Ivory Coast. Still, Group E was nearly as tough.

Costa Rica, my wife's team, was drawn into Group A. Ecuador and Poland were assigned to that group, and I believed the *Ticos* had a fair chance of beating both of them. The big news, however, was that the opening game for the *Ticos* was also to be the inaugural game of the tournament. They were to play Germany, the three-time World Cup champions. In Germany. With the eyes of the world upon them. It dawned on me that I could have bought the Costa Rican World Cup package and been assured of a ticket to the opening match. Hindsight always has twenty-twenty vision.

I had already booked our trip, so I knew we'd be watching the inaugural match on television in some pub in Berlin.

Hannia got on the phone with her family in Costa Rica. Everyone was amazed that tiny Costa Rica would assume such a prominent position, right out of the proverbial gate. They were also confident they'd get hammered by their hosts. "*Salados,*" was the term applied, which, according to Ernest Hemingway, "was the worst kind of unlucky."

Still, there was a silver lining. Costa Rican players would be on everyone's radar. Anyone who played well could get noticed by some European scout or other, and contracts might be in the offing. Additionally, it could be a big boost for tourism in the tiny republic, since all the Europeans would be paying attention to the "Switzerland of Central America."

I received calls and e-mails from around the globe. Attila, my one-time assistant editor in the Czech Republic, e-mailed and congratulated me on being his new sworn enemy. He said he might be able to get to the USA vs. CZE match. Louis Sterk, a former teammate from my L.A. metro league club, e-mailed from Holland to offer condolences. I offered my own, as they had to face Argentina (who beat them in the 1978 World Cup final). Louis' men in *oranj* were in the real "Group of Death." Gyosu Kum e-mailed from Korea, as did some friends from Italy. All my soccer buddies here in the States were lighting up the phone lines to offer reactions and opinions. I knew full well that this phenomenon was replicating itself a billionfold, as the soccer fans of the world contacted one another with the good, bad, and ugly news the draw had given them. I wished I'd owned telephone company stock.

Suddenly I knew which cities I'd be visiting. The U.S., in Group E, was to play in Gelsenkirchen, Kaiserslautern, and Nuremberg. I had studied the list of host cities since the beginning of the process, and I already knew a bit about these cities from their respective Bundesliga clubs. Former U.S. National Team star Tony Sanneh had played for Nürnberg FC, and I had tried my best to catch his games when they appeared on TV, so I had a basic idea about that *Bayerische* Burg. Kaiserslautern, though recently relegated to second division, was a famous and perennial Bundesliga club, and Gelsenkirchen I knew as the home of Shalke 04. A quick visit to the FIFA website revealed all the necessary tourist info, and I was able to coordinate the dates and venues into some vague image of an itinerary.

Since I'd purchased a ticket package, the details were out of my control. I'd been told by SoccerTravel that they could get me tickets to Costa Rica games, but they'd never confirmed anything. FIFA had another ticket sales period coming up in January, but considering the difficulties I'd had getting onto their site in the first couple of rounds, I had little or no hope of getting *Tico* tickets. And the opener against host Germany was probably out of the question. The demand for the inaugural game would be second only to that for the final.

Then I got a break. I received an email from U.S. Soccer. They said that since I'd been unsuccessful getting tickets from FIFA, I could apply for tickets to the U.S. games through the U.S. Soccer Federation. The fact that they knew I'd been unsuccessful meant that my original application had, in fact, gone through. I've never been so happy to be recognized as a loser. Since I had purchased first-round tickets as part of the package, I instantly downloaded the proper .pdf file, printed it out and filled out an application for "contingency tickets" for the later rounds, should the U.S. team advance from the first round. If the application were successful, I'd be able to follow Team USA as far as their talent and luck could carry them--conceivably to the World Cup Final.

I scrambled to fax the application on the first day it was permissible. The instructions indicated that the federation was renting banks of fax machines in order to avoid the sort of bottleneck that FIFA was experiencing on their website.

I went into work bright and early, and fed my application into the fax machine. It scanned the document and sat beeping and humming and dialing. I went into my editing room and started cutting scenes, blithely assuming that the application was a *fait accompli*. An hour or so later, after chopping and cutting and hacking away, I passed by the fax machine again, in order to pick up the receipt printed out. In fact, there was a receipt sitting in the receiving tray, which read, "Busy." I thought, "Well, it's just the first try." I got the original out of my briefcase and fed it back through the hungry apparatus. I again went about my business. And "busy-ness" was the order of the day, at least in telephone terms. I fed the blasted cover page and application through that blasted machine every ten minutes all day long. It looked to be a replay of my frustrating experience with the FIFA website. Around four p.m., I started to realize that there were more than enough U.S. fans to tie up those banks of fax machines indefinitely. I asked our post-production co-ordinator, Gabriel, if there was a FedEx office nearby. He sprang into action, asking, "What, when does it have to be where? Is it a DVD of the latest cut of the show for a producer, a director, or a writer?"

I reacted with as straight a face as I could muster. "Get a grip, man! Priorities! This is much more important than a DVD. We're talking about World Cup tickets!"

Gabriel replied with his customary chuckling scowl.

It turned out that we used a nearby DHL office for most of our overnight deliveries. Gabe gave me directions, and I zipped out the door and to the parking garage. Thirty minutes and thirty dollars later, my application was safely in the hands of a trusted courier service. I had done everything possible to submit the materials as quickly as possible.

Within a couple of weeks, I got my response. The application had been successful. I was the proud owner of "vouchers" for these theoretical games. If Bruce Arena and the boys got there, Hannia and I would be with them.

JUNE 6, 2006 – PARADISE FOUND, BAGGAGE LOST

Hannia, in her usual pre-trip frenzy, insisted on getting the bags ready days before the trip. It seemed like a good idea, so I let her. Actually, I may have helped a bit, just to spoil my perfect record.

We got up around five a.m., ingested some strong Costa Rican brew, and called a cab.

I asked the cab driver if things were getting busier with the summer coming on. He replied that LAX was always busy, but that yes, it was starting to heat up for the summer vacation season.

I noticed an accent, not uncommon among cab drivers in Los Angeles, and asked where he was from originally. He said he was from Georgia—not from Atlanta, but the former Soviet Union. "Ahhh," I replied, "Shota Arveladze."

The driver brightened immediately. He looked in his rearview mirror and grinned broadly. He was obviously not used to anyone knowing anything about Georgia.

"Arveladze, yes, from the old days."

"I watched him play a lot for Ajax and Glasgow Rangers," I said. "He was one of my favorites."

"He was good. You are a soccer fan?"

I launched into the whole spiel, of how we were going to Germany for the World Cup, and he was obviously interested. He asked which games and cities, and everything else he could think of. I said that since the break-up of the Soviet Union it was more difficult for the small, individual countries to qualify. I pointed out that the Ukraine probably got the best of the former Soviet players. I brought up the fact that wine was first invented in Georgia. I remarked that most everyone's name in

Georgia ended in "-adze", like Shota Arveladze, and Georgian President (and former Soviet Foreign Minister) Edward Shevardnadze.

"My brother used to drive for his family. A very powerful, corrupt family," remarked our driver. I chuckled. We talked about his kids, both of whom attended UCLA. One was pursuing a degree in international relations. Georgian is a very different language from Russian, but his son had studied in Russia and was fluent in both. I remarked that his son's language skills would put him in a good position in his chosen field. Here was a cab driver for whom the American dream had paid off: He had come to the States, got a job driving a cab, and was managing to put two kids through a great university. He was obviously proud of that last detail--and anyone who's taken on the mantle of parenthood knows that he's damn well entitled to be.

By 5:40 a.m., we were at the American Airlines terminal at Los Angeles International Airport.

When we arrived, there were two lines. One had a huge number of people waiting for two attendants to check them in. The second was a self-service line for eTickets. We milled around the large line for a bit, looking for someone to ask which line was appropriate for us. No one was available. I thought I might approach the counter and ask a quick question while the workers checked in other customers, but when I tried this, one woman in line went ballistic, and began demanding to see a supervisor, yelling at the clerks, and then directing her ire at the man who was called from backstage to deal with her. Her anger was over the top, but she had a legitimate beef. The airline had grossly underestimated the number of clerks needed to handle this crowd--a crowd, I feel compelled to point out, whose size was entirely predictable, assuming that the airline knew how many tickets they'd sold.

To avoid joining the human chaos, we went to the self-service lines, and waited for an electronic kiosk to open up. When I inserted my credit card in the machine, and punched a few buttons, it informed me in its digital way that it was not possible to check in there for an international flight. The American Airlines leg of the flight was LAX-JFK, with a connecting flight in New York. I had a bad feeling about this. We made our way back to the huge line with two open counters. Now an airline employee at the entrance to the line looked at our eTicket printout, and made dismissive sound. She wrote "6:05 a.m." on our print-out. We had clearly been given a demerit. Had the woman been in position when we arrived, we could have saved fifteen or twenty minutes wrangling with the self-service kiosk.

The clerk's task appeared less helpful than legalistic, as she was giving the airline a written record of when we arrived—in front of her, that is. I realized that American Airlines was treating the domestic leg of our trip as an international flight. They wanted us there two hours before departure. This was in sharp contrast to our many post-9/11 experiences. Two years earlier, we flew to Italy via New York, and showed up dutifully about about two and a half hours before the flight. We were informed that the first leg of the trip was considered entirely domestic, and we would have to reclaim and recheck our baggage before each leg of the flight. There was no way that we could check bags through to Rome's Fiumincino airport directly from Los Angeles. It seemed like a prudent idea, but I wished we'd have known in advance. We ended up sitting in the airport drinking extremely expensive coffee for two hours.

This time, the opposite was true. American Airlines considered us international travelers on this domestic flight, and thus late and irresponsible. Additionally, it began to dawn on me that airlines like the early check-in time for reasons of economy as well as security. This way, they can understaff the boarding gates, while you stand in line for an hour or two.

After waiting in one spot for twenty minutes or so, without any movement at all, I approached the counter and asked if they could get more windows open. I was told to approach a supervisor, identifiable by a grey jacket. I said, "I know, it's not your fault, it's a management issue." I looked up and down the row of employees—two check-in clerks, and two others talking on telephones. I recognized the American Airlines employee at whom the woman had been screaming earlier. He was in shirtsleeves now, his grey jacket sitting on the counter beside him. He was either very warm, shirking his responsibilities, or perhaps both. He was on the phone, but I asked the woman standing next to him if they could open more windows, or if, since my plane was soon to leave, my wife and I could be shuffled through out of sequence.

I was told to wait in line. Which we did.

When I reached the counter, the woman attending us looked at our eTicket and said, "There's no way you'll make this flight. You should have gotten here earlier."

I started to explain our previous experience but was cut off. "This is an international flight. You have to arrive a minimum of two hours before," she insisted. I protested that we were about to board a domestic flight, but that if they considered it an international flight, we still had twenty minutes before it left.

"Well, what? Do you want me to check your bags just to New York?" she asked.

"That would have made sense an hour ago, but we've been standing in the line in the interim. Is there a later flight you could book us on?" I replied.

She checked the eTicket, and saw that the second leg of the flight was with Delta.

"You booked this through Delta. You'll have to talk to them about re-booking a later flight. We can't do anything for you."

"No," I replied, "I booked it through Orbitz."

"You'll have to talk to them."

"Could I talk to a manager?"

"There isn't one here."

"How 'bout that guy over there who took his grey jacket off?"

She looked around, then went and conversed with another employee. She came back and very silently proceeded to book us on a later flight. There was, after all, ample time to make the New York connection.

We made our way up to the gate, and as we were waiting in the security check line, a couple and their son in bright-yellow Ecuador jerseys ambled past.

"¿Van al Mundial?" I asked. ("Going to the World Cup?")

They looked at me with characteristic shock. The red-haired fellow that speaks Spanish is always a curiosity.

"Sí. Vamos para Alemania." ("Yes, we're going to Germany.") The gentleman of the family responded at long last.

"Nosotros también," I replied. *"Y esta es Tica,"* I went on, pointing at Hannia. *"La enemiga."* ("We are, too, and this one's Costa Rican. The enemy.")

They looked to her and back to me and laughed. It was our first competitive encounter, and it was warm and friendly. We could only hope that the rest of our encounters would follow this early pattern.

As they went on their way, I made my parting shot, *"¡Costa Rica y Ecuador a la segunda ronda!"* ("Costa Rica and Ecuador to the second round!") They laughed and gave me the thumbs-up, both of us knowing that the two teams that would emerge from Group A would include Germany.

We scrambled to make our connection to New York, which worked out fine. In fact, the lady at the counter took one look at me and insisted on changing our seat assignments to an exit row, which would provide more legroom. "When my husband flies, I always ask for the exit row, his legs are so long," she added. So we had the full spectrum of customer-service experiences in our two check-ins. One clerk went out of her way to be snippy, and one made a point of being helpful. Luck of the draw. In the waiting area around the gate we were starting to see more and more travelers in the colors of their countries. Red, white, and blue of the U.S., the Czech Republic, and Costa Rica, the red, white, and green, of Italy and Mexico, English red, Holland orange, French *bleu*, and the picnic-table-like red checks of the Croatian flag. We could all feel the gravitational pull toward Germany. We were leaning in that direction, as if connected to the old continent by a magnetic thread. We all looked like we just needed a little push to magically slide across the water, *Deutschland* bound. Luckily, there was an airplane to facilitate things.

JUNE 7 – ARRIVAL

Berlin Tegel is a large, modern airport, as one would expect in a major German city. When we left the plane, we found the baggage retrieval is right at the boarding area. Immediately we were impressed by German technology--but not in a positive way.

The baggage retrieval system, a smallish loop of conveyor belts and rollers fed by a chute from the tarmac, seemed shoehorned into the space of the waiting area. The airport was fairly new, so it was probably designed with this machine in mind. As the bags careened upward from the tarmac out of the chute, every third suitcase or so had trouble making the very tight transition from chute to conveyor belt. There was a skirt of metal attached to the edge of the conveyor, obviously intended to give bags a little extra room to slide around the corner, but it wasn't enough. Each time a bag couldn't negotiate the transition, it blocked the rest of the luggage. One dutiful passenger, an energetic young man in his twenties, observed the logjam and grabbed the offending bag. He slid it along the metal skirt onto the conveyor belt, where it caught traction and moved along. A few couple more bags clunked through the juncture, then another got caught. The lively young man hoisted the errant bag onto the belt, and all was right with the world. A few bags later, it happened again. The young man looked a little less energetic, but performed his civic duty. After hoisting five or six more bags through the turn, the young man looked a little less enthusiastic and a little more annoyed. Still, he stuck to his guns and was hovering over the danger spot as though it were his natural destiny. Finally, a couple of bags hung up so badly that the young man had to step onto the belt to get them free.

A blatantly loud alarm horn sounded. The entire crowd lurched in unison at the sonic assault. An airport attendant suddenly appeared, a man with an official-looking tan cap on his head and a cigarette dangling from his mouth. He looked around the group for the perpetrator. Everyone averted their eyes, not wishing to shoulder the blame. The attendant stomped his way across the still conveyor belt, kicking the occasional bag for emphasis. He halted in front of the hung-up bags and stared at them as if they were petulant, unruly children. He looked up at the passengers, knowing that one of them had wantonly roused him from his daily routine, and shifted his gaze back to the luggage. He hoisted the bags out of the logjam, and plopped them back onto the belt with indignant force. He surveyed the crowd again with the sort of disgusted look that let us know he did not appreciate that the enjoyment of his cigarette had been interrupted. He brushed some imaginary dust from his tan uniform and stepped back to the center of the baggage retrieval system and off the conveyor belt. With the eyes of his spectators upon him, he very ceremoniously hit a large red button and, after a loud buzzer sounded, the conveyor belt rattled and hummed back into operation. Three or four bags spewed forth onto the belt and then--you guessed it—it jammed again. The energetic young man stared at the bags with apprehension. Dare he exercise his civic duty yet again and risk the wrath of the cigarette-smoking attendant? Another young man beat him to the punch, and we were back to square one.

As we watched the drama of the baggage retrieval system play out, our own drama unfolded unpleasantly: Our baggage did not show up.

Each passenger spotted his or her bag and, with a smile of recognition, felt the warmth of fulfillment at being reacquainted with their possessions in a strange and distant land. As the ranks of passengers thinned, we felt more and more deeply the pangs of impending separation anxiety. Our T-shirts, socks, underwear, and toothbrushes had been wrenched from our grasp by the cruel fates of intercontinental travel.

Yet the German functionaries were not indifferent to our plight. We were directed to the lost-baggage booth in the nearby terminal, where a charming older man with half-moon reading glasses and a grey goatee assured us that he spoke enough English to help us. He looked at our luggage tags and typed some numbers into his computer keyboard. He showed us the universal menu of lost luggage: a laminated chart showing a variety of the most popular bag types. We pointed enthusiastically to photos of the bags that most closely resembled ours.

The computer before him beeped, hummed, and refreshed its glowing LCD screen.

"Your bags are in New York," he said in a very Henry Kissinger-like accent. The gentleman gave us the proper paperwork to fill out, and assured us that our possessions would arrive at our doorstep no later than noon the following day. We thanked him and proceeded to the taxi stand, realizing that for perhaps another day, we would have no other clothes than the ones we had been wearing for the better part of twenty-four hours. Such are the joys of travel.

We had a few options: We could go out and buy a new wardrobe, or hang out in our hotel and de-jetlag until the clothing showed up. Hannia favored the latter, preferring to relax before the World Cup whirlwind began.

We gave the cab driver the address of the hotel and he looked confused. He was obviously familiar with the principal tourist hotels, and this address didn't quite fit his preconceptions. The place we were to stay, Miniloftmitte, was a sort of apartment-hotel. Located in the residential area of *Mitte*, literally the middle of Berlin, this part of the city formerly had belonged to the eastern, walled-off portion of the city. It was an interesting, modern-looking architectural confection—or so it appeared in its photos on the Internet—and not the usual tourist destination. That, of course, is why I picked it. The driver looked for our bags, and was even more confused. International travelers with just a backpack and a purse? When I explained that the airline had lost our luggage, the driver was sympathetic, and soon we were on our way.

It was a short drive into downtown, ten minutes or so, and I started chatting up the cab driver about the World Cup. I asked how far he thought the German national team would go. He thought they were going out early. He told me he was originally Iranian, so he didn't care about Germany. I brought up the fact that Iran was to play Mexico, and that we wished his team luck in knocking out our CONCACAF rivals. He told me that six members of the Iranian team played in the *Bundesliga* in Germany. The rest were from the domestic league. I told him that since I knew the Iranian league was semi-pro, its international accomplishments were all the more admirable. He say that yes, the domestic players had to hold down other jobs to make ends meet.

He drove past the address, finding the next posted number, then turning back to find the previous number. The number we were looking for wasn't posted. Nothing looked like a hotel, or the picture on the Internet--until I looked up at the skyline. The gleaming metal and glass edifice stood out among the old brick and mortar structures. At ground level it looked like all the other buildings around it, but one story up it was a very different beast. We hopped out of the cab, I paid the gentleman and shouted, "*Forza* Iran!" The driver laughed heartily and waved as he drove off.

We went up to the door of the odd structure we were to call home for a couple of days, and rang the bell. The caretaker said she'd be down in a minute. We would be in the "old building" attached to the back of the modern one. She led us through a doorway into a hall, and into our room.

"This is like living in IKEA," commented Hannia. Our room resembled a spacious studio apartment, with high ceilings and a galley kitchen. We signed and paid, and told the young lady that our bags were to arrive the next day. She left us to our own devices.

Hannia was right. The entire place was furnished in the blonde wood and stainless steel of the Swedish chain store. We plunked down our few belongings, figured out the room's essentials—the coffeemaker, the television, the bathroom—and sat down to rest. I could feel the cobwebs of jet lag overtaking me, and knew that if we didn't get up and move, we'd be cemented to our seats for the next few hours. I roused Hannia to go out and have a look at our surroundings. The hotel provided a small map of the couple of surrounding blocks, showing the grocery stores, post office, and the *U-Bahn* station.

The neighborhood looked rather bohemian. Not in the operatic Puccini decadent *artiste* sense, but geographically. I had worked in Prague once, and this was similar to the neighborhood where our post house was. It was an urban residential area, filled with apartment buildings and small businesses crammed into the equivalent of brownstones. There was a university extension down the street, so we saw a number of twenty-somethings, most dressed in black, parading in and out of that building. We found a grocery store, and decided to stop by on our way back to the hotel.

Hannia proclaimed a powerful hunger that would not wait. I suggested that we return to a few of the places that we had just passed on the street, but she capriciously decided that the restaurant we happened to stumble into at that moment was the only restaurant that would do. It was a typical European street café with a bar and tables inside as well. It was a warm day, so we moved far enough inside to escape the heat radiating from the sidewalk. Judging by the exotic name of the restaurant, and the appearance of the waiter, I wondered if this would prove to be an authentic German restaurant. It turned out to be extremely German in the modern sense, which is to say, Turkish.

Hannia was delightfully confused by the menu. I helped translate a few things, but was also a bit lost. I ordered her a sampler, which included a couple of familiar items.

The owners of the restaurant, a middle-aged woman and man-- and, I assumed, the parents of our waiter--were in the bar next to us conversing with a very blonde and beefy German guy about a television set. He was installing a large LCD screen in the bar, and they were guiding him on its exact placement. The male owner kept taking up different positions around the room, scratching his chin and looking over the tables, seemingly imagining where patrons would be and what their view would be like. The woman kept a close eye on the installer, concerned with hiding the wires that led to the gargantuan TV set.

"Ist dass für den Weltmeisterschaft?" I asked in what was probably very flawed German. Luckily they understood. ("Is it for the World Cup?")

They smiled and answered *"Ja, ja."*

"Es ist sehr schön," I ventured. ("It's beautiful.") They were very pleased by this—obviously this was a big investment to keep their clientele happy.

The woman came over to me and asked what I thought of the TV's position. At least, I assume that's what she was asking.

I looked up at the TV, on which now a news show was flickering. *"Ein bisschen mehr..."* ("A little more...") I couldn't think of a word for "tilted," so I used my hands to get the idea across.

They both sprang into action, scrambling over to the hapless installer, who got a screwdriver out of his bag, and began tweaking the wall mount. The giant screen moved ever so slowly, but soon was in a more tilted, convenient position. The couple looked toward me with questioning eyes. I gave them the thumbs-up and a big smile. They were satisfied--obviously very proud of their new TV--and I was happy to have helped.

When Hannia's food arrived, suddenly I felt like we were back in Korea. She didn't recognize a lot of the stuff on the plate, and looked at it with consternation. With the help of the menu, and a little creative thinking, I was able to help her identify a few components of her sampler. Lamb, yoghurt, garbanzos, pilaf, curried something-or-other. A few other things remained mysteries.

Hannia ate very tentatively, but enjoyed it.

I had a chicken dish and a ridiculously tall beer in an ornate monogrammed glass. Hannia stared at the size of the glass. "Are you going to drink all of that?" she asked in an accusatory tone.

"Damn straight, "I replied, "I'm on vacation."

It was the perfect thing to start off my German adventure.

Hannia asked me about the Turkish presence in Germany. I didn't really know any more than she did. We'd both read about the Turkish population in *Deutschland*, but hadn't really anticipated how large it was. So far in Berlin we had seen Turks everywhere, seemingly performing most of the work. Virtually every restaurant, mom-and-pop store, hotel, and small business was run and staffed by people of Turkish descent.

As we asked for the bill, I put to the test something I'd read in guidebooks, that credit cards are not widely accepted in Germany. When I asked the waiter if I could pay with a credit card, his face looked a little panicked, but he said certainly, no problem. Once he took the card into the back and tried to run it, he came back out and said it didn't work. My limited German made it difficult to ascertain whether the problem was with my card, or with his card-reading system. I had the cash to take care of the bill, but generally prefer to put everything on the card when traveling, to avoid having to change money every time I turn around or pay exorbitant ATM fees to get Euros, *zlotys, colones* or whatever.

We returned to Miniloftmitte via the grocery store we had spotted earlier. A market is always an interesting place to start a visit to a strange land, and we wandered through aisles and aisles of unfamiliar and familiar products, trying to decipher what was what and how the prices compared with our own emporia back home.

We bought some bottled water, careful to find "*ohne kolensäure*" (not carbonated). This is a harder task than it might sound. Most Germans drink fizzy water, and it can be tough to come across the still variety when you are thirsty. This is one of those cultural differences that are insignificant, but can be very annoying. The upside of Germany is that fresh bread abounds, and it's excellent. We grabbed a loaf, our water, paid, and wandered out into the street.

We made our way back to our room and rested a bit. We could feel the effects of travel and jet lag still weighing on us. Before we became permanently anchored in our places, I insisted that we go out again. I had forgotten to pack a jacket of any kind, and was sure that I'd need at least a windbreaker or light, rain-resistant jacket. We again braved the street. I had seen an icon in the hotel-provided brochure that indicated a post office nearby, and also wanted to see about sending a package home, so we could off-load some of our souvenirs and junk toward the end of the trip, to lighten our load and remain more mobile.

We followed the route that the map indicated, but the post office was nowhere to be found. Instead we found a large grass expanse, Invaliden Park, in the center of which is a triangular "sculpture." It was, in reality a sort of stone wall, in the middle of a fountain. At first I thought it might be a chunk of the old Berlin Wall, but judging by the route of the wall, which formerly had stood a few blocks away, it didn't seem like anyone was going to transport that large of a section that far. The water of the fountain cycled up through the highest portion of the sculpture, and spewed down the top edge. A local woman at the bottom of the fountain had a toddler with her, and she stripped off his clothes. The little boy cavorted naked in the water, a practice we would see repeated throughout our stay.

We pressed on until we came upon the Berlin *Hauptbahnhof,* or main railway station. It was a huge glass-and-steel structure at which the region's rail travel converged. We wandered in, impressed with the building's size and style. The station contained many shops, and we thought they might have some World Cup-themed jackets for sale.

Inside, the building seemed even larger, a multilevel palace, all brand-spanking new, filled with shops, restaurants, and, of course, trains. There were *U-Bahn,* and *S-Bahn,* and regional trains and intercity trains and intercity express trains coming and going on all different levels, and people were flowing in and out in waves.

We went to a few shops offering menswear. Hannia steered me to the trendiest, youth-oriented stuff that would make me look tremendously silly. Luckily, nothing fit me. We saw many German men my size or larger, but somehow the stuff in stock at this place wasn't ample enough. We asked a couple of guys at a café for a good place to shop for men's clothing. They said *Alexanderplatz* was a shopping area, and that we could get there on the *U-Bahn*. I had already wanted to see *Alexanderplatz*, because of the *"Herzog"* miniseries and the book it was based on, so the idea appealed to me.

We deciphered enough of the subway map to figure out how to get to *A'platz*. Then we had to decipher the train station to figure out where the heck the train we wanted stopped. A giant video display showed that the *S-Bahn* #7 stopped on *gleis* (or "track") number 9. We wandered around until we saw a big number 9 posted, and rode the escalator up to the proper *gleis*. Still unsure that we'd figured things out correctly, I approached a very business-like, dark-suit-clad fellow, and asked in my most basic and sloppy high-school German, *"Deise Zug geht am Alexanderplatz?"* His response was positive, then his face clouded over a bit and he started looking at the posted routes and timetables on a nearby display. A station employee happened to wander past and the man asked him something. He walked back over to us. "Do you speak English?" he asked me. "I'm Belgian. I don't really speak German well. I'm just here on business." He explained that *A'platz* was the third stop headed east.

The Belgian fellow very kindly made sure that we were headed in the right direction, and boarded the same train. We talked with him a bit about the World Cup, and the fact that Hannia's cousin lives in Belgium. We'd considered visiting her, but she takes off for the beach in Costa Rica every summer as soon as her kids get out of school. He felt it was very logical for a Belgian to head for the tropics at the earliest opportunity, stressing, "It's very cold and rainy in Brussels."

We thanked him for his help and went on our little mission. Getting off at *Alexanderplatz*, we found that the main shopping center, right next to the station, was closed for the evening. The sun was still fairly high in the sky, but it was 8:30 p.m. It felt like afternoon. We found another shopping center on the other side of the station, and Hannia looked around while I tried to get our cell phone to work. I called Hannia's brother, Luís, who was taking care of our house and beloved Border Collie, Keiko, in our absence. I managed to dial the correct access and country codes. I gave Luís our cell phone number and tried to tell him how to call. Our prepaid phone charged an exorbitant amount for international calls, so I wanted him to call me back immediately. I told him what I thought the country code was and the procedure for dialing from the U.S.

What I didn't take into consideration, however, was the phone number in Germany. There is a country code: 49 for Germany, a city code: 31 for Berlin, and then the phone number itself, which was eight digits, starting with 0. What I didn't know was that the cell phone had its own code, instead of the city code. When I got that straightened out, I then didn't realize that when dialing into Germany internationally, you drop the leading "0" on the German phone number. It took a number of calls (and about $15 in phone cards) for us to get the procedure straight. On my final call, I asked if Luís had found the country code for Germany in the phone book--to confirm what we had been told. In Spanish, he told me that he had looked for *Alemania,* but couldn't find it. "They had Andorra, Angola, Australia, Austria, but no *Alemania.*"

"Germany," I replied. "Look under 'G.'" I could hear the nickel drop on his end of the line. "Oh, yeah, here it is." Finally, we had success. The cell phone rang, and Luís' voice came through loud and clear.

We gave up on finding a jacket. There weren't too many stores open, and the selection was not good. We figured the next day we'd have more luck. We wandered around *Alexanderplatz* and saw the sights. The most prominent feature was the *Fernsehturm,* or TV tower. According to my guidebook, the locals refer to it as the *Telesparge,* which they said was German for toothpick. *Zahnstocher* is the German word for toothpick, and *spargel* means asparagus, so I have a feeling that it's more like "tele-asparagus." It's a large spike that sticks up in the skyline some 365 meters (1,197 feet), with a revolving restaurant on top. The large sphere surrounding the restaurant had been overlaid with large octagonal panels made to look like a soccer ball. Thus the skyline was dominated by a huge *Fussball,* illuminated at night, as a constant reminder of what the top priority really is.

The Germans seem to have an unhealthy fascination with these phallic symbols. Every town you go to has its tower, right in the middle of the skyline, some sort of tribute to modern technology, or broadcasting prowess (spreading the German seed--don't spill it!), or as a monument to the architect, politician, and/or event associated with its construction. This one is supposedly the second-tallest structure in Europe. Even in Munich, in which the Alps nearby could have provided more than enough height for broadcast purposes, the Bavarians insisted on erecting a TV tower to prove they weren't in need of architectural Viagra.

The *Marienkirche*, close by, is an impressive old structure, especially in contrast to the stark, modern-looking needle of a tower behind it. A bit further away is the *Berliner Dom*, the main cathedral of Berlin.

We managed to backtrack to the train station, and take the *S-Bahn* back to the *Hauptbahnhof*. I stopped at the fan kiosk, a large, soccer ball-shaped structure, colored like the ball on the *Fernsehturm*, to ask about the route to the FIFA ticket center, in order to pick up the Costa Rica vs. Ecuador tickets we had purchased on eBay. The attendant gave me a brochure that showed the address and the train routes, and explained quickly how to make the trip. As I thanked him in German, a random German fan, proud to do his civic duty and show off his English, popped his mustachioed face up out of the crowd and said, "Have you been to the Fan Mile?"

We replied that we hadn't. He pointed toward the government buildings directly out the *Hauptbahnhof's* main doors. The sun was starting to go down, but I could make out the *Reichstag* in the distance.

"It is very fun," our helpful German insisted. We nodded to each other, not really having a firm reason to return to the hotel except to indulge in jet-lagged sleep.

We trekked out the front door of the *Hauptbahnhof* and crossed the street. As we wound our way through down the path toward the Fan Mile, we came upon two enormous soccer cleats on a grassy area. They were sculpted in what was described as "an innovative plastic material by BASF," a pair of cleats literally as large as a house. These monster cleats were part of a series of displays entitled, "Germany: Land of Ideas." Collectively, the displays were referred to as, "The Walk of Ideas, an edifying stroll through ideas in Germany."

Here's a bit of the inscription:

"Innovative Football Boots

"An idea by the Dassler Family, 1953, *Herzogenaurach*

"On their path to becoming the 1954 world champions, the German football team relied on talent, luck--and the right boots: Adi Dassler had developed football boots with studs that provided a firm grip even on rain-soaked ground. To this day, athletes the world over claim their victories in German sportswear. Eighteen of the thirty-two at the Football World Cup count on equipment by German manufacturers."

So it looks like Adi Dassler, whose name yielded the brand "Adidas," made his mark with removable studs in 1954, though already had been introduced to American gridiron football some time earlier. Oddly, the removable studs are not represented by the "Walk of Ideas" sculpture. The modern "blade"-style, baseball-like cleat is depicted. Poetic license, I guess.

We pushed past the "Walk of Ideas" between the impressive buildings in Berlin's governmental center. In front of the *Reichstag* was a faux stadium, built out of scaffolding and covered with giant tarps to look like a coliseum of sorts. Giant portraits of famous footballers, with the +10 logo decorated the structure.

Loud cheering emanated from within the faux stadium, and guards told us we had to have tickets to get in. We couldn't buy tickets, we had to win them. How to win them? No one knew. Only later did we find out that the +10 campaign was an Adidas-sponsored promotion.

The faux stadium appeared to be the broadcast center for many of the pre- and postgame World Cup interviews. We would see the interior later, on television. We followed the endless stream of people toward the bright lights and loud noises coming from somewhere south of us. We came to several large lines of people awaiting entry.

We walked through one line, and Hannia was directed to a separate line which a female police officer was patting down female spectators. We were in the Fan Fest.

Inside the chain-link confines of the Fan Fest were hundreds of thousands of people. There were booths selling beer, bratwurst, memorabilia, and company representatives handing out promotional goodies by the shovelful. I was amused to pass by a large display sponsored by automaker Hyundai, nearly identical to stands we'd seen in Suwon, South Korea, at World Cup 2002, and outside the Rose Bowl in Pasadena for the Women's World Cup in 1999.

Then we hit the Fan Mile. The stretch from the Brandenburg Gate to the Triumph Tower is approximately one mile long. Into this mile were packed some half a million people, all watching giant LCD screens of a World Cup-related stage show. A blonde woman was on screen doing a stand-up routine in German, and the crowd was eating it up. Ripples and torrents of laughter flowed, collided, and bounced all around us. Virtually everyone was sporting some sort of soccer gear, and most were clad in *Deutschland* jerseys or other paraphernalia. An obviously very beloved entertainer came on screen and joined the blonde woman comedian. He led the crowd in a song, whose chorus was *"Zum finale!"* ("To the final!"). Of course, the final was to be played in Berlin, but the second meaning of the phrase was that the German national team would arrive at the final. Generations of beer-hall culture paid off, and the crowd rocked and sang along enthusiastically, in a way American crowds are usually too self-conscious to do. The beer flowed as it only can in Germany. Okay, maybe the Czechs could give them a run for their money, but there are only ten million Czechs, compared with more than eighty million stein-holding Germans.

We moved through the crowd, discovering that no matter how huge the crowd looked, there was another one mob on the other side of the next big screen, and then another, and then another. We finally reached the end crowd, in front of the Brandenburg Gate, and realized that the stage show was being put on right there. The crowd was loud and raucous and very friendly. We decided then and there that this would be where we would watch the opening game.

The duo on stage and screen then led the crowd a song to the tune of *"Volare,"* with *"Finale,"* substituted for the title lyric. Though nobody with whom I'd spoken so far harbored great hopes for the Teutonic Eleven, here you could feel the vehement support of the crowd. As I've said on many occasions, Germany can never be counted out, and in front of their home crowd, they would be particularly formidable.

We left the festivities behind, thoroughly tired from our trip and the time change. Though it was about ten p.m., the skies had just gotten dark, and it was disorienting that this happened so much later than back home in Los Angeles. We walked back toward the *Hauptbahnhof*, our only known landmark. I looked at the face of the building and figured we could follow the road that ran along the front of it to *Invalidenstrasse*. A street in front of us ran parallel to that road, so we followed it. However, in my eagerness to cut corners, I'd gotten a little turned-around. We followed the street in the darkness until it went under a freeway overpass.

Then it started to look a little weird. We were in a residential area, filled with nice-looking apartments, but the street we were following seemed to veer off oddly, not paralleling the guiding street, which was the wrong street to begin with.

A woman came by walking a dog. I asked her, in German, where we could find the *Invalidenstrasse*. She pointed in a direction that made absolutely no sense. I continued on, crossing the street in question and coming to another street that wasn't the one I was looking for. Getting a little paranoid, we doubled back to ask someone else for directions. A small contingent of police, taking a break from Fan Fest duty, were doling out take-out food from an official van, to compatriots who were smoking and drinking and relaxing at the side of the road. When I approached, they tensed up and put their hats back on. They could tell we were tourists with a question, and looked a little "pre-flummoxed" in anticipation of a few questions in English. I asked them in German where the *Invalidenstrasse* was, and they relaxed again, exchanging smiles--either out of relief, or because my attempt at a question in German was pretty laughable. They pointed in the same direction that the woman had, and told me to cross the street and turn right. The angle of the street still seemed totally wrong to me. I then pointed at the street I had been using as a reference and asked if the street that ran by the *Hauptbahnhof* was *Invalidenstrasse*. They replied no, *Invalidenstrasse* ran along the <u>other</u> side of the train station. Thus it ran perpendicular to where I thought it did, and the section that the woman and the policemen pointed to was in fact *Invalidenstrasse*, but the section of it on the opposite side of the train station from where I thought it was. I thanked them profusely.

We retraced our steps back under the overpass. and turned onto the correct street. We had to walk past the *Hauptbahnhof* and found *Hessischestrasse*, where Miniloftmitte awaited us. The misguided route had thrown us off and panicked us, but it also had succeeded in exhausting us a bit more. Not what we'd expected, but this was perfect ammunition in the fight against jet lag. We collapsed in our bed like bags of cement falling off a truck.

I woke up at three a.m. or so, but was able to doze off again with little difficulty. Had I beaten the Goliath of jet lag at long last?

JUNE 8 – WAYNE ROONEY'S FOOT

We awoke a little early, around six a.m. We looked into each others' eyes and smiled. It felt like we were we in sync with the sun god. We hoped for a prompt delivery of our bags to continue of our Berlin adventure. I popped out of bed and fumbled through our kitchenette. I fished out an aluminum stovetop espresso pot, the kind that screws together in the middle. A snap-top IKEA-issue jar contained the magic grind. I fired up the electric stove, and in just a few minutes, the steam blasted through the grounds, giving us a good, black brew.

I poured out two cups and took them back to the bed, where Hannia was fiddling with the TV remote. "The freakin' thing won't turn on" she complained, pushing the button harder and harder.

I took the remote from her and fiddled. No luck. I examined the television. The main power button had to be pushed in for the TV to turn on. The screen leapt to life with a news story that rocked the entire world, keeping human beings of all ages and ancestries glued to their media outlets, or engaged in the fiercest of debates known to the soccer-loving world.

Wayne Rooney's foot: What sort of shape was it *really* in? A damaged metatarsal in his right foot was threatening the hopes and dreams of the limey legions, the hooligan hordes, the teabag troops across the globe. The Sun Never Sets on the British Bunion. Experts in cheap suits blathered away on our TV set about the match fitness of the twenty-year-old Manchester United striker. This was especially true of the English broadcasts, but the local German channels, TV1 from France, and RAI International from Italy—the entire world, it seemed was contemplating this athlete's foot, and not the itching, burning, chafing variety of athlete's foot. Wayne Rooney's drama involved the flesh-and-broken-bone kind of foot, and the fungus among us be damned.

I didn't really want to think about this young man's foot while I ate my breakfast, but anything for the cause. The reliance on Rooney was a little dangerous, I thought. One player can certainly make a difference, but he cannot carry a team. I remembered the 2002 drama surrounding Beckham's metatarsal, and the special cleats he was fitted with to protect his injured hoof. Finally, even with Beckham--some would say *because* of Beckham--the British succumbed to Brazil. One player among eleven doesn't comprise a team. But the consensus at that stage was that Rooney's Right was fine, or at least good enough for play. An MRI scan had come back and been examined by legions of physicians in white lab coats with clipboards and pocket protectors. They scratched, and sniffed, and finally opined that all was well with the Liverpool product. He was fit to play.

Manchester United, however, issued a more cautious statement, which most interpreted as wanting to undercut the national team in order to protect their most important asset.

France, however, was not so lucky. Djibril Cissé, France's bleached-blonde striker of Ivorian descent, had been knocked off balance by a defender in a friendly against China on June 7. He crumpled to the ground as his right leg buckled under him, broken. Few people thought the French had much of a chance anyway, so the absence of Cissé was considered perhaps the last nail in the team coffin.

We flipped from channel to channel to channel. Most broadcast extensive World Cup reports, with news of teams and players, feature pieces on the Fan Fests--anything and everything imaginable related to soccer.

We had had our fill of TV and coffee, so I offered to go pick up some bottled water (*ohne kolensäure*), along with soap. Since this was an apartment rental, there were a few amenities we had to provide. I also thought I'd find a map of Berlin so I could navigate the big city.

I quickly put on my clothing from the day before--our lost luggage had yet to arrive--wincing appropriately, as I could feel that it was not nearly as clean as it should be. I strolled down *Hessische Strasse*, made a right on *Invalidenstrasse*, sauntered past the Humboldt University outlet and onto the next street. I spotted a small convenience store on the other side of the street, so I crossed and entered.

It was a typical urban store, filled with staple items: beer, snacks, and the like. The two guys working there looked to be Middle Eastern. I figured they could be Turkish.

"*Haben sie ein Stadtplan?*" I asked. The man behind the counter showed me three different maps, the first two of which were simplified tourist maps with only the usual points of interest indicated. "*Mit alles Strassen?*" He opened the third map to reveal a complete street map. "*Ja, diese,*" I decided.

He told me that map had too much detail, and might be very confusing, but I insisted. I always prefer to be confused.

As he rang up my purchase, I asked him which team he thought would win the World Cup.

Without hesitation, he shot back, "*Turkiye.*" His companion chuckled.

"But Turkey isn't even in the tournament," I protested.

"It doesn't matter," he responded. "They are the best team. They lost out in qualifying by goal differential to the Swiss. This was a great injustice." His colleague was grinning ear to ear. I'm sure he'd heard this rap thousands of times before.

"What do you think of Germany's chances?" I asked. "No, no way. They have no chance," he scowled.

"But you live here in Germany," I persisted. "Aren't you for the German team?"

Something awoke in him, perhaps a little shame or fear that I was questioning his loyalty to his adoptive land, and he instantly changed his tune: "Yes, yes, I like the German team. They have a wonderful history, but I don't think they're very strong this time." His buddy shook his head in agreement.

I thanked them and left, giving a parting shot of, "*Forza Turkiye!*" They both laughed and waved.

Back on the street, I tucked the map into my pocket and moseyed to the subway station. I motored down the stairs to the track area, looking for a map of the system. No one was around, and the little brochure-holder on the employee kiosk was empty. I looked at the map posted behind Plexiglass on by the tracks, then decided to leave. As I started back up the stairs, two men in official-looking smocks came past me, chatting away with each other from beneath their handlebar mustaches. I turned and followed them to the kiosk in the middle of the two tracks.

"Haben sie ein Plan fur den System?" I asked. They snapped out of their little social moment, like two kids caught passing notes in school. One realized he was carrying a stack of just such maps, and handed one over to me. In fact, they had three different maps, one of the entire system, one of just the *S* and *U-Bahns*, and one that showed all tram and bus lines. They forced all three on me with an enviable enthusiasm. They were very happy to have helped me out. I now had to assault them with my new standard question: *"Und Deutschland? Was denken sie? Zum Finale?"*

"Ja, ja," the one said, while the other shook his head glumly. The smiling one caught himself. He had been reacting positively to the familiar phrase from the song, *"Zum Finale."* His smile dropped. "No, I don't think this German team will make it." His partner in crime nodded in agreement, now happy that his friend had returned to his senses. *"Warum nicht?"* I asked. *"Deutschland ist immer stark in den Heimspiel."* They both smiled politely, but with a hint of condescension. *"Vielleicht,"* one of them said, "Perhaps."

I thanked them for the maps, and scurried up the stairs.

Using my new Berlin street map, I navigated my way down the block, turned left and ventured out into the reality of Germany. It was a mundane exercise, but an exercise just the same: I could orient myself as I marched down the streets, and though I saw nothing worthy of mention in a guidebook or travelogue, I was able to see a few blocks of apartments, small businesses, and people going about their daily lives. I got a bit of the flavor of the neighborhood. After twenty minutes or so. I decided that Hannia might be worried about me if I were gone too long, so I cut back toward my familiar market, quickening my step.

I bought some soap, some water (*ohne Kohlensäure*), and zipped back with the feeling that I'd actually accomplished something—however modest--with or without my luggage. I arrived at the apartment and

Hannia informed me that the bags still weren't there. I downed some water, made some more coffee, and lay back down on the bed to watch TV. I grabbed my cell phone and called the Delta stray-baggage people. The gentleman who had helped me the previous day answered the phone, and when I provided him with the tracking number, he was able to tell me that my bags had arrived in Tegel Airport and would be delivered sometime between noon and three o'clock.

I arrived back at the loft hoping that the bags would have beaten me back to my destination. No such luck. But with soap in our possession, however, we were able to bathe like civilized human beings. Civilization is overrated, of course, but bathing is not. Especially when it's ninety degrees outside, with ninety-percent humidity. If the Roman Empire performed one good deed among its many rapacious brutalities, we must thank them for teaching the world to bathe.

We thoroughly enjoyed getting clean and fresh, and all we needed was some clothing, since the errant luggage had yet to arrive. We decided that we would give in to the remaining vestiges of jet lag and nap a bit. Of course, we could have rinsed out some clothing in the sink or tub, using dishwashing detergent from the kitchen, but it would probably take longer to wait for the stuff to dry than for the bags to arrive. We drifted off watching television. The yammering German hosts of news and sports shows provided the perfect cacophonous aural pillow to support us as we drifted in and out of consciousness.

Finally, the phone rang. The loft manager called to let us know that the bags had arrived. I put on my dirty clothes once more, and made the trek to the office. It was pretty silly to have carried the bags up the elevator to the fourth-floor office, so that I had to haul them back down again, but I was so happy to see my luggage again that I really didn't care. The manager, a young woman who spoke good, precise English, was also pleased to see us get our goods. I manhandled the bags into the tiny elevator, then out to the "old building" where our loft was. I struggled a bit with the door into the hallway where our room was, as it had an automatic door that apparently was designed for gorillas. The door forced me to take extreme, athletic measures to keep it open while juggling two rather heavy suitcases. The small but useful victory was complete as the loft door snapped shut behind me like a bear trap. Hannia was ecstatic to get her goodies. She leapt at the nylon zippers, noisily opening her bag and rifling though its contents. She extracted some mysterious containers and dove into the bathroom to avail herself of the cosmetic marvels that had been held hostage overnight. I made sure my camera equipment was intact.

I bathed again, having worked up a sizable sweat slinging bags in the humid heat of Berlin in my grubby clothes. It was well into the afternoon now. I had hoped to go to the stadium ticket center to pick up the Costa Rica vs. Ecuador tickets, leaving the afternoon open for some sightseeing. I had also hoped to go to the *Gemäldgalerie*, which houses some of the great German and Nordic art as well as renaissance Italian stuff. I double-checked the hours of operation of the ticket center, and figured that I should take care of that first. If there were time left, we'd go to the gallery. Once we had the tickets in our hot little hands, I could relax a bit.

I rifled through the train maps and timetables I had acquired that morning, in order to confirm the routes to the stadium where the ticket center was. First was the foot journey to the *U-Bahn* station. We bought two all-day passes, which would allow us unlimited mischief anywhere in the greater Berlin transit system. We hopped on the U6, then transferred to the musically named (or spy plane-themed) U2 line, and were soon hurtling through the great city at breakneck speed. The stadium is way out of the center of town, so we got a good introduction to Berlin, zipping in and out of tunnels, over and under streets and apartment buildings and offices, until the train wound its way to a more open, grassy, tree-lined region. When the train came to a halt at the *Olimpiastadion* stop, we emerged into a pretty much empty station. I'm sure that on game day, it is packed and raucous and loud and lively, but today, it was like a tomb.

We followed the walkway to the street. There were some painters on a cigarette break by the exit, so I asked one where the "ticket center" was. I showed him the address. He was totally nonplussed, as though I'd asked him for directions to the Great Wall of China. His companion waded in, made some gestures, and said a few things that allowed me to orient myself a bit. I grabbed Hannia's hand and dragged her out into the street, which also were pretty much empty. Looming in the distance was the huge *Olimpiastadion*, with its distinctive towers. It brought back memories of films I'd seen growing up of the 1936 Olympics. For the uninitiated, I recommend renting Leni Riefenstahl's landmark propaganda film, "Olympia." It is a chilling reminder of Hitler's use of the Olympics for political and self-promotional purposes.

The *Finale*, which had been sung about in the Fan Mile, was to be held here. If the USA somehow stumbled its way in the final match,

Hannia and I would be here, decked out in red, white, and blue. But now, we had the more practical and pressing issue of ticket acquisition to attend to. We turned on the *Jesse Owens Allee*, again a reminder of the history of the place.

We rounded a corner and saw a yellow building in the distance that we knew to be the ticket center. As we came closer we saw that the line to get in was maybe eighty people deep--not bad considering that this was the principal stadium in the principal city of the host country. The size of the building made it appear that the facilities were ample to attend to what was not a huge number of people. We made queries to make sure that this was the proper line, and assumed the position. In a few moments a couple of guys got in line behind us. I noticed red, white, and blue paraphernalia. They were speaking Spanish. I asked them if they were *Ticos*. They lit up. They had come from New York, where they'd lived for a few years.

One guy was fortyish, the other in his twenties and and a bit more gregarious. They were traveling with a group of five *Ticos*, but the others had stayed in the hotel to get some sleep. They planned to drive that night to Munich for the opener against Germany. I never really understood why they'd come to Berlin if they had opening-game tickets in Bavaria, but I'm sure they had their reasons.

The drive to Munich was a huge, long, arduous journey. I wondered if they had known how long it took to drive between cities when they booked their flights. It's always mind-boggling for Costa Ricans to travel such vast expanses and still be in the same country.

Of all the people we could bump into, it amazed us that the ones standing right next to us in line would be from the same tiny Central American republic as my wife. We conversed and compared notes on travel, German beer, and the difficulty of obtaining tickets. They said that they had been fortunate, that a family member had ordered tons of tickets, and couldn't make the trip from Costa Rica. They had all the paperwork in shape, they said, and it would be no problem to pick up the tickets. It sounded to me like they had bought tickets from a scalper and were practicing their story to get past the security and anti-scalping procedures. I thought that because that was precisely what I was doing. Everyone selling tickets on eBay said to claim that it was a family member who had given them the tickets. I really didn't think it would be an issue, because my seller had done the proper things to get title of the tickets transferred to my name. We had provided him with passport numbers, addresses, and phone numbers to facilitate the process, including a ten-Euro transfer fee. He had sent me a .pdf of his ownership certificate and screen grabs of the transfer transaction. There in black and white was the "new ticket holder," namely me.

The line moved very, very slowly. Ahead of us was a Japanese woman, chatting in English with a German guy. We joined the conversation about tickets, procedures ,and things of World Cup interest.

It turned out that the Japanese woman, who spoke English very well, had lived in Berlin for several years. She had been interested in tickets, not because of any desire to see games, but as a method of luring relatives from Japan to come visit her in Berlin. She had bought several tickets for family members who decided at the last minute that they couldn't come. She had sold her tickets online, and was there to transfer the tickets officially to the buyers' names. We all wondered aloud if it were really necessary to go through the official transfer process. In Korea, they had patted everyone down and made a show of checking the name on tickets, but many people had filtered through just fine with scalped or gift tickets.

The German fellow outlined the security measures that were in place. He said that a friend of his worked with the organizing committee, and had assured him that everything would be done to the letter. He had see reports on television that showed how the tickets had an embedded computer chip that contained the owner's personal data. At the entry gates, the chip could be scanned, and then the ticket holder's passport could be scanned to make an instant match. The television report demonstrated that the scans were performed easily. Yet his friend in the organization had warned him that he should get to games a good three hours early, because passing through security might require it. We were glad to get the tip, but we all agreed that we'd pay attention to reports from the first few games, to see how things were done in actual practice. We could imagine the system crashing, with 60,000 beer-soaked fans stuck in line for the entire day. It seemed likely that they would probably spot check at best.

We discussed the strengths and weaknesses of our national teams, agreeing that while the U.S. was in a very difficult group, their showing at the previous World Cup gave us some hope. While the German fan spoke highly of the U.S. team, I couldn't help but feel he was just being polite. Like most Germans, he'd picked the Czechs as the only European team that had a chance to go all the way.

When I asked him about Germany, he laughed and shook his head. "No way," he asserted. "This team is very weak. They are way too young and inexperienced, and Klinsmann is a beginner as a coach."

I pointed out that Germany was always tough in big tournaments, especially playing at home. With the home crowds behind them, they'd be tremendously pumped up. He thought that the team would sneak through the first round, and be eliminated in the second.

We quizzed the Japanese woman about her experiences in Germany. She married a Brit, and had lived in England for a time before moving to Berlin.

I asked her if she had learned German. "I took lessons when I first moved here, for a few months," she said. "Then I gave up. It's hard enough to speak English, and German is very, very difficult. Almost everyone in Berlin speaks English anyway. Sometimes when I'm in the eastern section I'll be out of luck, but in West Berlin it's usually not a problem."

I hadn't really thought about the division in those terms. I would imagine that the residents of what was formerly known as East Germany had been encouraged to learn Russian instead of English. Certainly the Germans are very diligent about education in general and language study in particular, but the majority of those who grew up in what was then East Berlin were much less likely to speak English. Certainly their children had been at a disadvantage learning, if *Mutter* and *Vater* couldn't help them out with their homework.

Even with the good conversation diverting us in line, waiting became a tedious affair. We had been standing in the hot, muggy Berlin air for at least two hours, waiting for perhaps eighty people to be processed ahead of us. And yet, I've gotten frustrated in the "will call" line at the Galaxy's stadium when it has taken fifteen minutes to admit twice as many people. I could feel my legs cramping up.

As we progressed to a bend in the line, we could see inside the ticket center, a facility with more than thirty ticket windows—only four of which were open. No wonder things were moving slowly! In addition, people who clearly held VIP status were ushered into the lines ahead of the rest of us. Not good.

When I finally reached an open window at the head of the line, a pretty young blonde German woman asked me to prove my claim. I opened my notebook, in which all of the documentation had been laid out in impeccable order: our passports, photocopies of our passports, the original owner's certificate of ownership, and photocopied "screen grabs" of the transaction conducted to transfer ownership of tickets to the two of us, including one clearly stating the identity of the new ticket holder, identifying me by name and passport number.

After reviewing the documents, photocopying one, she looked at me with the most sincerely forlorn expression a human being has ever directed at me. "Where is the power of attorney?" she asked.

"He said we wouldn't need one, since the transfer already went through online," I explained. The seller had told me that if the transfer had been denied, he would have sent me a power of attorney, but since the transaction was successful, we assumed we didn't need it.

"To pick up the tickets, you need a power of attorney from the original owner," the clerk stressed.

"But our names and passport numbers are already on the tickets, aren't they?"

She clicked and pecked at the keyboard in front of her.

"Yes," she said, "The transfer was completed successfully."

"Good."

"Your name and passport numbers are here in the computer."

"Great."

"But you need a power of attorney to pick the tickets up. I'm terribly sorry."

She was not nearly as sorry as I was. But her furrowed little brow told me that I'd run headlong into the Teutonic need for every conceivable form of proper documentation and she wasn't going to budge. After consulting with a supervisor, she returned with the same response. "We will accept a fax," she offered.

"I don't know where he is. I think he's traveling right now to come to the Cup."

"There's a power of attorney form online, or he could just hand-write one, as long as it has your names, passport numbers, his name, passport number, a statement that you are authorized to pick up the tickets, and his signature," she recited.

I backed out of the line a little dazed. A lost day, train ride, and hours of standing in line. had come to naught. Before I started to wander away, I remembered to ask one more thing: Would I have to stand in line for two hours again if I could come up with the proper document? The clerk very graciously asked a manager to give me a signed card that would allow me to come directly to the ticket window.

As I walked away, I saw the *Ticos* we'd met standing at another ticket window. One of them was talking feverishly, and looked a bit red and frustrated. He obviously was having problems similar to my own, despite his insistence that his was a simple familial transaction. The Japanese woman, with her stack of impeccably arranged documents in front of her, succeeded in receiving her tickets from the attendant at the third window.

Backtracking along *Jesse Owens Allee*, we found a place to eat. We were both starved, not having imagined that this process would take so long. Just outside the stadium, we filled up on food and beer.

Next, we scrambled back to the Miniloftmitte to e-mail our ticket seller to see if he could fax us the required power of attorney. Since he was from Australia, I figured that it was best to fire off the e-mail as soon as possible, since the time difference might cause delays. On arriving, I immediately whipped out my laptop, composed an e-mail, and fired it off. I had no way of knowing if the seller would pick it up in time, or would be motivated enough to fill out the proper form, and to go to the time, trouble, and expense to fax it to me. Since we were about to change hotels in Berlin, and then would be flying to Mainz in a few days, I wasn't sure where I'd be, if he decided to send the fax.

I sent the seller every fax number I could find, and the corresponding dates we'd be at each number, just in case. I checked the time, and figured it was around one a.m. in Australia. We hoped that he'd read the e-mail when he got up in the morning, and respond quickly. If he got back to me in the next two days, I'd be able to use my "get out of line free" card at the ticket center in Berlin. I didn't relish having to sit in line again in Frankfurt, the nearest stadium to Mainz.

We rested a bit before going out to see the sights. I wanted to see the *Reichstag* building, which was not too far from the Loft, so we hoofed it to the *Platz der Republik*, or Republic Square.

Since it was nearly nine-thirty in the evening when we arrived, it didn't seem likely that a government building would be open, but I thought I remembered seeing a sign that said it was open until midnight. I definitely remembered seeing people in the dome on top of the building at sunset, and lo and behold, my ever-faltering memory had been correct. The last group was allowed up the elevator at 10:30, but the dome atop the building was open until midnight.

As we shuffled through the entryway, under the giant inscription *"Den Deutschen Volke"* ("to the German people"), through an enormous glass wall, we could see the plenary chamber in which the *Bundestag* meets. If we came back during the day, we could see the hustle and bustle of legislative madness carried out in all its glory and splendor, in the great Teutonic tradition beneath the "fat hen," the popular nickname for the federal eagle, symbol of the German republic. I wondered how much the World Cup was affecting governmental offices, with everyone trying to sneak off for a glance at a clandestine TV at three, seven, or nine p.m.

According to a brochure handed out at the entrance, the legislative calendar was detailed on an hour-by-hour, day-by-day basis. I doubted that business proceeded as optimistically as the document suggested. I wondered how many staffers would have hand-held TVs hidden in or under their desks. If Germany were the victor in any game, I was sure the hangover count would be substantial, and productivity would plunge as a result.

We proceeded through metal detectors and were herded into a huge elevator, finding ourselves on the top floor, where the giant glass cupola known as the *Reichstag* dome, stood before us, like a crystal orange juicer awaiting a giant half-orange. It was truly impressive, as was the view from atop the *Reichstag* building. Berlin was laid out below us, and clearly visible for miles.

Unfortunately, my capacity to enjoy the beauty was hampered by the fact that my eyes were watering, and I was starting to sneeze. The *Platz der Republik* is located at the end of the *Tiergarten*, a vast expanse of greenery, formerly a hunting preserve, in the midst of Berlin. Something or other was blooming, and the wind carried the pollen or other irritants right to the top of the *Reichstag*. As my bags had arrived late, my usual routine of taking allergy medicine after showering had been interrupted. I was without defenses against the invisible foe. Hannia was looking at me, concerned I might explode from all the sneezing. I insisted we continue up the stairs, an interesting architectural feature. They are arranged in a gently sloping spiral, following the interior contours of the dome.

As we got up higher, we looked down to see the plenary chamber through the glass bottom of the dome. Hannia started feeling a little dizzy. She and many of her siblings suffer from vertigo, often getting disoriented in high places or moving vehicles if the conditions aren't just right. She wanted to stop her ascent and return to the base of the dome, but I convinced her to continue climbing.

The dome is open at the top and bottom, allowing air to filter through, and in fact, the body of the structure is made of horizontal ribs of glass--Plexiglass, I'd image--with gaps in between to allow the free flow of air. Normally appreciative of ventilation, in this instance I felt oppressed by it. From my narrow, afflicted perspective, the dome's design served as an extraordinarily efficient pollen-delivery system, sucking up far too many irritating particles up from the *Tiergarten* and depositing them in my sinuses.

The view from atop the dome was extraordinary, judging from what my watery eyes would allow me to appreciate, between rhythmic sneezes. It was magic hour, and the setting sun bathed the Berlin skyline in a light pink glaze. Hannia and I stretched out on a bench that allowed us to look up and out from the top of the dome. We imagined aloud how it might appear later at night, when the stars were out. This would have been wonderfully romantic, if it were not for my incessant sneezing and Hannia's vertigo. Despite our pathetic mortal frailties, the view was still impressive.

We found our way back to the Loft much more easily this time.

June 9 – Let the Games Begin!

We got up early and swapped hotels, now opting for something on *Lützowplatz*, just south of the *Tiergarten*. I checked first with the management of the Loft to make sure my fax hadn't arrived, and it had not. We took a cab to our new digs, dropped off our bags, and set out to the south to explore the new area. On *Lützowplatz*, we passed five or six big tourist hotels teeming with cabs and patrons. We made our way to *Nollendorfplatz*, where the *U-Bahn* station was, along with a large assortment of shops and restaurants. We walked up and down the main streets to make a mental inventory of what was available. It was a very pleasant tree-lined area, with smallish, stylish cafés and homey little mom-and-pop stores. We passed all kinds of restaurants, notably one billed as an "American café," specializing in burgers, fries, and 'Fifties diner-style fare.

We finally stopped at a sidewalk café for lunch, where we both ordered a spaghetti and chicken dish.

We strolled back to the hotel, rested up a bit, and donned our Costa Rican gear. It was time for the inaugural game: Germany vs. Costa Rica. The game was to be played in Munich, but we knew that the Fan Fest in Berlin would be a happening spot. We were a little farther from the Fan Fest in our new digs, but since we'd found the *U-Bahn* station, it'd be easy to make it back for the party. We both wore Costa Rica jerseys, Hannia had a flag, and I had a hat and scarf, showing our support for the team. We Tiny *Ticos* were ready to cheer on the squad daring to take on the Teutonic Titans on their turf.

We strolled out into the lobby, our affiliation leading the way. I stopped at the front desk to ask about the fax. The young woman behind the counter checked the message box. "No, sir, nothing," she said, unable to take her eyes off the Costa Rican emblem on my cap.

On our way to the *U-Bahn* station at *Nollendorfplatz*, immediately we saw the evidence of German boosterism. Every second passing car flew a German flag, either the small, plastic variety that clamps onto the car window, or the full-blown banner, waved out the window by fanatic youths, mostly young men. Every other pedestrian was wearing a jersey, or cap, or T-shirt, or scarf, or any combination of the above, all swearing their allegiance to the German national team.

Pedestrians groups were traipsing down the sidewalks, beers in hand, headed to a friends' houses, pubs, or public squares to watch the national *Mannschaft*. They invariable became quiet as they saw the two lone representatives from the tiny Central American republic that was to be their foe of the day. We may have been the only Costa Ricans (in my case, an honorary Costa Rican) most of them had ever seen, and they seemed palpably embarrassed. Obviously, they had been chattering away with one another about how they were going to thrash these unworthy opponents, and laughing and joking about the prospect. Suddenly, confronted with actual, unretouched human representatives of their opponents, and unable to be sure we hadn't overheard them, or that we hadn't somehow divined their thoughts from their posture and body language (which wasn't hard), they were suddenly torn between being good hosts--which I'm sure had been drilled into them since FIFA announced they were to hold the tournament--and being normal, partisan sports fans, enjoying the nationalistic surge of emotion that could feel so good. Germans, too, have had a precarious relationship with unbridled nationalism in the last century or so.

As often as not, the German fans passed us in silence, gulping and stumbling and looking away, or trying to smile to make up for what they had been thinking or saying only moments before.

As I passed one group I called out, *"Zum Finale!"* The group paused, laughed, and responded in kind, showing visible relief that I had broken the silence.

At the *U-bahn*, even more groups of flag-bearing, national-team-jersey-wearing Germans flowed in and out and up and down and all around us. They eyed us oddly as they passed.

We got on our train and headed for the *Hauptbahnhof*. Groups of slightly buzzed, beer-wielding Germans surrounded us, many of them singing supporters' songs, or chanting, *"Deutschland, Deutschland, Deutschland!"* like good Hun hordes.

At the train station, we were carried out with the wave of German supporters. This time, we had been wise enough to go to the *Unter den Linden* stop, which put us out just behind the *Pariser Platz* and *Brandenberger Tor*, where the festivities would be centered.

The *Pariser Platz* was filled with television crews, setting up equipment. We had purposely arrived an hour or so early, since we figured that a half-million or so people just might show up. The buildings on the *Pariser Platz* were the headquarters for the television commentators, and on one balcony, you could see where the panels of broadcasters would be sitting, tables and microphones and lights already in place. From a fleet of production vans, frantic crews pulled cables from the vans' open doors like sailors pulling entrails out of giant beached whales. A huge replica of a soccer ball stood in the middle of the plaza, housing a small museum in which replicas of the World Cup were on display.

We wandered around the plaza a bit, taking in the energy and atmosphere and peering at the huge cranes that held television cameras a hundred or more feet above the ground. If there was this much activity in Berlin, we could only imagine what it was like in Munich, where the game was actually being held. After a while, I told Hannia we should stake out a place by the big screen.

"Are you kidding? It's still early."

"There were 500,000 people here two nights ago. And there wasn't even a game that night."

She nodded her head in affirmation. We passed the Brandenburg Gate and found the line. Luckily, it wasn't too long. The most obvious and logical entrance was the one we had used on the prior night, coming in from the *Reichstag* side. I imagined that entrance was impossibly glutted, while the entrance we chose was only obnoxiously busy.

Hannia got in the ladies' line to get patted down, and I got in the guys' line. I made it through first, and looked around at the crowd as I waited for her. The area in front of the stage was packed, but there was a side area that was surprisingly empty. Some people had sat down in that area to stake out a claim, and I thought that it would be great to have a place to watch the game seated. There was also a beer concession to the right as you entered that was doing a bang-up business. In fact, there seemed to be more competition for beer than for seating space--at least more enthusiastic competition. I admit that I felt compelled to join in, and did so with great gusto, elbowing my way to the counter to hoist a plastic mug of *deutsch* suds in honor of the inaugural match. It was a hot day, and noisy, crowded, and sweaty. The cold beer felt great going down.

Hannia made it through security as I finished my beer and asked where we should go. I pointed out the open spot near the stage. It was in the direct sun, but there was still space to be had, and it was possible that we'd be able to sit through the game. We staked out some territory and sat down for a while. Germans filtered in, doing double-takes at the Costa Rican regalia. We had yet to see any compatriots.

There was a bit of a wait before kick-off, and the space began to fill up. I was discovering that many Germans are less than shy about invading the personal space of others--not uncommon in any country in crowds like this--but a couple came and sat down in front of us, and then proceeded to lean back on top of us in a way that invited us to move. We held our ground and I hoped that they were very uncomfortable leaning against my sweaty leg. The odd thing was that there was space on the other side of them, but they insisted on crowding us. Other people were practically stepping on us as they blithely made their way through our area, more concerned about their beer than where they were walking.

On the big screen in front of us, the usual pre-game show was grinding away. It was hard to hear what was being said, but there were the usual pieces about players and coaches and line-ups and strategies. We could see the faces of Paolo Cesar Wanchope, Gilberto Martinez, and Andre Guimaraes flash by in big blocky pixels on the towering monitor.

Finally, the Costa Rican national anthem played, and the crowd stood at attention. The Germans were very quiet and respectful--not always the case in international soccer matches--as the cameraman walked down the row of expectant players. One jerk in the crowd was yelling, "*Deutschland, Deutschland!*" over the anthem, but as no one joined in, he shut up after a few rounds. When the German national anthem played, the crowd sang loudly and enthusiastically, culminating in a gargantuan round of applause and "*Deutschland*" chants.

Germany kicked off, and the 2006 World Cup was under way. The *Tico* players looked nervous to me, and were very tentative in their passing, but the Germans looked far from potent, either. After some indecisive play, Gilberto Martinez held the ball way too long in the Costa

Rican defense and was picked by Lahm. My jaw dropped. Martinez was by far the best defender on the Costa Rican team, and perhaps in all of CONCACAF. He played his club football in Italy for Brescia, and had done phenomenally well against the likes of Ronaldinho, Ronaldo, and company when CR played Brazil in the 2002 World Cup. He had just made a very amateurish mistake in defense. Lahm advanced swiftly and took a powerful shot on goal, beating keeper Porras to the far post. The Germans were ahead 1-0 in the sixth minute. Saying that the crowd went wild would be a vast understatement. They went gonzo berserk. All the tension hosting the tournament, with the eyes of the world upon them, with the German public and *Fussball* association openly criticizing head coach Klinsmann and dissing the team at every opportunity had built up to this moment, and the release was joltingly electric.

Hannia and I stood, glum, in a boiling sea of red, yellow, black and white exuberance. We exchanged long-suffering looks. A goal this early could foreshadow a dismal rout. Germany was now all fired up, with the home crowd behind it. Anything could happen. The chants were rising to a fevered pitch and the phrase, *"Zum finale,"* now had great resonance.

Six minutes later, Costa Rica's beefy forward, Ronald *"La Bala"* Gomez, poked a beautiful through ball past the German defenders. Paolo Cesar Wanchope, the lanky, mercurial striker, who had played in England, Spain, and Qatar before returning to Herediano in Costa Rica, made a diagonal run onto the ball, beating the offside trap perfectly. He looked up, very calmly settled, and slipped the ball past Arsenal goalkeeper Jens Lehman.

The fan mile in Berlin was dead silent. Except, of course, for the two Costa Rican fans: Mark and Hannia. We screamed and cheered and flapped our flags like the happy maniacs that we are. Then we looked out at a sea of 700,000 Teutonic faces, all staring at us, and none too happily. Suddenly, all the fears of their team's frailties, all the insecurities, all the suspicions about their Los Angeles-based coach flooded into the German *Zeitgeist*. Everyone suddenly remembered that Costa Rica scored two goals against world champs Brazil in 2002. They may have remembered that Wanchope and Gomez were the goal scorers in that match. They may have suddenly remembered that the *Ticos* beat Sweden and Scotland in 1990. The Costa Rican team was largely unknown to those outside CONCACAF, and suddenly represented a fearsome, unfathomable threat.

"*Olé, olé, olé, olé, Ticos, Ticos,*" Hannia and I wound down. Unhappy eyes were latched upon us. Still, the crowd was palpably more shame-faced than hostile. The silence was deafening. There were no German chants.

Five minutes later, however, the nightmare shifted. It was Schneider to Schweinsteiger to Klose. Miroslav Klose, a clinical finisher, and tied for second in goals in 2002, put the ball away from a couple of yards out. The Germans had gotten back on top, and the mile of fans united in a single, joyous, screaming howl of relief. Hannia and I were again the silent ones.

The crowd was again on a roll, chants, applause, and "oohs" and "aahs" filled the air as the game proceeded. There were dangerous plays in both directions, and when halftime hit the score was still 2-1.

The crowd was abuzz. I made a beeline for the beer line and recharged my glass. People were really staring at my Costa Rican jersey now. Hannia was melting in the sun, and we decided to move back into the shade. Immediately, our spaces disappeared as we moved to a spot just in front of the beer tent. Farther back, we had a better view of the crowd, and it was quite a sight. It was a sea of people that flowed back as far as the eye could see... farther, in fact, as the big screens and their concomitant scaffolding obscured vision after five or six hundred yards.

Hannia commented on the beer consumption. Everywhere we looked, virtually everyone had a beer in hand: men, women, and, yes, children. We had noticed a bunch of young kids guzzling beer on the street, on the train, in the Fan Fest and some, we thought, might well have been twelve years old. Still, the crowd was very orderly in spite of the alcohol consumption. They were as co-operative as space allowed if you had to squeeze your way through. Periodically, however, we did see the crowd part to accommodate a stretcher transporting an unconscious or semiconscious person--usually a young female--overcome by the heat, or, more likely, by a combination of heat and fermented hops. The Germans, though they love the warm weather, are not accustomed to it. Those of us from the southwestern United States know to hover in the shade whenever possible, to conserve strength, skin, and bodily fluids. The Nordic tribes go to the sunshine like moths to flames, with similar results.

As the second half started, we were a little farther from the big screen, though still in a pretty good position. There were a couple of young, muscle-bound, shaven-headed guys close by who were screaming obnoxiously, so I guided Hannia away from them. They seemed to be the only people in the crowd who were on the edge of losing control.

Immediately, Podolski was on the attack, letting off a powerful shot that was just high of the Costa Rican goal. The *Ticos* returned fire, and Danny Fonseca sent a flying header just wide of the right post.

In minute 61, Klose again made his mark. Defender Michael Umaña failed to clear Lahm's cross, and Klose headed the ball well. Costa Rican keeper Porras valiantly parried it, but Klose snapped up the rebound and put it away. Again the home crowd screamed its collective head off. Hannia and I were feeling low. Now with a two-goal lead, the Germans were smirking a little. The pressure was off. Costa Ricans weren't much of a threat. The old cliché popped into my head, "a two-goal lead is the most dangerous." It's frequently true. With a one-goal lead, you can't relax. With a three-goal lead, you can afford to. With a two-goal lead, you have a tendency to feel the game's over, especially in the second half. But if the other team scores a goal, they can catch you deflated. Suddenly, you feel vulnerable. The other team is pumped up and smells blood. They have the momentum, and I can't tell you how many times I've seen a team come back from being two goals down and win. Or tie. A tie would be devastating to the hosts.

Walter Centeno chipped a ball past the German defenders and once again Wanchope was one on one with the keeper. 'Chope deftly crossed Lehman up, and the score now stood at 3-2. It was a marvelously executed play, very much like the earlier *Tico* goal. The Germans hadn't learned from their earlier lapse. Hannia and I made a point of yelling loudly and holding our flags high. The crowd was again deflated. A guy in a Brazilian jersey walked past, saw our Costa Rican regalia, and congratulated us.

"That was a beautiful goal," he said. I can't for the life of me remember if he said it in English, German, Spanish, or Portuguese. The people around us heard the compliment and stared at their shoes. If Germany couldn't stop some podunk Central American team from scoring, how would they do against Brazil, Argentina, or Poland for that matter, who was to be their next opponent?

But Germany was still in the lead, and there were only seventeen minutes remaining. The two teams continued to duke it out. I would have to say that Germany had the edge, but the plucky Costa Ricans were giving them a rough time. All the *Ticos* needed was one goal. Just one little goal and they'd come out of the battle with a point. They'd confound the pundits and prove their worth. If not giant-killers, they'd be giant-stoppers.

In minute 87, however, Torsten Frings cracked a powerful shot from around twenty-five yards out: an unstoppable blast to the upper right corner. It was 4-2 with three minutes left in regulation. All Germany had to do was play keepaway, and the game was in the bag. That's exactly what they did. When the final whistle blew there was ecstatic pandemonium. Flags fluttered, friends clapped each other on the back, and chants and songs and cheers rent the thick, humid air. The smell of beer and perspiration, combined with bratwurst and pretzels, made the perfect accompaniment to the sounds and sights. My cell phone rang. It was Hannia's brother, Luís. "*E, maje, que goleada que nos metieron,*" he started. ("Dude, they really stuck it to us.") I assured him that scoring two goals against Germany was no mean feat, and that the first two goals given up by Costa Rica were flukey mistakes, especially Martinez's giveaway. That had us both perplexed. We both agreed that if Costa Rica could score twice on Germany, someone like England or Brazil or Italy would give the German defense fits. I passed the phone to Hannia who chattered away with her brother for quite some time. At length she put me back on the line to talk to Chris Dill, who had watched the game with Luís.

"It was an entertaining game," Chris said with audible enthusiasm, "but Luís is disconsolate. He was really bummed by the four goals they gave up."

Chris quizzed me on the ambience in Berlin, which I assured him was amazing. I told him of the 700,000-to-two fan mismatch and he was concerned on our behalf. Chris spent some time in England, the inventors of soccer hooliganism, and that's his only European benchmark.

"They treating you okay?" he asked. "That might not be the safest place for you."

"Everyone has treated us wonderfully," I said.

Some random boy came up to Hannia, and in Spanish, started to compliment the Costa Rican team's play. I heard a Castilian *"theta"* sound, so he had to be from Spain.

Hannia was buoyant enough. She had expected a rout, and was pleased that the Costa Ricans at least had shown some offensive firepower. We wandered out with the crowd, who continued to chant and sing and cheer.

We found our way back to the *U-Bahn* station. While waiting for the train, we observed all sorts of celebrating Germans, most notably a group of ten or twelve young men at trackside who lined up and did "the wave," culminating in a unified, raucous shout of *"Deutschland!"*

We arrived back at *Nollendorfplatz* and headed up the main street toward *Löwenplatz*. Cars sped by waving flags and honking horns.

We arrived back at the hotel in time to see the Ecuador-Poland match in the hotel bar. I ordered a beer, which they brought to me in a ridiculously tall glass.

The hotel bar, just off the lobby, with a large lounge, two big-screen televisions and black leather furniture, was an inviting venue, though I noticed that none of the chairs really faced the TVs. I had to slide both chairs into radically different angles to view. One of the bar waitresses gave me a dirty look as I rearranged her furniture. Normally, I'd be sensitive to this, but if you're going to host the World Cup, and virtually all your patrons are there to see the event, I think it's within the limits of reason to adjust the seating for optimal viewing.

We ordered an appetizer from the bar menu, and settled in for the match. Poland had played a friendly against Ecuador in Barcelona the previous year, just before the World Cup draw. They had beaten them 3-0 in a rainstorm. I'm sure that Poland's players had to feel deep down that Ecuador wasn't going to be a problem. They were wrong. The Ecuadorans were outrunning them, out-passing them, and out-thinking them. I had read a quote by the Polish coach, Pawel Janas, just after the draw. He had said, "Germany is obviously going to be very difficult, but we can find a way past Ecuador and Costa Rica."

In minute 24, Augustín Delgado ran onto a throw in, flicked it to Carlos Tenorio, who deftly headed the ball into the back of the net: 1-0 Ecuador. The Poles were rattled. Ecuador continued to attack.

In the second half, the Poles started strong, controlling the game for perhaps fifteen minutes. But try as they might, they just couldn't generate opportunities. The Ecuadoran defenders were big, skilled, and organized.

The South Americans kept up the heat. In minute 80, Edison Mendez gave the perfect through pass to Ivan Kaviedes. He squared the ball to Augustín Delgado, who easily passed the ball into the back of the net.

The Poles had made a big error. Chances were that they'd lose to Germany anyway, so they'd have done well to throw everything they had at Ecuador. Instead, they took the South Americans lightly. Ecuador had shocked them, and was now in pole position (no pun intended), along with Germany, to make it into the second round.

After the U.S. had lost so badly to the Poles in 2002, I halfway hoped they'd put on a good show this time, to prove what a good team we'd lost to. But they looked lackluster and less than world-class. It was odd, this being nearly a home game for them, that they hadn't seized the opportunity and shown some spark. You had to hand it to Ecuador. They had played a very strong, smart game, and had proven that they could win without the extreme Andean altitude of their native country as an advantage.

Along with us in the hotel bar were a number of soccer fans from around the globe. One woman wore a U.S. T-shirt, so I asked if she was going to the U.S. games. She said that she and her husband had tickets, but that they wouldn't be able to go to the third match against Ghana in Nuremburg on June 22. She asked me if I knew anyone who would like to buy tickets. I immediately thought of Gabriel Dill, Chris' son, who was traveling to Germany but didn't have any tickets. The woman said to get in touch with her husband.

I raced upstairs and e-mailed Chris to see if Gabriel might be interested in tickets. I didn't know how quickly he'd get the e-mail or get back to me, but figured I'd hear something before the ticket holders checked out.

JUNE 10 – OVER THE WALL TO ENGLAND AND PARAGUAY

The first thing on my mind when I awoke was… well, it was coffee, if the truth be known, but the second thing was the fax that I was expecting from my Australian friend, with the power of attorney that I so desperately needed. I got up, got ready, and guided Hannia downstairs for breakfast. As we passed the desk, I again asked about the fax. They remembered me from my last inquiry, and assured me that they'd call me in my room the second anything came in. I had really hoped to get my hands on the document before leaving Berlin. I could have everything wrapped up and not have to worry about finding my way to the stadium in Frankfurt, or wherever the heck I had the opportunity.

We went to the buffet breakfast, and we loaded our plates with eggs, sausage, bread, and all the other heavy fare that the Germans are so fond of. A group of six or eight older Germans sat down next to us. We ignored each other while we ate, creating a bit of privacy despite being a bit too close to each other. After a while I could hear them discussing soccer, so I chimed in with my usual, *"Was denken sie? Deutschland zum Finale?"* ("What do you think, Germany to the final?") The most talkative gentleman in the group, obviously the leader, probably in his late sixties or early seventies, was soon asking us about our trip. I tried my best in German to recount our comings and goings so far, and when I ran out of German, he was very pleased to wade in with his English, which may not have been exactly fluent, but was very crisp and comprehensible. It was obvious that he was showing off his English for his friends, none of whom ventured to speak to me in my native tongue.

His response about Germany was resoundingly negative. He didn't like Klinsmann as a coach, and said that the team was too young and inexperienced. They really had no prayer. I brought up the Germans' edge from playing at home. He was not impressed, and continued with his little diatribe.

I asked if he had tickets to see games, and he said no, he and his friends were in Berlin as tourists. They were from Münster, a relatively small city.

Finally, he asked me how we were enjoying our visit to his country. We told him that we were very impressed, and that we'd been treated wonderfully.

"I think this is a very important opportunity for us to show the world that Germany is a very friendly, open place," he said earnestly.

I agreed with him.

"When you talk to most people from England, they still seem to think Hitler is running the place and we're some sort of savage imperialist nation," he added.

I said that many people in the U.S. still had a World War II-era view of Germany, and that a mention of Germany was apt to bring out a fascist joke or reference. "It's hard for a lot of people to get past," I said, tactfully refraining from telling him about my numerous Jewish friends who were petrified to even think about setting foot in Germany. Some of them had parents or grandparents who had survived the death camps. I didn't mention my English friend, John, whose parents had been bombed out of house and home in the Blitz. These people had trouble accepting Germany as a benevolent entity.

I did some mathematics in my head. This guy was around seventy years old, so that meant he'd been born around 1936. Certainly he wasn't a participant in the war or the Holocaust. In fact, he probably suffered from the war more than anything. You can imagine being ten years old when defeat in global war came crashing down around the Germans' collective ears. Most of the country had been bombed into oblivion. A quick review of photographs from Germany in 1946 show endless rubble and burnt-out buildings--Somalia, Bagdad, Kabul, and Beirut had nothing on Germany. Privations, hunger, and poverty were the norm in the postwar German world. With the advent of the Cold War, the Soviets and western powers were endlessly haggling over Germany. NATO and the Warsaw Pact actively debated how to roll tanks through Germany, and who would nuke whom in the event of hostilities. Germans were the butt of all jokes, the bad guys in all the Hollywood movies, the biggest pariah in history.

I can imagine how it felt to be a young boy, subjected to the propaganda of the war, believing that the *Vaterland* was virtuous and wonderful, only to spend the next sixty years of your life in a constant state of guilt and universal reprimand, hearing about how evil your parents, government, and culture were. I can also imagine the despair of knowing that the world was correct in this judgment.

The man at the table across from me had been through this, and it was apparent in his tone and demeanor that he was eager for it all to change. He was desperate to be able to feel patriotic and a little proud and nationalistic without the fear of condemnation. I think he overestimated the power of the World Cup, but I hope he gets a modicum of relief. It is hard not to believe that Germany had something in it that had conjured up the demons of World War II, and that this something was cultural and idiosyncratically Teutonic in nature, and should be kept in check. On the other hand, it had probably been enough penance for this obviously reasonable and intelligent retired gentleman and his friends to endure. For the people who actively participated in the madness, I have no similar sympathy.

After breakfast, I checked my email, and our ticket seller had written me to say he would fax the power of attorney to our hotel in Mainz. I phoned the hotel in Mainz, where I was told they had the fax, but no reservation in our names, and that there were two Hilton hotels in Mainz. I was sure that this was the one that SoccerTravel had indicated. I double-checked, and it was the link they had sent me via e-mail when the accommodations were confirmed--Hilton Mainz City. That's where I had gotten the fax number to send to our Australian friend. I told the hotel desk to please hold onto the fax until tomorrow, since I'd be arriving there about midday. They assured me it was no problem.

With that thoroughly mucked up, we decided to shift into tourist mode.

Perhaps the major point of interest in Berlin is what used to be the Berlin Wall. Though it no longer stood, its remnants and history loom large in the public consciousness. Just sixteen years before, on November 9, 1989, crowds thronged to the Brandenburg gate to whack away at the structure and let a turbulent river of democracy, capitalism, consumerism, and Western imperialism flood through the cracks.

To me, the place to hit was Checkpoint Charlie, the fabled passage through the Iron Curtain of yore. I shuffled through my maps and *U-Bahn* diagrams, and figured out how to get from *Nollendorfplatz* station to the *Stadtmitte* exit on *Friedrichstrasse*. Believe me, it is no mean feat to keep all these street and place names in a cluttered and disorderly head like mine, compounded by the fact that many streets change names every block or so. *Zimmer Strasse*, where the Checkpoint Charlie museum stands, is *Niederkirchenstrasse* as you travel west, and turns, veers south, and becomes *Kothener Strasse*. *Friedrichstrasse*, a major artery, retains its name through the *Mitte* district, but when it hits the *Oranienburg Tor*, it bends westward and becomes *Chausee Strasse, Müller Strasse*, and so forth. If you're looking for a well-planned grid of easily recognizable thoroughfares, which you might reasonably expect from the Germans, you are out of luck. Berlin is Byzantine in more ways than one.

The sight of the guard shack, flagpole, sandbags, and soldiers standing at Checkpoint Charlie immediately took hold of my Cold War-steeped memory. It looked exactly as I remembered it from news reports, documentaries and *LIFE* magazine. The sign over the guard shack reads, "You are now entering the American Sector." A couple of German youths dressed in military uniforms held the American and Soviet flags respectively. Everyone took pictures with the two, and snapped up kitschy memorabilia, faux passport stamps, postcards, and the usual bric-a-brac required for the acquisitive tourist.

Hannia, whose Cold War memories were very different from my own, marveled at the checkpoint and was full of questions about the formerly divided city. While she was certainly aware of it growing up, she had been subject to less reporting and anecdotage than I had. I explained the British, French, American, and Soviet partition of Berlin as best I could, and provided her with a few dates and historical landmarks. I had grown up hearing about the fabled Berlin airlift, an exercise in American organization, "can-do" attitude, benevolence, and anti-communism.

This, of course, was no mere exercise in historical babbling. We were standing in front of the real deal, and it was bizarre. A decade and a half ago, it was impossible to do what we had just done, namely cross the city freely and walk across a particular street. It seemed ludicrous that human beings would be so vehemently opposed to people wandering around their own city, but there it was. While the North and South Korean division lives on, at least it's not within the same city.

The *Mauermuseum*--Wall Museum, not to be confused with Walmart--laid out the historical timeline and commemorated the efforts of Germans to cross, some of which proved deadly. The building houses displays of items used in clandestine crossings: subterranean, aerial, amphibious, and automotive. While the wall was up, human drama abounded.

From the upper floors of the museum, I looked out a large plate-glass window at where the wall once had stood. There was no perceptible difference between the two sides, but there remained an empty space in the middle, where the wall had been, now barren, with patchy grass and mounds of dirt. I was sure that in a few years it would all be built up, but for now, the vestiges of the wall were still very palpable.

As we came out of the museum and took our requisite photos in front of an old wall segment, we went in search of a cold beverage. Nearby we found a small market, and dove in. It was run by a Turkish family, and most of the patrons seemed Turkish as well. Hannia examined the produce to the right of the entrance, and surveyed the canned and boxed products on the shelves to the left. Most was familiar, much was not. She grabbed some grapes for the trek to the *U-Bahn*. We got a few interested stares as we plowed through the crowd, speaking Spanish, the redhead and the Central American, seeking out some bottled water (*ohne Kohlensaüre*), and some snack crackers. Veritably in the shadow of the Checkpoint Charlie, the new generation of immigrants was sprouting up from between the chunks of the old wall, filling the gaps in commerce and culture, and doing so with a blithe and lively indifference to the past.

Our next stop was the *Museuminsel*, or Museum Island, where the River *Spree* decided to split in half and leave a triangular slice of land for the Germans to build museums on. It is one of the most picturesque spots in Berlin, with grand buildings and classical architecture.

We visited the *Berliner Dom*, the main Protestant church of Berlin, where we discovered that they wanted to charge us to enter. I guess this is the chief difference between Catholic Italy and Protestant Germany. Martin Luther not only nailed his tenets to the door, but he built a ticket booth as well. Though appreciative of the entrepreneurial spirit in evidence, we declined the invitation. After we'd been welcomed into St. Peter's, the Pantheon, and the Florentine *Duomo*, it stuck in our craw a bit that our cash was more important to them than our interest. Our apologies to the Hohenzollerns buried therein--I'm sure they'll get along fine without us.

There was a wedding going on, so we stood out front and marveled at the huge, ridiculously ornate baroque edifice with its large, green copper domes. A happy couple and its complement of festive family members, dressed in their finest, streamed down the stone steps, and ran the gauntlet of photographers, both professional and familial. The newlyweds plunged headlong into a maroon sedan, decorated with all the silly ornaments available to the modern connubial celebrant, and drove off amidst cheers and catcalls to a new life. *Viel Gluck*.

"I wonder how far in advance you have to book this place for a wedding," Hannia pondered.

"And how well-connected you have to be," I added, giving voice to my cynical impulses. Any church that charges admission to the visitor off the street must be very judicious about who can and can't get married there.

We proceeded to the *Altes Nationalgalerie* (Old National Gallery) nearby, and enjoyed the exhibits of Degas, Courbet (odd landscapes with odd, stuffed-animal-inspired deer), Rodin, and more.

We timed our cultural exploration to accommodate the real priority: England vs. Paraguay. As the appointed hour approached, we got antsy, making sure to drink in every last ounce of painting, sculpture, and tapestry the gallery afforded. Finally, unable to contain our anticipation, we bolted from the marble halls and made a beeline for the nearest television set.

Backtracking from the *Museuminsel*, we walked past a corridor between two large office buildings, where a food court offered several semi-fast-food restaurants and open-air dining. Large plasma and LCD screens were set up. We found the section in which the sunlight created the least glare and had a seat. The tables seemed to be available to one and all, but were in fact claimed by the restaurants on either side. We happened to be in the zone controlled by Happy Sushi, a Japanese restaurant. An Asian girl popped out of the restaurant and handed us menus. "*Nihongo wa wakari mas-ka?*" I asked her with one of the seven or eight phrases I can manage in Japanese. She looked confused and frightened. "*Sprechen sie Japanisch?*" I tried in German. She looked horrified.

"*Mein vater ist von Vietnam,*" she replied, at long last. "But I speak English."

I glanced into the restaurant and saw some people of Asian descent working behind the counter and in the kitchen.

"Are the owners Japanese? " I continued.

"No, they are also from Vietnam," she informed me.

So much for trying out my Japanese. And so much for a legit Japanese meal in Berlin--it serves me right for not sticking with the national cuisine: Turkish.

I ordered an assortment of sushi and some yakitori. Hannia had a noodle dish. I ordered a beer.

The English and Paraguayan teams strode onto the big screens that littered the food court.

England had high hopes. They felt they were real contenders to hoist the trophy. The country that invented the game felt it was ready to climb back into supremacy. This might be their opportunity. Spice Boy David Beckham was still near the top of his game. The likes of Joe Cole, Ashley Cole, Owen Hargreaves, and Steven Gerrard were in their prime and arguably among the best in the world. Michael Owen, fragile but explosive, could always blow a game wide open at any moment. Rooney was still nursing a bad metatarsal, but the bizarrely proportioned Peter Crouch, six-foot-seven, 155 pounds, a stork of a man, whose twig-like frame seemed ready to snap at a moment's notice, was on fire. He had scored six goals in eleven caps. He had a nose for the net, and world-class skills you would never associate with a man of his proportions.

Paraguay was the perpetual overachiever. A tiny South American republic of just under six and a half million inhabitants, they have always been a solid, scrappy squad. Since the retirement of José Luís Chilavert, their stellar but volatile goalkeeper, few thought they'd have the moxie to qualify in the competitive South American confederation. Their lone star, Roque Santa Cruz, who played for Bayern Munich, was surrounded by competent players, most of whom played in Paraguay, Argentina, Brazil, and Mexico. They had a few players based in Europe, but no real standouts. Still, somehow they managed to qualify, beating out some pretty impressive squads like Colombia, Chile, and former world champion Uruguay.

Not only did they qualify, they managed to beat Argentina in Paraguay and to tie them in Buenos Aires. They couldn't be taken lightly, but few expected them to survive the first couple of rounds. Most observers figured England and Sweden to take top honors in this group.

The match started out hard fought, but in the third minute, Beckham bent one in on a free kick from the left. Defender Carlos Gamarra, Paraguay's captain, got his head on the ball, but only succeeded in redirecting it enough to fool his own keeper, Justo Villar. The ball bounced around the back of the net and the Brits were on top. It seemed they were in a position to rout the hapless *Guaraní*. Five minutes later, goalkeeper Villar challenged Michael Owen for a ball, and though he managed to clear it, he also managed to injure himself. The Paraguayans found themselves a goal down, with their second-string keeper between the pipes. They still had 82 minutes to go against the inventors of the game.

But the Paraguayans weren't about to roll over. England mustered some good attacking play, but the South Americans held firm. Substitute keeper Bobadilla played admirably, making several impressive saves.

Both teams sagged in the second half, presumably wilting in the Frankfurt heat. Still, both sides created opportunities. Paraguay showed grit and character, but couldn't find the back of the net.

When the final whistle sounded, the result was as expected. The real story, however, was that the English weren't going to win the World Cup in 2006. If they had their hands full with Paraguay, and only won on an own goal, they would have serious trouble with such teams as Brazil, Argentina, Italy, Germany, and Holland.

Paraguay, though defeated, could be very proud of the show they'd put on, despite having abysmal luck in the opening minutes.

My own luck had also been abysmal. The beer I had ordered from my Japanese-Vietnamese Restaurant was sweetish, and awful. I figured I'd get the taste out of my mouth with a cappuccino. The cappuccino was just as bad as the beer. Beer and coffee were two items I never thought I'd have trouble with in Germany, but it proves that surprises will always find you, no matter where you go.

We returned to our hotel room. I called my parents back in scenic Walnut Creek, California. My father loudly asked, "Hey, what happened to Costa Rica?" knowing that this would nettle his Costa Rican daughter-in-law. Hannia, who could hear the squawk of the earpiece, scrunched her face up in displeasure. "Our team's not going anywhere," she growled. I repeated my defense of the *Ticos*. They'd scored two goals against a world power, and had they not given up a couple of stupid goals, they could have sneaked away with a tie. I sincerely felt they had a good chance against Ecuador and Poland, and who knows, they might just squeak into the second round.

Hannia and I whined about the weather and lack of ventilation, and anything else we could think of, but generally admitted that we were having a wonderful time. My mom and dad were veterans of years of youth soccer, as Dad had coached numerous teams, while Mom did a yeoman's job as a chauffeur and personal manager for her soccer-playing son. I had taken them to a few MLS and U.S. national team games, and they were jazzed to watch the World Cup on TV, especially since they had family in attendance.

We turned on the TV in the hotel room and watched Sweden play Trinidad and Tobago. Of all the participants, T&T were expected to be among the worst. Not only did they come from what most consider one of the "weakest" confederations--our own CONCACAF--but they didn't even qualify in the normal run of play. They had to go into a consolation round against Bahrain. They tied the first leg 1-1, and then won the second, 1-0. Trinidad has produced some great players, most notably the aging Dwight Yorke, who lit it up for Manchester United for a number of years. Playmaker Russell Latapy played for Porto and Boavista in Portugal, as well as Hibernian in Scotland. Shaka Hislop, their long-time goalkeeper, also plied his trade in the land of teabags for Reading, Newcastle United, West Ham U, and Portsmouth (as well as NCAA soccer for Howard University), but was now relegated to the backup slot. My favorite of the bunch was Stern John, whom I'd seen play in MLS before he jumped the pond to play for Nottingham Forest, Birmingham City, Derby County, and Coventry City. John was an explosive and creative forward, and was one of those guys who just oozes enjoyment of the game. Another player on the radar was Cornell Glen, who had recently been acquired by the L.A. Galaxy, but hadn't yet gotten much playing time.

John was in his prime, but Yorke, Latapy and Hislop were all well on the downward slope. The team had hired Dutch coach Leo

Beenhakker and got perhaps more organized than a T&T team ever had been. The highlight of their qualifying run was beating Mexico 2-1 in Port of Spain. Stern John scored both goals for the Trinidadians. For anyone who knows anything about CONCACAF, this is nothing short of amazing. Mexico, a country of more than 100 million people, and arguably the most impressive soccer history in the region, versus an island republic of 1.3 million souls--this should have been a walk in the park for the Guacamole Guys.

The Scandinavians boasted a stellar lineup including forward Henrik Larsson, who most recently had helped Barcelona win the European Champions League. The other forward was Zlatan Ibrahimovic, of Italian champions Juventus (champions until their title was removed for match-fixing), one of the best strikers in the game. Midfielder Freddie Ljundberg of Arsenal was another dominant player from a top team. The rest of the squad featured solid players from Sweden's domestic league, with a few who played in France, Belgium, Greece, and Germany. As Sweden took the field against the islanders, very few people were in doubt about the outcome.

Those few people, however, happened to play for Trinidad and Tobago.

In the stadium in Dortmund, the yellow shirts in the stands announced a staunchly pro-Swedish crowd. Since Germany was a short hop for their Nordic neighbors, this was virtually a home game for the Swedes.

Ljundberg, Larsson, and Ibrahimovic came out strong, creating chance after chance. But somehow, their finishing was off. The Soca Warriors were holding tough on defense, and suddenly counter-attacked with abandon. Thirty-seven-year-old Shaka Hislop (first choice Kelvin Jack was injured) made some excellent saves, and the game held at 0-0 at the half. No one expected the T&T squad to hold out so long against such impressive firepower.

In minute 46, Avery John received his second yellow card for a two-footed challenge. The Soca Warriors were down to ten men.

The Swedes smelled blood and poured it on in the attack, but the Trinidadians held their shape in the back, covered the gaps--even though they were a man short--and went after every ball with fire and courage.

Cornell Glen got off a tremendous shot, which bounced off the Swedish crossbar.

Ibrahimovic had a few excellent opportunities, but couldn't get off a decent shot.

When the final whistle blew, T&T were undefeated. They were ecstatic. The Swedes were shell-shocked. It had been an exciting game: yes, 0-0 draws can be exciting. And the Soca Warriors had done it against a very good European team, playing a man down for virtually the entire second half. I would have loved to be in Trinidad at that moment. I'm sure some very spirited celebrating was breaking out all over the island.

Dwight Yorke, so long denied the chance to shine on the world stage, could retire satisfied that he'd filled all the spaces on his resume.

We popped down to the bar to watch the next match: Argentina vs. Ivory Coast. We settled into the seats we had occupied the night before for Poland vs. Ecuador, and ordered a drink. We were looking over the appetizer menu when the game began. The sound was turned down on the big screen, so we asked them to turn it up for the game. The waiter informed us that the manager of the bar had decided he didn't run a "sports bar"--a term uttered with utter disdain--and they'd put the picture on, but with no sound. Hannia and I looked at each other for a long beat.

"But we watched a game in here last night with the sound up," I protested, thinking there was some miscue. I looked around at the patrons, all of whom were staring raptly at the silent screen.

At last, Hannia said, "This is the World Cup. We wouldn't be here if it weren't for the World Cup."

The waiter shrugged apologetically, "I'm sorry, but the manager...."

We popped up out of our seats at the same time.

"Okay, "I said, trying to sound as cheerful and positive as possible. "We'll go elsewhere."

All the staff in the bar seemed shocked and dismayed to see us go. We'd order a fair amount of food and drink in our previous visit, and had tipped like… well, like Americans. As we strolled out, we saw a few more couples taking a cue from us and clearing out.

We walked out into the *Lützowplatz* and Hannia asked what I had in mind. I'd seen a restaurant down the street as we'd strolled to *Nollendorfplatz* before, perhaps a block and a half away.

As we walked, a nice-looking sedan pulled up to the curb and a young lady hopped out. As the sedan pulled away Hannia and I both noticed her mode of dress--or undress. She was a tall, slender, twentysomething brunette wearing high-heeled boots, a mesh bodysuit, and bikini. She strutted provocatively to the corner and looked searchingly into each passing car.

Hannia's jaw dropped open. We were in a very upscale neighborhood. It featured a number of hotels, but they were large, classy hotels. Hannia finally asked the obvious, "Is she….?"

Just then a car stopped. She opened the passenger door conversed a moment, then hopped in and sped off.

"Yep," I replied. "She is."

We looked up and down the street and saw a second, then a third young lady, similarly attired, standing around on the street corner.

Hannia reacted. Certainly this was something you didn't see in Los Angeles. Streetwalkers there were relegated to certain scuzzy neighborhoods, not that there isn't clandestine prostitution going on in the better areas. Prostitution was even less obvious in Costa Rica. But these ladies were soliciting business right out in the open, in a fairly elegant part of town. How tremendously European.

We followed *Einemstrasse* south toward *Kurfürstenstrasse*. The restaurant, Ambrosius, was on a corner and had sort of a small *biergarten* outdoors, but the chairs were up on the tables. We approached the door of the restaurant carefully. It looked all but closed. Despite the large banners outside proclaiming that it was your best choice to watch a game, no one seemed to be doing that. The lights were on, but one could only distinguish scant activity inside. A busboy scurried with a tray of dishes, a waitress folded napkins. A man seated at the bar played a little game with matchsticks on the counter, seemingly waiting for his girlfriend or whomever to get off work. We looked for someone to ask if they were open, and finally came across a waitress, who insisted we come in and sit down. I asked if they had the game on, so they steered us to the back portion of the restaurant, where the only occupied table had four employees eating their dinner and watching a large LCD TV. They looked a little embarrassed as we settled in, as though they had been caught slacking off, or breaking protocol. I felt that probably they were on the brink of closing, but figured they'd get another two plates worth of cash into the till, and have an excuse to relax and watch the game.

The menu was odd, to say the least. All of the dishes had semi-biblical names: the Sermon on the Mount, the Noah's Ark, the Multiplying Fish. I scanned the restaurant to see if I'd missed something. It didn't seem to be an overtly religious establishment. I wondered, considering the commerce on the street outside, what I'd get if I asked for the Mary Magdalene.

I ended up ordering the Tenth Apostle, which was a herring dish. Luckily the beer was easily recognizable by name.

The game was interesting. Argentina was, as usual, one of the favorites, and the Ivory Coast was an underdog African team that many were expecting to produce surprises.

Affectionately referred to as "The Elephants," the Ivorians boasted the likes of Didier Drogba, a talented forward who plays for Chelsea, Kolo Touré of Arsenal, his brother Yaya Touré of Greek side Olympiakos, and Bonaventure Kalou of Paris Saint-Germaine.

Argentina, of course, has a stellar lineup, with names that are featured in legendary club rosters around the globe: Pablo Aimar and Roberto Ayala of Valencia, Juan Riquelme and Juan Sorín of Villarreal, Gabriel Heinze of Man U, Javier Saviola of Sevilla, Hernán Crespo of Chelsea, Carlos Tevez and Javier Mascherano of Corinthians, Esteban Cambiasso, Nicolás Burdisso, and Julio Cruz of Inter Milan, Lionel Messi of Barcelona, Gabriel Milito of Zaragosa, Leandro Cufre of AS Roma, Maxi Rodriguez and Leonardo Franco of Atlético Madrid, and Roberto Abbondanzieri of Boca Juniors.

It would be prudent for anyone with an ounce of soccer knowledge to be scared to death of this list of names and teams. The Ivorians, however, were not scared in the least. They were young, hungry, and talented, and knew instinctively that on a good day spirit can easily trump skill in soccer. And I don't think anyone was fooling him or herself: the Ivorians were pretty damned talented and skilled themselves.

The Argentines also had to have, looming in the deep recesses of their brains, the memory of another African team they played back in 1990. Cameroon had come into its first ever World Cup as a virtual unknown, led by thirty-eight-year-old, "just out of retirement" Roger Milla, and had exited with the appellation of "giant-killer," though Argentina still managed to squeak through to the next round as one of the best third-place teams. Many pundits were expecting the Ivory Coast to be this year's Cameroon. Drogba was lusting for blood, and was not at all intimidated by the South American roster.

It turned out to be the Crespo, Saviola, Riquelme, and Drogba Show. Riquelme fed the ball, and Crespo and Saviola finished. Riquelme created many more than the two goals that went in for his side, but these were the two that found twine. Drogba created many opportunities, unselfishly setting up his compatriots, but ultimately, it was up to the Chelsea man to get on the scoreboard himself. The final 2-1 score was reflective of play, but Ivory Coast could have easily ground out a tie if the ball had bounced a little more their way.

The restaurant workers at the table across from us were clearly favoring Argentina. These four women were obviously much more familiar with the European-based players, and they cheered loudly at every opportunity the South Americans produced. I think they were also a little enamored of some of the pretty-boy Argentine players.

My Tenth Apostle dinner had settled in well, especially behind a couple of mugs of beer, and we said our good-byes. We braved the prostitute-lined streets of Berlin as we walked back to the hotel, relishing the contrasts. Here we had sullied ourselves by going to a lowly "sports bar"--which was anything but a sports bar, and possibly some sort of establishment with religious ties--and traipsed back into the noble halls of the chain hotel that had stooped so low as to admit us as guests, before they knew of our disturbingly proletarian tastes.

Back in our room, I got on the Internet and planned our escape. I confirmed our flight to Frankfurt the following day, and reserved a spot on the train to Gelsenkirchen for--could it actually be?--the first U.S. game of the 2006 World Cup. Visions of sugarplums danced in my head as I lay it down on the pillow next to Hannia. The real event was about to start for us.

Our Berlin digs.

The *Fernsehturm* a la Fussball.

The Brandenburg Gate dwarfed by a giant soccer ball and red-haired guy.

L: Hannia contemplates the Bundestag.
R: For the World's Largest Headache. The World's Largest Aspirin.

The dome atop the Bundestag.

The dome view: a faux stadium below.

500,000 of our closest friends.

Keeping things under control.

Fans watch the inaugural ceremonies.

June 11ᵀᴴ – TO THE Treffpunkt!

We popped out of bed at the first light of dawn, not waiting for the alarm to sound. We had to get our act together and take it on the road, to the airport, to Frankfurt, then Mainz. We felt the rush of adrenaline even before the rush of caffeine, though we were pretty quick to seek out the complimentary coffee in the lobby. We showered swiftly and headed out to *Nollendorfplatz*. No streetwalkers at this early hour. It was so early, in fact, that the American café we had seen on our earlier outing wasn't even open yet. We wouldn't get the unbridled pleasure of a pancake breakfast--Hannia was gravely disappointed.

We strolled the boulevard until we found a coffee shop. It was a glass-fronted, corner building, a student hangout, with lots of loitering, Mac-toting bohemians with funny hats. Of course, in this part of the world, when you say "bohemian," you could be talking about real Bohemians from the environs around Prague, just a few hundred miles away. But of course, I mean the good, old-fashioned figurative bohemians: pseudo-hip, non-conformist, *artiste* types with scraggly beards, who nowadays dress in black, have piercings and tattoos, and try extremely hard to act morose enough to appear as though they have the salvation of the world constantly on their minds. We sidled up to a table, looking very much the dorky U.S. tourists. Then we started speaking Spanish to each other. I detected some sideways glances up from the stanzas of romantic poetry that patrons were pretending to labor over. They looked us up and down. Yes, shorts, tennis shoes, baseball cap, but wait, what language is this very Irish-, Scottish-, or German-looking fellow speaking? We flouted convention in a number of ways. If we were American, why were we here for the World Cup, and why on earth did we speak Spanish? If we were Latin American, why did I look like Matthias Sammer? If we were European, why was I wearing white tennis shoes, white athletic socks, and a baseball cap?

So much confusion, and all this in just a couple of glances. Silent, furtive, instinctual, synaptic activity.

I ordered in German, and pretty well-pronounced German at that. (Or so I've been told.) This prompted even more furtive glances. These terminally cool hipsters were on the verge of crossing into very uncool territory, by being visibly intrigued or surprised by something.

Hannia ordered the New York breakfast, and I ordered the Frankfurt breakfast. It was very good. The Germans, unlike the Italians and French, enjoy a hearty first meal, and the offerings are substantial. Hannia's plate held bacon and eggs with various types of bread, and mine displayed an assortment of meats, including sausage, meatballs, and salami.

We lingered over the plates and enjoyed our meals, ordering seconds on cappuccino.

Bidding the *Nollendorfplatz* farewell, we trudged back to the hotel to check out, asking again about our errant fax. Still nothing. We caught a cab back to Tegel International Airport, arriving early enough to wander through the shops. The modern airport has become something of a mall. One section was entirely devoted to shops: gifts and gewgaws and magazines, of course. Personal hygiene items, cold remedies, and snacks, it goes without saying. Postal outposts? Banking facilities? Cell phone stores? Well, it makes sense, after all. But the jewelry stores, the clothing outlets, the T-shirt stores, and the video-rental houses make you wonder a bit, possibly enough to forget about a flight altogether.

Hannia was on a mission to pick out goodies for our many nieces and nephews in Costa Rica. All sorts of World Cup paraphernalia was available: little semi-rigs with the flag and team of each country on them, key chains, kerchiefs, action figures, banners, flags, glasses, cups, plates, in fact, virtually anything you could imagine. In addition, all of the stores' decorations were soccer-themed: giant balloons with octagonal, soccer-ball-like patterns, giant posters of Oliver Kahn, Michael Ballack, and the rest of the *Mannschaft*. Window displays were framed in plastic goal posts and netting.

Hannia was loading up, and I admonished her to restrain herself a bit so we wouldn't have to carry our gifts all around the country. She agreed, but still couldn't contain her generosity entirely. She filled a couple of bags with toys and books: Santa Claus in June.

We finally boarded the plane and took wing. It's a short flight from Berlin to Frankfurt, much like the commuter route between Los Angeles and San Francisco. The plane rose to cruising altitude in time to level off briefly, turn off the seat belt sign, have a cup of coffee, and descend. We might have been in the air a total of fifty minutes.

Frankfurt airport is immense, but we retrieved our baggage quickly enough. It was all compartmentalized and well organized, and also, we'd been there a couple of times before. We got our bags off the conveyor belt and looked around the baggage retrieval area. Numerous tourist-guide-looking people were holding up signs with company or individual names in order to collect their charges. We expected one of them to say "Soccer Travel." We didn't see one. I told Hannia to keep an eye on the bags while I made the rounds. I threaded my way through the ample crowd, staring intently at any and all placards that might help my cause. A couple of times I looked at a travel representative and he or she at me, thinking for a brief moment that we were meant for each other, only to be disappointed by the big block letter that spelled out something other than what I sought. Another passenger and I looked each other over. He was wearing the same U.S. national team cap I'd been sent by Soccer Travel, and carried the same kind of red bag they'd sent filled with tourist brochures and tickets. We asked each other if we were waiting for Soccer Travel. Why, yes, we both were. We both brightened. Upon further interrogation, however, it turned out that he was going to a different town with a splinter group. He had to take a bus. I hung my head with disappointment. I returned to Hannia and the bags. "Find 'em?" she asked.

"Nope" I said.

"You?"

"Nope."

I whipped out my cell phone and rifled through my papers to find the local representative's number. The first number I dialed was answered by a guy who listened to my predicament. He told me he was on the road to another venue, and I should call another young lady who was taking care of today's arrivals. I called her and she took my information down. She asked me if I knew where the meeting point was. I felt like I had missed something, maybe I misread the instructions or something, saying, "I didn't know there was a meeting point. No one told me of a pre-determined place to meet."

"Where are you?" she asked.

"I'm in front of baggage claim," I replied.

"Look toward the exit."

"Okay," I said, and looked toward the exit, expecting to see a group holding a sign. Instead, I saw a huge sign hanging from the ceiling, a metal and Plexiglass monstrosity featuring, literally, a giant spot. It was emblazoned with the word *Treffpunkt,* or "meeting point." Ah hah! This was a pretty intelligent feature in an airport. In fact, I was surprised that it hasn't been adopted in other airports I've visited. Or maybe they've been there all along, and I was just unaware.

"Wait at the Meeting Point. We've got somebody on the way," she said.

We dragged our luggage under the *Treffpunkt* sign and waited, looking searchingly at anyone who showed up searching for arrivals. Many had signs with the names of their prey. One gentleman caught my attention. He was a dark-haired, mustachioed, and rumpled man holding up a laminated sign that was illegible. It almost looked like the characters scrawled on it were Cyrillic or Arabic, or something else unintelligible to me, which considering the huge Turkish population, and the enormity of the international event that surrounded us, made this likely, as did his appearance. He almost looked like an older relative of Borat Sagdiyev. I looked at him a couple of times wondering if he was in fact our ride, but he wasn't too concerned about finding anyone.

Finally, after scanning all the souls in the *Treffpunkt* area, I repositioned myself to see his sign a little better. I noticed that it was a recycled sign. He was holding it upside-down and backward. I could see the back of the sign, where a name was neatly printed in big, legible block letters. I swung around to read the front of the sign again. I squinted at the name on the "front" of the sign, scribbled in smeary ballpoint pen on the slick plastic lamination. It read, "Mr. Baldwin."

I greeted him and introduced myself, grabbing Hannia and pulling her along. The gentleman seized her bag, and tried to take mine, but I insisted on pulling it myself. He apologized, in heavily accented German, for the time it had taken for him to get to us. They were inundated with arrivals and he had been sent to the wrong place in the confusion. I assured him it was no problem, and we zipped out of the terminal into the parking lot where a large, black sedan awaited. It was a shiny new Mercedes S-class, which struck me as odd for a tourist company, but I thought, what the heck.

He started to load the bags into the trunk very, very slowly. I pitched in--he was a large, strong-looking guy, but I felt he could have been my father--and we settled into the back seat of the very comfortable sedan. He asked which hotel we were headed to, and I responded that it was the Mainz Hilton, but that there was already some confusion, as there were two of those. As he pulled out into traffic, he fired up his cell phone and clarified our destination. We merged onto the freeway, and he remained in the far-right, slow lane. Cars were flashing past us on the left, in typical *autobahn* fashion. They were passing us like we were standing still. After a bit, I looked down at his speedometer. The kilometers per hour were more prominently displayed on the device, but on a separate, smaller ring under the KPH, miles per hour were indicated. We were doing eighty-five. Miles, not kilometers.

I suddenly realized how smooth the pavement was, and how quietly the Mercedes rode. And I realized how ridiculously fast the cars were traveling as they blurred past us on the left. I made a point of not bringing the fact to Hannia's attention. She would have been a little flipped out, and rightly so.

After our speedy trip, we arrived in Mainz. Our driver rolled us into the circular driveway of the Mainz Hilton and started getting the bags out. Once again, feeling like a schmuck for letting the old guy hoist the bags, and also a little impatient, I pitched in, pulled them out, and gave the driver a tip.

We waddled up to the counter, checked in, and found our room. Luckily it was well air-conditioned. Mainz was even warmer and more humid than Berlin, and carting the luggage around had made me more than a little sweaty. We lay down on the bed for a few moments to relax. After cooling off a bit, we realized that there was a game about to start. We charged out into the hall and the lobby and asked where there was a communal place to watch. On the second floor, in front of the restaurant, we found a bar, and staked out a place on one of the sofas, where we had a good view of the big screen.

The game was Serbia and Montenegro vs. the Netherlands. S&M. part of the ever-shrinking former Yugoslavia, had declined in years past. The Yugos were once considered the "Brazil of Europe" because of their flair, but when Croatia split off, they took the majority of the stylish players with them. Still, you can find any number of Serbs on big European club teams. In Italy, for instance, many squads have players with names ending in "-vic." Frequently, they are tough guys, known to be enforcers or hard defenders. There were also a few good Serb strikers sprinkled around European clubs, including Nikola Zigic, at six-foot-eight, the world's tallest professional soccer player.

The Netherlands is, of course, one of the top-flight teams. Though they have a history of folding at the wrong moment, or not playing up to potential, they still possess some of the best players in the world, and the 2006 squad was no exception. The coach had neglected to call up some of the aging stalwarts, such as Davids and Kluivert, and the rumor was that they finally had a man at the helm capable of standing up to the big stars and whipping the team of prima donnas into fighting shape.

A couple of Americans were seated next to us, and we fell into conversation before the game. Sean, a young fellow with dark hair, insisted that he only followed European teams, but when I mentioned a few things about the MLS, he knew all about it. His rap seemed a bit defensive, in anticipation of confronting Eurosnobs. Sean's friend seemed to be at a loss when it came to soccer conversation, but they were both brimming with excitement as the game kicked off.

The Dutch were in control for most of the first half. Arjen Robben, with his blistering speed, was dangerous from the outset, putting a goal in at minute 18. He threatened a few more times, but couldn't get in a second one. The second half saw Serbia and Montenegro come to life and threaten a few times, but they couldn't find the finishing touch. The Dutch sagged visibly by the end of the game, but held on for a minimalist victory.

We said our good-byes to Sean and his buddy and wandered off into the town of Mainz, to get to know the place a little, and to find the train station, from which we'd depart for our first game the following day. I got rough directions from a map and the concierge, and we crossed the street and headed into town.

It was Sunday, and most of the stores were closed, but we made mental notes of the businesses we'd need to frequent during our stay: photo processing, department stores, stationery stores, groceries, and all kinds of restaurants.

The town was tranquil and smallish. Cobblestone sidewalks wound their way between buildings and streets. We passed a park that featured the ruins of the earliest church in Mainz, probably where Guttenberg worshipped. I navigated as best I could, using the map the hotel had provided, as well as my guidebook, which had a rough diagram of the city.

We made it to the main drag, where we happened past the Euro store—like the dollar stores back home, everything imaginable for one Euro. We found a laundry and a fish restaurant and traveled west, which lead us past the post office and up to the train station. The station was, naturally, a hub of activity, and we saw more people there than during the rest of our walk. The station was a mildly ornate *mitteleuropa* structure with a plaza in front of it, in which buses, taxis, and streetcars vied for space on the periphery. Arrivals streamed out, their wheeled luggage bumping on the cobblestones of the plaza. We made our way into the building and up the escalator. The interior of the building was strikingly modern: chrome and glass and convenience stores, all off which pulsed with activity. There was a bakery on the bottom floor, and a different one at mezzanine level. Up top, there were a couple of drugstore-like emporia and, of course, the ticket office, open and full of patrons.

I moseyed into line, waited my turn, and showed my reservation printout to the clerk. She examined it with a characteristically German grimace, trying her best to read every last detail as quickly as possible. She frowned at the page and typed a few aggressive keystrokes into her computer. "Aaaaaaaaah!" she purred at long last, "*Das ist schlecht.*" ("That is bad.") This got my attention. It turned out that the time of the train had changed by half an hour, and it would be arriving on a different track. I was glad that I had checked. I thanked the woman profusely in my very best high-school German, and we headed out.

On the way back, we took a different route, heading down a tree-lined boulevard past a large church until we met the river Main as darkness fell. Turning right, we followed the road past the *Kurfürstliches Schloss* (electoral palace), an impressive group of reddish structures huddled against the street. These were the government offices of old, and worthy of touristic inquiry, but not tonight. We found the hotel again, having traced a great circle on our journey. Having successfully navigated the city of Mainz for the first time, we were glad to get back in at a decent hour to ready ourselves for the next day's trip. We hit the sack and tried to get as much rest as we could.

JUNE 12 – GAME DAY #1, USA vs. CZE

We got up early to get ready for the train ride to Gelsenkirchen. The breakfast buffet area was teeming with fans, stoking up on hot grub to fortify them for the day's challenges. Where before the pace had been leisurely, today it was harried. We shoveled as much food as possible into our faces, packed up, and made the trek through town to the train station. Despite our plans and preparations, we arrived a minute or two late. Our train had departed. We hurriedly scrambled to the ticket office and consulted with a woman behind the counter. She was a little shocked that we'd missed the reservation—this was such un-Teutonic behavior!--but then focused on helping us figure out how to re-route us, though without reservations on the first leg. We could take a train up the Rhein ("Quite beautiful this time of year" she assured us), and transfer at Köln. We thanked her and hopped up onto the platform.

The train arrived and we boarded hurriedly, hoping to get a seat. Hannia always insists on facing the direction the train is traveling—to thwart those vertigo problems again--and there was only one seat that fit those specifications in the car we entered. Other passengers were streaming in, so I plunked her down in that seat and grabbed another seat I'd spotted at the other end of the car that faced backward.

Across from me was a young couple who seemed vaguely Hispanic and oddly familiar. They nodded amiably as I sat down. I noticed the young man wore a T-shirt with a flag in red, white, and blue, though it was obscured by his partially zipped sweatshirt. I kept my eye on the shirt for a while, and as he shifted in his seat, a little more of the flag was visible. I still couldn't be sure, but it looked like a familiar Central American banner. He and his mate started to converse in Spanish in low tones. I couldn't place her accent exactly, but for a moment it sounded South American--dropping an "s" in the middle or at the end of words is often a giveaway. When her husband started chattering away, I heard the telltale signs of a familiar accent.

"*¿Sos tico?*" I asked. Their heads swung up and they looked at me, confused. "*¿Sos tico?*" I repeated. They looked at my U.S. national team jersey and cap, my red hair and beard, and my painfully pallid complexion.

"*Sí,*" the young man responded. "*Soy tico.*"

"*¿De San José?*"

"*Sí*"

It turned out that he was from Desamparados, where my sister-in-law and her husband live. His name was Esteban, and he was there with his brother Alberto, and his wife.

As I was facing the back of the train, I could see Hannia at the other end of the car, craning her neck to see just who the heck I was speaking to in Spanish.

They were excited to meet someone from home, even if it was someone who was not a native, and Costa Rican by marriage. We talked a bit about Costa Ricans and Americans and the prospects for both teams in the World Cup. It turned out that Esteban's sister had given him the tickets. They had been to Munich for the opening match, and were still recovering from the festivities. They were taking a different route to the game, had accommodations on the way, and were changing trains before we were. When the train finally stopped, Hannia made a beeline for us, but barely got to say hello to her countrymen as they hustled out to make their connection.

We finally arrived in Gelsenkirchen. The U.S. throngs poured out of the train, as did the Czech supporters: Red, white, and blue versus red and white. The gringos were chanting and strong. The Czechs were characteristically a little cautious, but they were having fun as well, and displaying some raucousness. They all remembered when the former Czechoslovakia beat the living daylights out of a basically collegiate U.S. team in the 1990 World Cup in Italy. They seemed to know that the U.S. had progressed, but still felt very confident. Many Europeans, Germans included, were handicapping the Czech team as the only Euro team capable of going toe-to-toe with Brazil.

We chanted, "*Olé, Olé, Olé*, USA, USA," with our contingent as we shuffled down the steps and into the station. It was an odd sensation to have such a large group on our side. Everyone wore U.S. national team jerseys or a U.S. flag draped around their shoulders like a cape. Suddenly a Dutchman was in my face. It was Louis Sterk, a friend of mine from Los Angeles. Louis was all smiles, happy to see us both, as well as to be in the midst of World Cup madness. "Hey, what the hell happened to you?" he called out, referring to our later train. I had text-messaged him with our change in schedule. He led us out of the station to an adjacent shopping area, a cobblestone promenade in which throngs pulsed around, singing, yelling, chanting, and snapping pictures like mad.

"Where is Gabriel?" I queried.

"Right over here" Louis said, pointing to Chris Dill's son, who was floating around, drinking in the ambience. Gabriel was very happy to see us. He had gone for a while without any native English speakers to converse with. He was wearing a San Francisco Giants baseball cap, but I was happy to see him anyway, despite my Los Angeles Dodger upbringing.

We took a few pictures together so I could send them to Chris, to prove that his son was alive and well. Right opposite the train station was a large official-looking building, a post office or municipal offices or something, with large steps leading up to the entrance. The steps were filled with a few hundred U.S. and other fans, chanting "USA" or some odd song based on, "Clementine." We realized that if we stood there, the chanting and screaming and yelling would be going on the entire time.

We plowed through the crowd up the promenade. A street celebration was in full swing. There were tons of vendors, with food and souvenirs, soccer paraphernalia, and, of course, BEER.

We found a sidewalk café and staked out a table for the four of us. Behind us, in a large plaza, was a bandstand, where a musical group was setting up. We chatted with Louis and Gabe about their trips and experiences. I had originally met Louis when I was editing a PBS documentary in Sherman Oaks in 1997. He was in the U.S. on a lark, a young guy looking for an interesting experience and wanting to improve his English. He had an American girlfriend who was a production coordinator, and the two of them were working on the show together. I used to chat with him when he came by the cutting room to drop off tapes or whatever. It had dawned on me at one point that he was probably a soccer fan. I asked what he thought of the Dutch national team's prospects. He responded that they had some good players, such as Davids and Bergcamp, and that he thought the best prospect of the era was a guy named Kluivert. "Oh, the rapist," I responded flippantly. He had been accused of sexual assault recently, but was later absolved.

Louis' reaction at the time was priceless. He was incredulous that an American knew anything at all about soccer, let alone a fairly esoteric detail like that. His face betrayed total shock.

"So if you're from Amsterdam, you must be an Ajax fan, "I proceeded. I could tell from his expression that I'd hit pay dirt.

"Why do you know about soccer?" he quizzed, a little panicked.

"I've always been a soccer fan. Ajax was big when I was a kid. Johan Cruyff and total soccer and all that. I was shocked they lost in both '74 and '78. I thought they were the better team in both cases," I explained.

You could have knocked Louis over with a feather. From that point on we were fast friends. He asked me at one point if I knew of anyplace he could play soccer. He was too young for my team, but I promised to keep my ears open for other options. Louis was a tall, rangy, athletic-looking guy. It turned out that he had played in the same youth league as the famous Bergkamp twins in Holland.

A few years later, when a friend called me looking for players for a metro league team, I called Louis and gave him the information. Nothing came of it, but when Chris Dill got involved with a team in the municipal league and wanted to take it into the metro league—a big step up, from recreational to a notch below semi-pro--I told him about Louis.

Louis turned out to be an excellent central defender. When we played on the same squad we frequently paired up as a sweeper-stopper combo, Louis being the "*libero*." He was certainly more skilled than I, and a hell of a lot younger, so I was very happy to have him behind me. When Louis got injured, it fell to me to be the last man.

After a few seasons, I dropped out. Louis and another player went into the Pacific League briefly, but ended up drifting out of it. Finally, Louis announced he was returning to Holland, and he, Chris, and I had kept in touch via e-mail.

We talked about his new job for a casino outfit. who actually sponsored the Dutch League. Louis was a computer guy, and designed and maintained systems. He was doing well with the new job in his native country, and had married and had a daughter. He told Chris and I in earlier e-mails that he had tried to find a soccer team back in Holland, but the camaraderie and fellowship were lacking. He was now a solid citizen with a family.

Gabe was having a ball as well. He had started college about a year before, and traveled to Costa Rica to study Spanish and do some heavy surfing on the Pacific Coast. Hannia, who was visiting home toward the end of his stay, had helped him negotiate a dicey moment when his plane connection was in jeopardy and he had to seek accommodations for himself and his surfboard in San José at the last minute. Hannia had also been a teachers' aide at Mar Vista Elementary when Gabe's sister was there, so there was all sorts of common ground among us. Chris, Louis, Gabe, and myself had all played soccer together at one time or another as well.

As we reminisced and caught up, we heard music behind us on the bandstand. The music was pre-recorded, but soon a singer appeared. He was a Turkish-looking guy in a white, sequin-studded jumpsuit. He sidled up to the mike and started singing, "Jailhouse Rock." He was an Elvis impersonator, and a pretty damned good one. We hoisted a few beers in honor of the Turkish-German-American confluence of divine *kitsch*. He performed a long set, with all the standard Elvis pop tunes. Between "Love Me Tender" and "Blue Suede Shoes," he yakked away into the microphone to set up the next song.

We determined it was time to mosey on to the stadium. Louis and Gabe didn't have tickets, and the prospects of getting some without mortgaging a house or two seemed remote. They were headed to the Fan Zone, which, as we had discovered in Berlin, was almost as good as being at the game, and in some ways perhaps more fun. For a teenager like Gabe, it seemed an excellent opportunity to find himself some female companionship, and we teased him about that mercilessly.

We pushed our way back through the pulsating crowd to the train station where we found the line to the #302 Tram, the route to the stadium. We said heartfelt good-byes to Louis and Gabe. Louis had to get back across the Dutch border to reunite with his family, and Gabe had plans as well. We briefly strategized about meeting up after the game, but we were scheduled to hop on a train shortly thereafter, and it was going to be pretty late already to make it back to Mainz while the trains were still running.

We oozed into the crowd. And "crowd" was exactly the right word. There was barely space for a piece of paper between the bodies crammed into the chute that led to the tram platform. Everyone was pushing to get forward, and you could feel the common expansion and contraction of the hundreds of lungs pressed against one another. When a tram pulled up, a loud cheer rang out, a big exaggerated sense of gratitude and victory that the line would at least move forward a bit. The tram filled up to what was probably over capacity, and when it chugged out of the station, everyone left in line felt abandoned. It was hot and sticky anyway, and being surrounded by that many stressing and straining human bodies was nearly as comfortable as, say, digging a ditch, or working in a coal mine.

A second tram arrived soon. When we looked up and saw the welcoming #302 on its front, we all applauded and cheered again. It was a small victory. Our prayers for motion--any motion, just let us get a move on--had been answered. Hannia and I popped loose as the people in front of us scrambled for seats. We managed to park our butts in convenient spots, resting a little while the tram glided along its tracks, full to bursting with U.S. and Czech fans. The tram passed gaggles of people who were hoofing it to the stadium, and finally we could see the stadium, or at least a glut of automobiles and humans that suggested a stadium. We could see down the street that bordered the stadium to the south, and could make out an entrance. We hopped off the tram prior to reaching the stadium stop, and headed down that street to a parking lot and a trail that led up the hill to the stadium. It was a bit of a climb, but we reached the entrance in a few minutes, and made it through the security surprisingly quickly. I had wondered about getting my video camera in, but it passed with flying colors, as did my extra lens for my still camera, though the guard asked me what the heck that bizarre cylinder in my bag was. I had looked for the phrase specifically in my phrase book, and was able to say, *"Das ist die Linse für diese Kamera."*

At any rate, they sped me through and were very polite and helpful as they patted me down. There was a separate line for women, with female guards, and Hannia entered without incident.

Once inside, I made a beeline for the beer vendor. I was happy to discover that though Budweiser was the official beer, a German beer, Bitburger, also was available, though much less prominently displayed. As

I crossed to the Bitburger stand, I notice a little knot of people around a guy with long hair. He was obviously someone famous, and seemed to be working the crowd as people asked to have their pictures taken with him. It was Frankie Hejduk.

For those of us who follow U.S. soccer, Frankie has been a fixture on the national team since the mid-1990s. Flamboyantly long-haired, wiry, and fast, Frankie has always played a sort of 110-percent, wild, and energetic soccer. Often he looks less than elegant, flailing away and running all over the field, but his play is effective and his spirit contagious. I remember clearly watching the U.S. play Brazil in the 1998 Gold Cup at the L.A. Coliseum. Frankie was playing his usual game, balls out. He'd come out to confront a wily Brazilian. A couple of times he lunged at the ball, got faked, and ended up on the ground. The Brazilian player continued on down the field to find the next challenge, when suddenly Frankie appeared again, having gotten back to his feet and caught back up with the Brazilian, who had been moving at a full gallop. The look on the Brazilian's face was priceless, something like, "What are you doing here? Didn't I just leave you in the dust?" Frankie then lunged back in, harassing his opponent until he coughed up the ball, or made a bad pass, or beat him again, which wasn't really beating him. He'd sure enough be back up in his face ten seconds later. My friend Chris Dill attributes Frankie's tenacity to his being a surfer, saying, "After you've been pounded by a fifteen-foot wave, you're not afraid of anything." Frankie was a UCLA product--one of "Sigi's boys"--and had appeared in the 1998 and 2002 World Cups. He would have been in the 2006 Tournament too, but had blown out his ACL only a month or two earlier. Now he was working the crowd, with his eight-year-old son, and the U.S. crowd was mobbing him, ecstatic to see him.

I took a picture of Hannia with him, and told him how bummed I was he wasn't in uniform.

We climbed to our seats, and "climbed" is an accurate description. It was a huge stadium, very elegantly designed, but we were up in the rafters. When I examined our tickets, I noticed for the first time that we were in different rows. This didn't make me too happy, and made Hannia downright furious. Weren't we paying a pretty sum to have to sit separately? She pouted and whined, but what were we going to do? We found our way to our seats.

Next to me was a young blonde kid, who looked extremely German. It turned out he was an American, here visiting German relatives in order to follow his team. He was very bright and outgoing and asked me all about my stay in Germany, and which club teams I followed. His knowledge of the game was inspiringly complete.

As I breathed in the atmosphere, something in the stadium struck me as strange. It took me a while, but finally I figured out what it was. The American fans were as numerous as the Czechs. And we were louder. Much louder. The Czechs are characteristically a bit reserved. Not so the Yanks. Of all the international matches I'd been to, this was perhaps first one where the U.S. really felt like the favored club.

I watched the players come out onto the field to warm up, and the U.S. guys looked shocked. After so many years of being nobodies, or villains, here we were in the heart of Europe, next door to the opposition's home country, and we had a better crowd than they did. I saw Oguchi "Gooch" Onyewu talking to Claudio Reyna on the field. They were both looking up at the crowd in awe. "USA, USA, USA," reverberated throughout the stadium. Gooch and Reyna were dumbfounded--were they dreaming? I got a little choked up myself.

The game started, and the fans were raucous.

In their initial play, the U.S. team looked lackadaisical. The Czechs looked sharp and determined and focused. It smelled bad.

As I said before, many Europeans felt the Czechs were the best team in the tournament. Aging but potent Pavel Nedved was the engine of the team—he had been voted Footballer of the Year in 2003. With his trademark blonde mullet flopping as he ran, it seemed he could be everywhere at once, attacking out of midfield, or setting up his compatriots with enormous skill and vision. Jan Koller, the six-foot-seven-inch giant, roamed the front line like a giraffe, ready to pick balls out of the air with impunity. It would be interesting to see him match up against Gooch, who though a bit shorter at six-foot-four, was a big, ridiculously muscular youth with a great vertical leap.

Four minutes into the match, Gooch received a yellow card for a foul on Nedved.

Five minutes in, the U.S. lack of intensity paid off for the Czechs. Poborsky took the ball down the wing--left back Eddie Lewis entirely absent--and Jan Koller got on the end of his cross to put one away neatly.

He hadn't really needed his height, it was timing and a little feint that got him between Gooch and the equally talented Eddie Pope. They were uncharacteristically caught with their pants down. The Czech fans were suddenly not so reserved. The U.S. fans kept up their chants, however. After all, it was only a one-goal deficit, and you could easily forgive being beaten by a Koller aerial attack. They could certainly adjust and get back in the game.

A minute later, Claudio Reyna dribbled to the top of the box and was tripped--no call. In addition to a one-goal deficit, the refereeing wasn't helping us, either.

At minute 16, Landon Donovan beat Rozehnal, who then tripped him, resulting in a yellow card. So the ref was awake. The resulting free kick was not dangerous. The U.S. had some good possession, but through balls to the forwards just didn't connect.

In minute 28, Claudio Reyna bounced a rocket of a shot off the left post. Woulda, coulda, shoulda.

Pavel Nedved was all over the midfield, scooping up the ball and setting up his countrymen. Eddie Lewis just looked horribly out of his element.

The U.S. crowd was wonderful. The chants went on and on, pounding out a constant rhythm.

At minute 36, the U.S. lost the ball at midfield. Nedved moved it down the left and crossed it. Gooch rose and cleared it out of the box, but it fell straight to Rosicky. He was at least thirty yards out, but unleashed an unstoppable shot into the right side of the net past a fully extended Casey Keller. It was a screamer. We were two goals down before the end of the first half.

Beasley and Convey switched sides. Somehow that didn't strike me as the solution to our problems.

The Czechs absolutely dominated the midfield, picking up most of the loose balls and moving freely.

At minute 42, Koller, went down with a hamstring problem. He was replaced by #12, Lokvenc, who was also very tall.

Halftime was a welcome break. Maybe the U.S. could catch their collective breath, regroup and threaten the Czechs.

To start the second half, Eddie Johnson and John O'Brien came in for Steve Cherundolo and Pablo Mastroeni. I couldn't believe that Eddie Lewis was still in the game. Eddie's a guy I like a lot, but he was playing defense (he's traditionally a winger), getting on in years and getting beaten badly. This was precisely where we needed the injured Frankie Hejduk.

The U.S. established lots of possession, but every time they tried to go forward, they ran into a brick wall and had to pass backward.

Around minute 68, Lokvenc received a yellow card for foul on Gooch. Then a minute or so later, Claudio Reyna got a yellow for a slide tackle from behind.

The U.S. continued to play without urgency, while the Czechs still hustled to each ball. The Czechs remained sharp on attack, executing precise, penetrating passes.

Bobby Convey tried to take things into his own hands, and started dribbling at the Czechs, but he got stopped every time.

At minute 68, a totally unmarked Rosicky ripped another one from outside, and hit the crossbar.

DaMarcus Beasley made his way to back to the right side, but he remained ineffective. At minute 71, Eddie Johnson got off a good shot from outside, but it went wide left.

Donovan and Convey combined well on one play, putting a nice ball across the goalmouth, but Eddie Johnson arrived just a hair late.

Around minute 76, Nedved split the defense with a beautiful through ball, Rosicky ran onto it, and scored.

At minute 77, Arena brought in Josh Wolff in for McBride. Johnson had another good shot, this one a little high.

It was all to no avail. The addition of Eddie Johnson was too little, too late. The hunger and urgency that the Americans had displayed against Portugal four years prior was absent in 2006. Tough, scrappy players like Tony Sanneh, Cobi Jones, and Earnie Stewart had retired in the interval. The U.S. team looked lethargic throughout. But the Czechs weren't the Portuguese, either. The Portuguese had been arrogant, looking past the first round. They had bought the "Golden Generation" hype hook, line, and sinker, and had arrived full of hubris, expecting a walk in the park. The Czechs were a different story. They were tactically a very solid side, and since they were used to being also-rans--usually to Germany--they weren't taking any chances. They played strong and smart, hustling to every ball, making clean and smart passes and ceding nothing.

This time it was the Americans who had probably taken too much of the hype to heart. Landon Donovan and DaMarcus Beasley, who had graced the cover of *Sports Illustrated* (almost always a jinx), looked bad. Beasley at least had the excuse of being played out of position, Coach Arena had the natural left-footer stationed on the right side of the field, but Donovan was invisible most of the time. It was a failure at midfield-- as it usually is in soccer. The U.S. couldn't hold the ball in the center, and we couldn't find our forwards with any meaningful service. This, of course, puts tremendous pressure on the defense, which made a few bush-league mistakes as well, and left the forwards twisting in the wind. The initial goal was a breakdown on the left (hello, Eddie Lewis and Bobby Convey), and then bad coverage in the middle, an uncharacteristic miscue by the usually rock-solid Eddie Pope.

There was plenty of blame to go around. Still, losing to the most highly-touted Euro squad wouldn't be so bad--playing like a bunch of flaccid wimps, however, is inexcusable. If they beat us on skill and flair, fine, congratulations. If they beat us through hustle and grit, there is something seriously wrong. There was something seriously wrong. It seems to me also that the U.S. team has a tendency to fold in Europe. Even the players who are based in Europe--or perhaps most especially those--seem to arrive with a fateful sense of impending doom. I think that they are so used to hearing about European superiority that the prospect of losing to a European squad in front of a European crowd weighs a bit too heavily on the Yank psyche.

Enough of that. The game was in the books. It left a horrible taste our mouths as Hannia and I shuffled out of the stadium. There is something about flying halfway around the world to watch your team lose that is especially depressing.

Hannia got a call from her brother Luís, who was watching the game back in Los Angeles at our house. *"Que aguevado, maje,"* was about all he could come up with. This is the approximate Costa Rican equivalent of "That sucks, dude." Luís put Chris Dill on the phone. I could hear the weight of disappointment on Chris' voice. "What a lack of intensity," he lamented, hitting the nail on the head. I offered that the prospects against Italy might be better. The U.S. has done well against them in recent friendlies, and they now had something to prove. "If they play like this, though, our goose is cooked."

In a daze we plodded with the crowd down the hill toward the tram stop. Caught in the river of humanity, we marched and mumbled. The one light spot was the Harlem Globetrotters, who appeared next to us suddenly. Of course, it wasn't the real Globetrotters, but a few crazed U.S. fans who had donned uniforms and Afro wigs and carried basketballs. One of them held a boom box that played, "Sweet Georgia Brown." They paused every few minutes to play the theme, throw the basketball around, dance, and mug. This delighted the legions of fans-- both American and Czech.

We made the mistake of following the crowd to the official tram stop for the stadium, which was swamped. Several trams arrived, already stuffed to the gills, and there were hundreds, if not thousands, of people ahead of us in line. There was no prospect of getting on a tram any time soon. We noticed that a small group of Germans, seemingly in the know, were peeling off and heading toward another spot. We followed. They led us to what turned out to be a bus stop, and we were able to board fairly quickly.

Back at the main train station and open-air mall, we found a sidewalk café where we could sit down and have some coffee and ice cream. The Czechs had come out of their shell a bit, and were chanting and singing and waving their flags. It was funny to watch them when they realized that there were Americans present, not sure how we would react. Would we behave like the Brits or the Swiss? We behaved—uniformly, I believe--with a very "un-European" equanimity. As our coffee arrived, a few musicians fired up their guitars on the bandstand. They launched into a rendition of the Willie Nelson classic, "On the Road Again." They all wore ten-gallon hats and were most certainly from the American southwest. My guess was Texas or Oklahoma. As if to compliment the cowboy motif, a band of Indians appeared--actually a group of roving Peruvians dressed in Cochise-style headdresses, leather-fringed and beaded jackets, and carrying toy tomahawks. They were the sort of street performers you find throughout the world, playing "*El Condor Pasa*" on panpipes and guitars. Drowned out by the powerfully amplified country-Western band, they had ceased playing and were dancing around the crowd in a faux-conga line with celebrating Czechs and resigned Americans.

We didn't feel much like dancing, but the joyous absurdity of the festivities cheered us up enormously. The Czechs weren't being jerks, they were just enjoying their victory and savoring their well-earned three points. We were fortunate enough to be at the World Cup, after all, and win, lose, or draw, we were the envy of billions.

At the train station, as we were waiting on the platform, I heard TV coverage of the Japan-Australia game wafting from the nearby bar. I ducked in and looked at the scoreboard. Japan was ahead 1-0 in the dying minutes of the second half. This surprised me. I thought that the Aussies, with a few Premiere League stars in their ranks and coached by Gus Hiddink, of South Korean fame, had a good squad. Still, the Japanese, coached by Brazilian legend Zico, were no slouches, and I thought, well, maybe the Japanese have hit their stride.

I returned to the train platform and told Hannia the score. "Hiddink's boys are done for," I said. Shortly thereafter I heard loud cheering coming from the bar. I wasn't sure what had happened, and was preoccupied with checking the train schedule and track number and the like. We heard another burst of cheering and applause as the train arrived. We boarded. It was a direct train back to Mainz, which was fortunate. It saved a little time, and it was late already. Unfortunately, the train was horribly hot. We noticed that the windows on one side of the compartment were open, but those on the other side were all closed. I walked over and slid one of the closed windows open. The stream of air, though not cool, helped alleviate the stifling humidity and heat in the compartment. All of a sudden, the windows began to pulse and quake and rattle and make a horrific racket. Somehow the force of the air rushing through caused some sort of sympathetic vibration that threatened to break the train in half, or at least our eardrums. I sprang back to the window I had just opened and slid it shut. I tried opening it a different amount, opening different windows on that side of the car, and all sorts of permutations of "openness" and "closedness" of different windows to see if I could "tune" the air flow to avoid the dreaded rattling, which was more like a thumping. No dice. The minimum or maximum opening of a window on that side resulted in a veritable earthquake. We resolved to endure the heat. I slammed the windows shut on the offending side of the car. Having a bit of cross-ventilation for a while had helped, but after the windows were closed again, the temperature and humidity soon reached the same annoying levels.

After I had resolved to suffer the slings and arrows of outrageous heat, the train conductor came on the loudspeaker and announced that Australia had beaten Japan, 3-1. I was dumbfounded. I could see them coming back and tying, or maybe, just maybe squeaking in another to win 2-1, but they had scored three goals in seven minutes to win decisively. Good for the Socceroos and Gus, I thought. The Aussies were scheduled to play Brazil and Croatia. It would be interesting to see how they progressed.

The train made a few stops, and our ranks thinned. We ended up being the only passengers in the car except for one other couple. They were, like us, obviously U.S. fans, decked out in jerseys and hats and red, white, and blue paraphernalia. We struck up a conversation and started discussing the game. We both commented that it felt like France '98. It turned out that this couple, older than us by perhaps ten years, had gone to the World Cup in France and Korea in 2002. They lived in Japan. This gave us some common ground, especially as my parents had lived in Tokyo for eight years or so. They were originally from New Hampshire, and were, obviously, huge soccer partisans.

Their observations on the U.S. game were quite similar to our own, so we had sympathetic ears as we rattled down the rails in the hot, humid car.

They also shared their Japan stories, being *gaijin* in the land of the rising sun, and as a result somewhat famous in the little prefecture in which they lived. They shared amusing stories about social and language miscues, and I related some of parents' experiences.

We also benefited from their touristic exploits. They had arrived in Mainz a few days earlier than we had, and had a few tips and anecdotes about sights to see. In particular, they mentioned a beer garden that sounded interesting.

We arrived in the wee hours of the morning at the train station in Mainz and shared the cab ride with our newfound friends. They had plans the next day and asked if we wanted to tag along, but we had to decline. Since we'd accumulated tons of laundry, the following day was to be a housekeeping and planning day, before we took off for Hamburg. And I had to go to Frankfurt's *Waldstadion* to get our tickets.

JUNE 13 – THE FOREST STADIUM BECKONS

The next morning we got up late. We were exhausted from travel and our late arrival. I'm sure that had the USA prevailed, we'd have felt much more energetic, but such is human psychology. We felt, as my brother David would say, like we'd been dragged through a knothole. We braved the buffet breakfast. It was tremendously bright and hot, and we were lethargic as we picked through the bacon, eggs, noodles, cereals, fruits, and heavy German breads. We munched morosely, hearing our fellow gringos kvetch and moan about the previous day's performance. We moseyed back up to our room and piled our dirty clothes into bags. We asked the concierge for directions to the Laundromat, and got organized so that Hannia would have everything she needed. I made sure she had adequate cab fare to get back to the hotel, and got her a card with the name, address, and phone number of the Mainz Hilton, so that in case of utter confusion and linguistic breakdown, she could direct her cab driver.

We made our way on foot to the Laundromat, stopping by an Internet café where we could buy phone cards for cheap calls to the U.S. The Internet cafés all seemed to be run by Turkish fellows, who were very helpful and interested in what we were up to. When we arrived at the Laundromat, it was full of patrons, mostly Turkish women. We tried our best to decipher the instructions in German. You had to buy tokens, and then at a central control panel, you selected which washer to pay. A Turkish lady helped us figure out the process, and offered some of her leftover laundry detergent to Hannia. I made sure Hannia felt comfortable with the whole set-up, then headed for the train station.

I went to the counter and asked about the route. Luckily it was direct. I scribbled down the train number and headed for the platform. Soon a modern double-decker train pulled in, and I boarded. It was larger and more streamlined than the commuter trains I'd ridden so far. I climbed the stairs to the second deck and sat down. I asked a couple of German gentlemen if this train went to the stadium, just to confirm that I was on the right track, so to speak. They said yes. I said I was happy. They said they were happy, too. They had tickets. I suddenly realized that there might be a game today at the stadium. "There's a game today?"

"Yes, Korea vs. Togo."

"Bad for me," I responded in my lousy German. They laughed. I asked if they had any tickets for the German national team's games. They both laughed loudly. "Those are just for the politicians," they replied with typically upbeat European cynicism. As the train progressed, it got more and more packed. At each stop, crowds lumbered in, many with Korean and Togolese banners.

We arrived and the crowds flooded out toward the stadium, passing lines of mounted police, and filing through a wooded (*Wald* means forest), park-like area. There were big crowds of Korean supporters chanting, "*Dae Han Min Guk*," and suddenly I was transported four years into the past. Koreans were snapping pictures madly, occasionally asking me to pose with them. "*Hanguk Chukku Choayo*," I said ("Korean soccer is good"), to their general amazement. I asked a few guards where the ticket center was, and they were a bit confused as to whether I meant the ticket booths, which were straight ahead.

I insisted that I needed the ticket *center*, and was directed to the opposite side of the stadium. The most direct route to the opposite side of the stadium was, of course, blocked for security reasons, so I had to take the long way around, along the edge of the wooded area on a dirt path. A stream of spectators zipped up and down the path, and there were people from all corners of the globe trekking through the leafy, green canopy. It was frustrating to have to go so far out of my way, but the pleasant forest path more than made up for it.

When I came out on the other side, I entered a pulsing crowd of festive lunatics. There were Koreans galore, some dressed in traditional garb and some in every imaginable costume, including cowboy boots, ten-gallon hats, and chaps. There were fewer Africans. I'm sure the passage and ticket prices are much more expensive to the average Togolese. As if to make up for this, many of the Germans present were wearing Togo's colors, and many of them had donned rasta wigs in solidarity with their African brothers and sisters.

I asked again for the ticket center, and got conflicting accounts. There was still confusion about "ticket booths" and the "ticket center."

When I finally found the ticket center, I was informed that since there was a game that day, I'd have to wait until kick-off time, three p.m., as their main priority was to service the ticket holders of that day's game. I had an hour or so to kill, so I walked out of the stadium grounds and bought myself a bratwurst sandwich. It was funny to me that so few places accepted credit cards, but they were also very hedgy about large, and even not-so-large denominations of currency. I handed the bratwurst vendor a twenty-Euro note for my four Euros-worth of brat and Sprite, and he spend forever examining it. He made a great ceremony of holding up to the light, rubbing it on his table, and then finally calling a co-worker over--a wizened old veteran of the bratwurst trade--who poked, prodded, examined, scratched, sniffed, and rubbed the bill in every way imaginable, until he was satisfied that I wasn't some kind of international trickster bent on taking them to the cleaners. It seemed to me that the older man really enjoyed playing the expert, and had all the clerks conned into thinking that only he could pass judgment on currency. In the time it had taken for them to perform this arcane ritual, I had already wolfed down my brat and guzzled my Sprite. The people in line behind me were squealing and growling at the delay, but I rather enjoyed that German dinner theater.

In the little corridor leading up to the stadium, where the brat stands were, groups of fans were parading, loudly pounding on drums, chanting, and singing. I followed a group of revelers, returned to the periphery of the stadium and found a shady spot on the edge of the woods to sit down on a log. The area was filled with groups waiting to get into the game. Scalpers made the rounds, inquiring if anyone was in need of a ticket, and sniffing at the paltry offers they were receiving. As game time approached, however, I could hear the scalpers' voices becoming increasingly agitated, and appreciative of lesser amounts. One couple, who had been seated in front of me, very calmly turned away scalpers until the last possible moment, and ended up paying just slightly over face value, where fifteen minutes, before they'd have been charged a two hundred-Euro premium for the same tickets.

The stadium was filled at long last, and the area outside had thinned. I could hear the roar of the crowd. The game was under way.

I made tracks for the ticket center, and found the corral that led to the entrance, delineated by movable metal bars that resembled like bike racks, it struck me. There were already a few people hovering about, so I staked out my ground and waited. A few minutes late, as they were still trying to help out the latecomers who had tickets on hold for the current game, an official in a styleless, official-looking jacket came out and bellowed, "We have no more tickets for today's game, this line will be for people to pick up reserved tickets for other games." I knew I was in the right place at the right time.

All the accumulated ticket-seekers tightened up their positions, to be sure they wouldn't be aced out of their rightful place. When the group began to move and filled the ticket corral outside the tent, waiting fans spotted the flow and charged over, thinking that this must be their last hope to get tickets to today's game. They had, of course, missed the official's announcement. Suddenly, pushy, last-minute hopefuls were trying their damnedest to shoulder their way into what had been a fairly orderly line. A few German gentlemen behind me took advantage of the press of the ticket-hungry to slide the movable barriers over a foot or two in order to squeeze past a patient German woman, and yours truly. I reacted quickly, by repositioning my formidable humanity strategically and forcefully in their path, thwarting the attempted claim jumpers. Instead of backing off and admitting defeat, one of the fellows stuck an elbow in my back and pushed athletically. I spun around and glared at him, expecting a bit of contrition on his part. Instead, I was met by an insolent glare that hinted of a desire for violence. I surveyed the group. It consisted of fifteen or so young men in suits and ties. There was something tremendously incongruous about their appearance. They were very elegantly dressed, but had the demeanor and posture of street thugs. It dawned on me that perhaps three-quarters of the group had shaven heads. Many were missing teeth, and had interesting displays of tattoos and scars on their persons. They pushed as a group. I held my ground, digging in my heels and tightening my grip on the fence.

I knew that great pains had been taken to exclude soccer hooligans and skinheads from the World Cup, and calculated the following possibility. These guys were denied tickets due to, shall we say, overzealous support of their teams in the past. The application procedure had required extensive identification and gave the authorities ample chance to check lists and records and whatnot to weed out the "undesirables." The resale, or ticket-transfer, process offered a loophole. Only one member of the group had to have an affidavit from the original purchaser of the tickets. Let's say there's probably one person in the "supporter's group" unknown to the authorities. He gets the passport numbers of fourteen friends who haven't been identified as problematic, shows up with the affidavit, gets the tickets at face value, and presto, they've circumvented the security procedures. By this time in the tournament, word had gotten around that they weren't really checking

IDs at the gate, so it was child's play to show up and pretend to be the person whose name was printed on the little cardboard, computer-chip-embedded, brightly colored and stylishly logo-ized tickets.

They continued to very rudely push and shove and try their best to weasel their way past me and the other fans who had been waiting patiently for quite some time. When the attendant sent away the ticket-seekers for that day's game, the skinheads saw their opportunity. The pressure on the line was suddenly released, and pathways opened up, albeit briefly. The thug behind me hooked his foot around my leg and gave me a shove in the small of my back. Had he caught me by surprise, I'd have gone over face-first into the fine dirt beneath our feet. But I was ready. I turned with the force of the push. With the sudden lack of resistance, the hooligan lost his balance. He went down hard and his black suit became powdered with dust. His stumble blocked his compatriots from making a charge. *"Enschuldigen sie bitte"* ("Excuse me"), I said as politely as I could. This really ticked them off, and I heard the murmur of angry *Deutsch* ripple through their ranks. Luckily, this whole distraction took about as much time as I needed to get to the head of the line. The attendant motioned me toward an open window, and I smiled at my new-found friends. I turned and went about my business. I was tempted to tap the attendant on the shoulder and ask if he thought these guys were skinheads, just to try to scupper their chances of getting tickets, but I thought the better of it.

I sidled up to the window and extracted paperwork from my pocket. The young woman behind the counter furrowed her brow as she examined the documents. She was looking, looking, looking for some flaw in my array of faxes and photocopies and application forms that would allow her to boot me out of her fiefdom, but alas, none was to be found. She smiled, disappeared into the printing area and returned with tickets for Costa Rica vs. Ecuador, emblazoned with the names of Mark and Hannia. My quest had been fruitful. I thanked the woman profusely *auf Deutsch*, of course, and tucked the tickets safely away in a buttoned pocket.

I looked up as I left, and saw the dusty-suited skinhead angrily arguing with the volunteer behind the counter. I could only make out a few words, but oddly enough, the fellow was having some sort of trouble. I wondered if it was merely a failure to provide the proper paperwork, or if the master computer had identified the poor soul as a less-than-well-behaved patron and had flagged his transaction. If my suspicions were correct, I hoped he had paid an exorbitant amount for the tickets he was now being denied. The whole group was so worked up with the drama of the counter that they had forgotten all about me, and didn't even notice as I walked out floating on air--my prize in my pocket. I was happy for the distraction.

I backtracked through the path in the shady, cool woods, passed occasionally by a frantic Korean or Togolese or German fan scurrying to get to the stadium. The frequent roar of the crowd filled the rhythm of my steps on dirt and gravel.

I took the #59 back to Mainz, and paused in the train station to make my reservations for the trip to Hamburg. I bought water and food and met Hannia, who had successfully negotiated the Laundromat and German taxi ride to the hotel.

Hot and tired, we both lounged around the room watching the remainder of the France vs. Switzerland game within the comforting confines of our little fortress.

The constipated French attack was thwarted by a very plucky Swiss team, which had been unusually good throughout qualifying. *Hopp Schwiiz!* Though I like the French team a lot, I couldn't help but pull for the underdog. The final goose-egg score line was a victory for the Swiss, against a former world champion and current contender.

Having sufficiently recharged our batteries, we decided to go out to the Mainz Fan Zone to watch Brazil vs. Croatia with the multitudes. It was a short walk from the hotel. Unlike the festivities in Berlin, it was held in a small public square, a grassy area that seemed like a park or athletic field. It was literally in the shadows of a church, *Pfarrkirche St. Peter,* and the *Kurfürstliches Schloß.* As the sun set, the large spires of the rococo church, almost onion domes, glowed orange against the fiercely blue sky.

There was lots of security to get into the Fan Zone, and we had to shuffle though a line and get patted down by some serious *Deutsch* officials. Once inside, however, it was very loose and festive. There were food and drink booths surrounding a large array of benches, filled with German butts. The beer was flowing and sausages, pizza, and assorted goodies were flying around. At the front of the crowd was a big-screen TV with a big sponsorship banner touting *Allgemeine Zeitung.*

We made the rounds, watching the crowd as much as the game. As I sat eating my bratwurst, the world's youngest Brazil fan, about a year old, came toward me, riding on his grandfather's shoulders. He had his little Brazil jersey on (he was number 10, of course) and had a green and yellow bandana wrapped around his head, in case anyone hadn't noticed the shirt. I said, "Hey, Brazil!" and he and his *Grossvater* turned and mugged, as the game and the festivities churned on around them. I snapped a picture. I wished I had gotten the grandfather's address to send him a photo, commemorating the occasion of their family bonding over the great sporting event.

The game was predictable enough. Brazil dominated, but in a languid, lazy way that let you know that they weren't too concerned about winning, but would anyway. Croatia, no slouch of a team, put on a good show, matching the Brazilians' ball control and passing. Still, when the Brazilians decided to turn up the heat, they did, and Croatia struggled to upset their samba rhythms. Ultimately, though the Croatian back line was solidly frustrating to Ronaldo and Ronaldinho, Kaká managed to get the *verdeamarilho* on top with a beautiful, curling strike. It was the youngster's first World Cup goal. Overall, Brazil didn't look up to a world championship, and Ronaldo was surprisingly static and heavy-looking. Still, Brazil is a notoriously slow starter (they especially were in qualifying) and you can never count them out. Croatia played well, but couldn't silence all the Brazilian weapons. The one-goal lead held up.

The German crowd in Mainz was more than happy to see Brazil win, and very happy to have the excuse to carouse and mingle. Still, even the most yellow-and-green-clad Brazil fanatics were shaking their heads. This did not look like a world champion team. If they played like this against France, Italy, England, or Germany, they would probably have a rough time of it.

We strolled out into the night with the crowd and wandered back to our hotel. We packed our luggage and got ready for the next day's journey.

JUNE 14 – TO HAMBURG

We were up early, made our way to the train station, and took a local train to Frankfurt's main station. The station was huge, perhaps second to Berlin, but still huge. We found the indicated track number, and there was, in fact, a train waiting. The doors of the train were shut, however, and the board on the side of the track read "*nicht umsteigen,*" or "don't board." I was getting a little antsy. When the train pulled out without letting us on, I got a bit concerned and went to the end of the boarding area to read the listings and track assignments again. I told Hannia to wait and find our car if a train arrived before I got back. I walked to the end of the track, near the ticketing area and looked at the endlessly changing list of trains on the big digital board. We were theoretically in the right place, so I returned to Hannia's side just as the train pulled in. We found our car and reserved seats, facing one another. We were seated next to two college girls. They chattered incessantly from the time they sat down until we arrived in Hamburg. It was a direct train, so we didn't have to worry about transfers. We were also revisiting some of the same country along the Rhine that we'd already seen on our trip to Gelsenkirchen. I deemed it a good opportunity to sleep. It was.

Once beyond the spot we'd been to before on the Gelsenkirchen trip, I started paying attention to the scenery. It was less temperate than the Mainz/Rhine valley area, a bit greener, and then we got into the Hamburg area. The city is dominated by water: inlets from the sea, rivers, canals. It's an old-world maritime burg.

We pulled into the train station, and I found an information booth, a giant FIFA World Cup, soccer-ball-shaped kiosk filled with helpful young Germans. I asked one of the young fellows behind the counter how to get to our hotel. He had the "deer-in-the-headlights" look of someone who knew he was screwed if he was asked anything outside a narrow range of information. He also said, a bit too quickly, that he didn't speak English. When I mentioned our hotel's street address, he became inordinately happy. He KNEW WHERE IT WAS! He smiled broadly, gestured wildly, and slicked his dark, straight hair back as though he thought I might take his picture. He told me in hurried German how to walk out the door, around the parking lot, and that it was diagonal to the train station. I asked if it was walking distance. "Oh, definitely, yes!" he enthusiastically proclaimed. Hannia and I thanked him and charged out into the street, our wheeled luggage in tow.

I thought I had understood his instructions, but the diagonal he had described led me to a street with a different name. We walked another block over, thinking we had misunderstood his instructions. I was getting frustrated and considered getting a cab. Then I asked someone. They pointed to a street at the opposite end of the parking lot--diagonal in the opposite direction. It was still a little deceptive because the street that came off the parking lot had a different name, but a block beyond, the name changed and we were on track. The hotel was literally seventy-five yards from the edge of the parking lot. I was glad I didn't pay for a cab ride.

As we approached the hotel, a nondescript number among the brownstones, or their slightly more baroque Teutonic equivalents (*Braunsteins?*), I noticed some women standing on the street corner. They weren't just loitering, they were looking us over in a funny way. Something inside me told me they were streetwalkers, but, having just seen their Berlin counterparts a few days earlier--slender young beauties showing lots of skin--I couldn't believe these women were part of the same occupation. They weren't ugly, but just ordinary-looking, stocky, blonde women in their mid-thirties, clothed in thick, unsexy jackets and pants that hid whatever contours their bodies had left. Their presence also didn't really fit the neighborhood, a clean, orderly urban area with shops and restaurants, and, yes, hotels.

Since I was accompanied, they didn't try a sales pitch or anything. I was still uncertain of their profession. Hannia, too, had a quizzical expression on her face. "Are those..." I finally asked her in Spanish, not wanting to offend anyone if overheard. "I don't know," she replied. "They seem so..."

"Plain?" I ventured.

"Dumpy," Hannia responded in English, using a word she'd always found amusing. It occurred to me that this was a centuries-old seaport, in which unlaid sailors abounded. After you've been out on the *Nordsee* hauling cod and sardines though the frigid waters, you might not be too particular about with whom you bedded down for the night, if the price was right. If these were, in fact, working girls, it made perfect sense.

We passed the gaggle of ladies and entered the hotel. It was a modern, roomy place on the inside, nothing fancy, but comfortable enough. In the entryway were a large-screen TV and a couch and a little bar where patrons were watching some soccer coverage. We made our way to the counter and checked in. Most of the counter help and bellhops seemed to be of Turkish extraction. They were very helpful and led us up to the second floor to a warm, smallish, but comfortable room. We threw the windows open for a little bit of ventilation.

We hit the street to walk around Hamburg a bit. We passed the ladies, still on the corner, and headed past the train station toward the historic center of town. We passed the hotel where the U.S. national team was staying--Hamburg was their training headquarters. We scanned the area for any of the Boys wandering about, but had no luck. We passed the *Petrikirche*, a beautiful old neogothic structure that was being renovated. There was scaffolding on one side, and I found it funny that they had sold advertising space on the scaffolding, which consisted of a huge poster for H&M, a department store, featuring the photo of a svelte young woman in a tank top being photographed by a stubble-faced young fellow, also in a tank top. The caption read, *"Tops ab 14,90"* (Tops from 14.90). Not the sort of thing you expect to find on the side of the church, but then again, very European, I guess. When you're a simple provincial like myself, you are easily confused.

We hit the very center of town to see the *Rathaus*. This is not, of course, a house of rats, but the town hall. Though, come to think of it, a building full of politicians? House of Rats might be appropriate. It is a beautiful building erected between 1886-97. Inside it had a soccer exhibit featuring the history of Germany's national team in the World Cup. The *Rathaus'* main chambers were closed to tourists at that moment, so we went back out to the square and headed toward the waterfront.

The city was immediately more picturesque and old world than either Berlin or Mainz. The waterways, which surround the downtown area, gave it a vaguely Venetian feel, though devoid of gondolas and filled with automobiles. The downtown area was very clean and orderly. All the buildings were of stone, many in an old baroque style generally associated with pre-war *Deutschland*. Beyond the downtown area were vast expanses of docks and industrial districts, but the center of the city is unmistakably old-world German, whether surviving or re-created. On one of the main thoroughfares, we stopped to eat in a sidewalk café. The handsome young waiter that popped out to attend us responded with mirth at my insistence on speaking German. To tease him, Hannia launched into some Italian, to which he responded very deftly and playfully.

We asked him about the chances of the German national team in the World Cup, and he very characteristically gave them a snowball's chance in hell. We mentioned the Germany vs. Costa Rica game and told him we were from Costa Rica. "Oh, you played very well," he insisted. We told him we were in Hamburg for the game against Ecuador. He wished us luck. The German team was scheduled to play that evening against Poland, and the young fellow was not hopeful. He told us that we should go to the *Heilige Geist* stadium (yes, the Holy Ghost) to watch the game. It was the site of the Fan Fest. We asked how to get there and he explained the *S-Bahn* routes. We resolved to hit the Fan Fest in Germany's second-largest burg, Hamburg.

We returned to our room to reconnoiter. We watched a Group H match, Tunisia vs. Saudi Arabia, in our room. Earlier that day, Spain had trounced Ukraine 4-0, in the same group, so theoretically the second spot was open for a dark-horse candidate. Tunisia had a very outside shot at passing Ukraine. It was a spirited game, something of an African Derby, with some exciting goals. Still, I didn't feel too invested in the outcome. Neither team was likely to reach the second round. All the Saudi players were from their domestic league, and unknown. The Tunisians had many players from familiar teams scattered throughout Europe, Germany, Holland, England, France, and Scotland, but none were widely recognized stars. Still, it was an enjoyable game to watch. It ended in a draw.

We headed out to take a subway ride to St. Pauli. Though we'd been given meticulous instructions by our waiter to get to the *Heilige Geist* field, we really only had to follow the mass of German fans pouring into the station, decked out in team colors, carrying banners, flags, and beer.

When we arrived at the St. Pauli stadium, the entire human contents of the train spilled out into the street. The Fan Fest was enormous, in contrast to the very homey Mainz gathering we had just attended. This was a big city celebration, right next to the St. Pauli stadium, where, it suddenly dawned on me, UCLA and L.A. Galaxy standout Paul Caligiuri had played for the local club. He started with a few lower division teams in Germany, but had been loaned out to St. Pauli from the L.A. Salsa in 1995. He was essentially the first modern U.S.

soccer player to have a European Career. He moved to the MLS in 1996 for the league's inaugural season, and played 'til his retirement in 2001.

The Fan Fest had booths representing virtually every country participating in the World Cup, offering food and drink from each nation. We made a beeline for the Costa Rica tent. They were selling *Gallo Pinto, plátanos maduros, cerveza Pilsen, carne asada a lo tico*, and many other native dishes. When we ordered our food, however, we were a little surprised that the workers in the booth had strange accents, and looked at us a bit oddly when we ordered in Spanish. It turned out that they were Brazilians, who had figured out a way to make a quick buck that summer. I would imagine they managed to convince the German organizers that they were Costa Rican. Still, it was a very festive environment, filled with Costa Rica fans in town for the CRC vs. ECU match, as we were. We made the rounds and had native beer and snacks from Brazil, Argentina, Poland, and Trinidad. As it got dark, a large crowd formed in the central field in which the huge big-screen televisions were showing pre-game preparations.

We decided to stake out our territory. We elbowed our way in through the crowd and discovered that there wasn't much territory to stake out. The grounds were crawling with fans, mostly German, who were enjoying themselves altogether too much. When I saw heads turning toward some grandstands to my left, I heard the English phrase, "She's topless." Lo and behold, in the distance I could make out a very attractive woman, partially wrapped in a German flag, her supple young breasts exposed for all to see. And she was attracting quite a bit of attention. I noticed that in front of her, a man was snapping away madly with professional camera equipment. He was directing her to move this way and that as he immortalized her mammary glands on celluloid, or the digital equivalent thereof. It was obviously destined for one of those racy magazine covers so prevalent in Germany. The crowd loved it.

As soon as the photographer was satisfied, the model covered herself with the flag and slipped away, escorted by a couple of extremely large fellows who had been at her side the whole time, ostensibly employed to keep overzealous young bucks from getting too close to our professional exhibitionist. The crowd returned its attention to the large screens, on which the pregame yammering continued: "Gee, Hans, will Germany win at home?" "Well, Fritz, it's either that, or Poland will win." "Or they could tie." "That's always a possibility, Fritz."

A large group of fans pushed past us to our right. There was an interesting ripple in the crowd around us, so we took a second look at the passing group. They were decked out in the red and white of Poland. I thought this showed either bravado or hopeless naïveté. The Poles and Germans have nothing if not a contentious history, and here the eastern neighbors were climbing right into the belly of the beast to watch the game. I thought it would be interesting to see how the Germans reacted to the *Polska* T-shirts and foreign flags. In a way, considering their illustrious footballing history, the Germans should be a little magnanimous. They have been dominant. Still, the Poles are a plucky lot (as we learned in USA vs. POL in 2002), and though underdogs, always field a strong, determined team. The Eastern European countries are famous for solid, organized defenses, and on a good day they could shut out just about anyone. And the Germans were very insecure about their team. It would do no good to their self-esteem to be beaten or held to a tie by their puny Slavic neighbor.

For the Poles, beating the Germans would taste sweeter than anything in the world. It was David vs. Goliath time for them, and even a tie would represent quite a victory. The Poles clearly were up for this game. A Czech friend of mine tells a joke that fits perfectly here: Soccer is a game in which twenty-two men in shorts chase a black-and-white ball around a rectangular grass field, and Germany wins. This is the *Mittel Europa* perspective. Considering how many times the Germans, Prussians, or Austro-Hungarians have rolled over the eastern countries, any defeat that can be handed to Germany would feel magnificent.

The Polish contingent camped out just ahead of us, and they were quite vocal, chanting and yelling and dancing. The German fans were obviously not in love with them. As the game commenced, I saw middle fingers lifted on both sides. Barbs were flying back and forth--at least that's what they sounded like, though I couldn't understand what was being said.

The game was a classic. The Poles held tough, playing a defensive game predicated on frustrating their opponent and counterattacking. Their goalkeeper made numerous brilliant saves as Miroslav Klose and Lukas Podolski--ironically both born in Poland, but German citizens--put some dangerous shots on goal.

The crowd in the main field became too raucous for us. It wasn't out of control or scary, but the press of screaming bodies made it hard to breathe. We retreated to the edge of the crowd, where we could see not only the big screen, but also numerous smaller ones in the various countries' tents. I went into the Brazilian tent for a beer, where the atmosphere was electric. There were scantily-clad Brazilians dancing and eating and celebrating, and plotzed Germans and Poles screaming and gyrating with every pass, dribble, or shot. Since it was such an exhausting enough game just to watch, I can only imagine the intensity experienced by the players on the field.

In minute 75, the Polish number 7, Sobelewski, commited a "professional" foul. He ran behind Miroslav Klose and bumped his back with a strong elbow, knocking him to the ground to break up an attack. This earned him a second yellow card, and hence a red. He was a thrown out. The crowds howled, both in the stadium in Dortmund and at the Fan Fest where we were. Underdogs to begin with, the Poles were now down to ten men with fifteen minutes to go. It didn't look good for them. But the Poles held on doggedly. They played smart and tough and relentlessly, not ceding a goal to the end of ninety minutes of play. But, of course, there's stoppage time to consider.

The Germans, who are famous for never giving up, brought the ball down the right flank in minute 91. Odonkor crossed it, and Oliver Neuville slid in and poked the ball past the keeper and into the net. The game was over, and Germany, the host country, had won. The German crowd in the Fan Fest showed their ecstasy with a huge buzz and rumble of incipient celebration. When I sidled up to the German tent, the fans were so happy and agitated, they were almost foaming at the mouth.

We took advantage of the frenzy to bolt for the subway. We knew that if we waited even fifteen minutes, a throng of drunken Germans would be crowding onto public transportation. While they were in the immediate throes of victory and celebration, we took advantage of our small window of opportunity. As we hit the subway station, we could feel the swell of a great wave of people behind us. We scurried down the stairs and boarded the *S-Bahn* to return to central Hamburg. Already we could hear Germans singing and screaming in the terminal as we settled into our seats. The train took off as though propelled by the arriving crowds, and we had successfully escaped the crush. When we came up out of the *S-Bahn* cavern and took to the street by the train station, we entered the midst of bedlam. Cars sped by honking their horns, passengers joyously waving German flags. German fans were running, singing, chanting, embracing, screaming, flailing their arms wildly, waving banners and flags and whatever else they could lay their hands on. We retreated to our hotel, which wasn't much of a sanctuary. The streets were filled with celebrants--very noisy celebrants. All night long, we could hear the wildness though the thick walls of our hotel room. Even though it was warm, we kept the windows closed tight in a futile attempt to screen out the festive noise. We managed to get some sleep--I know not how.

JUNE 15 – GAME DAY #2, COSTA RICA VS. ECUADOR

I awoke to the sound of a shower. I looked next to me in bed. Hannia was not there. I looked over at my cell phone, sitting on my nightstand. It read 5:45 a.m. I did a double take. If there's anyone who doesn't like to get up early, it is my wife. No mistake, it was 5:45 a.m. I wondered if something was the matter. I approached the bathroom.

"Hannia, what are you doing?"

"It's late. We better get going."

"It's 5:45 a.m."

"No, it's almost noon."

"No, it's 5:45."

"Wait a minute."

She poked her head out of the shower and regarded me with a quizzical look. The wheels in her head were turning, until a sheepish smile came to her face.

"Whoops," she said. "I've still got L.A. time on my watch."

I returned her smile, gave her a little look to rub it in, then collapsed back in bed.

"Sorry," she said from the shower stall.

We slept for another hour.

As we walked into the hotel breakfast room, we were immediately engulfed in a sea of bright yellow shirts. This was an Ecuadoran crowd.

We were decked out in Costa Rica's white, red, and blue, so there was a mutual recognition as we passed into the buffet line. We sat down next to a couple of journalists from *Radio Reloj* and *Radio Monumental* from Costa Rica. They were very curious about where we were from and what we thought about Costa Rica's prospects against Ecuador. We discussed the *Ticos*' performance against Germany, and concurred that they had a shot at making it to the second round. One of the journalists, however, adamantly stressed that Ecuador had an extremely strong team. I was a little skeptical. I really felt that Costa Rica's team was dominant, and that that Ecuador's success in qualifying was due in large measure to the altitude in their native country, which puts opponents at a disadvantage.

We made our way back to the historical center of Hamburg to see a few sights before the day's game.

Upon entering the *Petrikirche*, we were surprised to find an art exhibit with a soccer theme. Soccer balls that had been painted, carved, or adorned in different, odd ways were on display in the middle of the church. One ball was mounted on a camera tripod, another was enclosed in a cage suspended from the ceiling, and one "ball" was formed from tubing arranged in the octagon shapes of a traditional soccer ball. I snapped a couple of pictures, and noticed that two older gentlemen, guards, or attendants--they wore official-looking armbands--were watching me with a little bit of disapproval. I didn't know if they took exception to the use of photography in the church, or whether they felt the exhibit was inappropriate for the setting. Then I noticed that one of the "soccer balls" hanging from the ceiling featured an open section that was designed like a church, with a little devil at the pulpit. To my secular sensibilities it seemed funny, a commentary on the devoutly commercialized nature of the sports world in general, and the World Cup in particular.

The guide approached, pointed at the devil-bearing display, and remarked in German that it should not have been allowed into the church. He then changed the subject, showing us a painting on a pillar of the church, depicting Napoleon's occupation of Hamburg, a tremendous tragedy inflicted on the city. Many people, he noted, had sought refuge in the church while waiting to escape to Denmark. He pointed out some white stains on the pillars and floors of the church. They looked like the lime deposits that accumulate in a teakettle or coffeemaker. "Horse urine," he said. "Napoleon quartered his horses in our church." I'm sure the invaders had made a Catholic gesture of disrespect toward a

Protestant church, but I didn't feel that this would be a pleasant issue to pursue in front of my Catholic wife.

"No respect," I agreed. I explained the origin of the stains to Hannia, who predictably responded with disgust. "Can't it be washed out?" she asked.

"It has been washed out over and over and over," the guide replied. "It always comes back."

I misunderstood a couple of historical details, so he quizzed us on what languages we spoke. When we mentioned Spanish, he called over the other church guide, who launched into a description of life in Hamburg under Napoleonic occupation. He showed us the rest of the artwork in the church, as well as a model of the church at the pinnacle of its opulence and splendor prior to a devastating fire. This guide, who was probably in his early sixties, impressed me. He was tremendously proud of his church and took great pleasure in showing it off to its maximum effect. The centuries of history, turmoil, and glory were all his, and he radiated a sense of connection to a long chain of important events through the ages. And he wasn't the least bit pompous or officious about the history of his city, but engaged in bringing these stories to life, generously sharing his knowledge with his foreign guests.

Bidding farewell to our *Petrikirche* guides, we headed again for the *Rathaus*, to see how the *Rathaus* Race was progressing. Once again, it was closed to the general public. This time they informed us that the first organized tours wouldn't be available until Saturday, when we would be back in Mainz. We wouldn't be able to enter the inner sanctum of Hamburger politics, to observe *Rathaus* workers scurrying through their maze, seeking the cheese (and pork) that the process offers.

We proceeded down the picturesque cobblestones, past the Venetian-style canals, and paused a moment to regard the statue of an unknown dignitary of old. Affixed to the railing of the canal bridge, the *Trostbrücke*, the tall figure stood guard over the waterway, arm extended to support a scepter-like sword, obviously a symbol of kingly power. He was, unfortunately, named Adolph, which carries all sorts of baggage. But with his bushy beard, crown, and a splendid outfit resembling something that Ian Anderson might have worn while performing with Jethro Tull, this Adolph made a much grander impression than the nerdy, evil, little twit with the toothbrush mustache. He was Graf Adolph III of Schauenburg, and his sculptor, Engelbert Peiffer, had succeeded in presenting to the world the illusion of his subject's benevolent love of his maritime town. The Graf's sculptor clearly earned his commission handily. The inscription said that Adolph III had held his office from 1164 to 1203. His legacy included extracting a promise from Emperor Friedrich Barbarossa (who was king of a whole bunch of stuff--German, Italy, Burgundy--as well as Holy Roman Emperor, and my favorite: Duke of Swabia) to give the citizens of Hamburg toll exemptions for their ships on the Elbe all the way to the North Sea. This commitment to seafaring established Hamburg's reputation as one of the world's great ports.

While looking at this sculpture, I spotted something that I saw repeatedly in Germany. Any tall sculpture also had a tall spire in the background, complementing the vertical lines of the work. Whether this was a conscious philosophy of sculpture placement, or just a happy accident--Germany is full of tall structures--I couldn't help but feel that Germans either had gravitated spontaneously toward such visual arrangements, or some traditions or guidelines had inspired them to incorporate this kind of synergy into their sculptures. After a month in the country, I was to decide that this theme was far too pervasive to be just a happy accident.

Behind our new pal, Graf Adolph III, the spire that completed the composition attracted me, Hannia, and, in fact, everyone who walked down the street. We proceeded around a corner and stared up at the clock tower of the old *Nikolaikirche*. All that remains of the church is the 153-meter-high clock tower, as the main church was one of so many casualties of World War II. The surviving spire now stands as an antiwar monument. The church was established in 1353, and the tower was added later, reigning from 1874 to 1876 as the tallest structure in the world.

We craned our necks upward as we approached. We shuffled into line under the array of bells in the archway, paid our Euros, and waited for the elevator to carry us to the top of the tower. The grey-haired lady selling the tickets regarded us very seriously. The view from the top of the tower was spectacular. Despite the grey, cloudy weather restricting the view a bit, but we still were treated to an engaging panorama of winding waterways, city streets, the *Rathaus*, and industrial buildings. Inside the tower, a display tallied the destruction of World War II: Two-thirds of the buildings in this historic and picturesque city had crumbled under Allied bombing.

After regarding the city below from every imaginable angle, returned to mother earth. There we saw the ticket lady now playing with her dog in the cobbled open square. This terrier of indeterminate breed chased after a tennis ball with explosive, springy enthusiasm, shared by a group of schoolchildren on a field trip to the church, who frolicked with the dog, the, ball, and Hannia. The formerly serious-seeming German ticket lady was now smiling from ear to ear, doting over her canine charge. Hannia, who profoundly missed playing with Keiko, our border collie back home, made up for lost time, running around and mixing it up with this very happy *hund*.

Since it was getting close to game time, we wandered back to the *Rathaus* on our way to the train station. Tourist buses were converging, and big groups of spectators were gathering in the square to catch a ride to the stadium. Most of the group wore the bright-red jersey of Costa Rica, and suddenly we felt at home. A small band was playing. A few *Ticos* with a banjo, saxophone, bass, and bongos were churning out the Caribbean tune, "Rice and Beans". It was a very tasty and infectious rendition, and the whole crowd was chiming in with the Creole-English from Limón, "Gimme some a dat, gimme some a dat rice and beans." Typically raucous and jovial and inviting, this quintessentially Central American display, in front of the staid and venerated *Rathaus,* offered up the height of surreal contrast. We joined the festivities for a time, clapping and laughing and singing, until the *Ticos* crowded onto their various buses. We made tracks for the train station and zipped toward the stadium, surrounded by Costa Ricans, Ecuadorans, and Germans.

Just as I had discovered four years before in Korea, I found that while standing on the train, I couldn't see the signs at the stops. I guess this inconvenience must be a flaw of the public transit world in general.

Luckily, it wasn't hard to figure out which station was ours. Hannia was enjoying chatting with the many Costa Ricans around her, when suddenly, at one train stop, virtually everyone in the train stood up in unison and tried to elbow their way through the doors.

We followed the pulsing mass of jerseys through the large cement passageways that led to the stadium. It was like being in a large drainage channel with a few thousand of our closest friends. A clever promoter-- Chiquita or Dole?--was handing out bananas to the crowd. It suddenly dawned on me that this match also represented a battle of two banana republics. While Costa Rica is known more for its production of coffee (and computer software) these days, while Ecuador exports petroleum, if you buy some bananas from your local market, they are likely to have come from one of these two soccer-mad countries. We passed a few bright-red garbage cans overflowing with banana peels. It was the image of the day. Another funny note was the slogan emblazoned on the garbage cans, "*Ich bin der Cleansmann.*" This was a bilingual pun on Klinnsmann, the German coach, whom the press, with affectionate sarcasm, referred to as "*Der Klinnsman.*"

The cement channels led to buses, into which the crowd poured. Soon we arrived at the crest of the hill, and piled out in front of a beautiful, modern stadium, unique in that it has giant poles and rigging sticking out of its top and sides, almost giving it a nautical look. Appropriate for Hamburg, though probably inadvertent. The Stadium Ship was ringed by festive Ecuadorans and Costa Ricans, all clad in bright colors, carrying enormous flags and banners.

To the left of the stadium, surrounded by a lush patch of immaculate grass, was an enormous statue, attracting scads of fans. Did it depict a hero? A politician, soldier, or soccer player of renown? No, it was a statue of a giant foot. Perhaps the world's largest foot. Of course, I had to sit on its bare toes and have my picture taken, with the statue's giant toenails sticking out between my legs. *Fussball über alles.* And here was what the *Fuss* was all about.

Moseying back toward the entrance to the stadium, we got in line to go through security. Everything moved along with alacrity, as it had at the USA vs. CZE game, until an overzealous young guard started patting me down. In my backpack I carried my still camera, an extra lens, and a small video camera. The sight of my video camera turned the guard's face glum. "This is not permitted," he said, pointing to the video camera.

"They let me in with it in the USA vs. CZE game," I replied, trying my best to look hurt and confused, "and they let me into all the games in Korea with this four years ago." Here I was, a repeat customer, and they were persecuting me like this?

"It is not permitted. I am very sorry, but you will have to check it in," said the guard, pointing at a cargo container that had been fitted out to check possessions for the duration of the game. Already, a substantial line was forming, and I knew that after the game, when 60,000 or so fans were all leaving simultaneously, I might have to spend an extra couple of hours trying to get my palm-sized JVC camcorder out of hock. The young fellow was not about to budge, obviously a bit too proud of his starched uniform and his position as guardian of world-class football to relent to some contraband-toting philistine like myself.

I protested, but he insisted. I thought, "Well, the Teutonic character has finally surfaced." In a way, though, I had been surprised that we hadn't such encountered strict security before this. Another guard came by and grabbed me by my arm.

"I'll take him over there," he said to the first guard. The first guard nodded his assent, handing him the article in question.

The second guard escorted me to the check-in kiosk.

"Let me see your backpack," he demanded.

"Great," I thought, "what else is he going to take exception to?"

I slipped my pack off and handed it to him. He glanced back at the first guard, who was otherwise occupied. He opened my backpack, stuck the video camera inside, closed it up, and handed it back to me. He nodded conspiratorially. We both smiled. "*Viel dank*," I offered. He clicked his heels officiously and sped off into the crowd to save some other hapless soul from his colleague's fastidiousness. So much for my preconceptions about our German hosts.

Once inside, we mingled with the throngs of festive *Ticos* who ringed the stadium. Everyone was decked out in the white, red, and blue of the tiny republic. Many women modeled traditional *campesina* dress, men wore Cat-in-the-Hat-style top hats emblazoned with the colors and names of their country, and several revelers wore oversized heads of Costa Rican forward extraordinaire Paolo Cesar Wanchope, as well as Brazilian phenom Ronaldinho, although in CR colors. Always ready to celebrate with abandon, in a raucous, friendly, inviting sort of way, Costa Ricans were dancing around to boom-box music, and taking pictures of one another in front of the stadium: with Germans, with Ecuadorans, and even with a certain big, red-haired gringo.

The Ecuadoran contingent clung to the periphery of the stadium, taking the rivalry a bit more seriously. They were having their fun, too, but were much more standoffish to anyone not clad in yellow.

We grabbed the obligatory beer and giant pretzel and headed to our seats. The teams were warming up on the field. Next to us sat a German fellow, in a German jersey and cap, who spontaneously and for no particular reason started screaming, *"Deutschland! Deutschland! Deutschland!"* Of course, his team wasn't playing that day, but he had to make his presence felt, in as obnoxious a fashion as you can imagine. The attitude reminded me a little of that of some Mexican fans I've encountered, who can't stand to see anyone support another team, or give anyone else props.

We were in the very center of the end zone, directly behind the goal, at the back of the bottom section. Above us was the upper balcony, and a Costa Rican banner flapped in the breeze, the light shining through it giving off a red and blue glow. We surveyed the stands, and the biggest group of *Ticos* was to our right in the corner. We moseyed down to the *Colonia Tica*, and blended right in. On of the Wanchope big heads was right beside us, and someone else was waving large, inflatable bananas, printed with the slogan,"World's Best Bananas." The logo on the inflatable bananas looked very much like the one I'd spotted on one of the banana skins I'd seen earlier in a "Cleansmann" garbage can. It looked like some trade organization was eyeing both the German and world banana market.

We watched the Costa Rican team run and warm up on the field. They looked good and confident. Wanchope trotted the length of the grass, stretching and turning backwards, sideways, sprinting for stretches. We were looking forward to a good game.

Shortly after kickoff, things didn't look good. The *Ticos*, always skilled and creative, were somehow way too lax. Ecuador looked hungry. Their play showed real urgency. They were stealing the ball from the languid *Ticos* and making dangerous runs and combinations. They looked sharp. The *Ticos* looked hungover. Additionally, Costa Rica's most talented defender, *"El Tuma"* Martinez, who plies his trade in Italian Serie A, was out due to injury, which explained why he'd had such a bad game against Germany.

In the eighth minute of play, Luís Valencia crossed the ball in from the flank. Carlos Tenorio zipped past defender Douglas Sequeira and headed the ball home. Augustín Delgado scored after chesting down a pass from Edison Mendez, then beating both Marín and Michael Umaña (whom we'd seen play—lethargically--for the L.A. Galaxy) before shooting near post. The score: 2-0 Ecuador. The *Ticos* were stunned.

Ecuador was a team they traditionally had been able to beat comfortably, but they were now getting their butts kicked. Their play never improved. They were being outhustled by the more aggressive side. Also, they were abandoning the typical Central American style of short passes and tight control over the midfield in favor of an almost English-style long ball attack. In theory, this might make sense. Their forwards, Paolo Wanchope and "*La Bala*" Gomez were both big guys, at six-foot-five and six-foot-one respectively, good in the air, and Wanchope had played a number of years in England. Unfortunately for them, the Ecuadoran defense was filled with big bruisers, too. The back line was easily as big as the *Tico* offense, and they were swarming them enthusiastically. Additionally, the *Ticos* weren't delivering the long balls with British accuracy. It wasn't hard for Ecuador's defenders to track soft and errant incoming balls and blast them out of the danger zone. And they were fast. Wanchope had trouble getting in behind them, which is how he'd scored two goals against Germany. As I had said in the past, the loss of their legendary distributor, "*El Pato*" Lopez, had left a huge vacuum in the middle of the field, and it was all Hail Mary going forward.

Ecuador was on fire. Their passing was crisp, they were intimidating, and they forced the *Ticos* to make uncharacteristic mistakes. Pressure and hustle are formidable weapons.

Finally, in the second minute of stoppage time, substitute Ivan Kaviedes received another cross from Mendez, got past Marín, and poked the ball into the net. It was the final nail in the coffin. Kaviedes pulled a Spiderman mask out, put it on his head and danced for joy. It was a tribute to Otilino Tenorio (no relation to Carlos), a teammate who had been killed in a car crash in 2005 shortly after playing with his National Team in a friendly. Tenorio, whose nickname was "Spiderman," was famous for similar celebrations. The Ecuadoran fans went... well, they went BANANAS. This was huge for them. They were going to the second round in only their second World Cup.

The *Ticos* were devastated. This was their most promising match-up, and they had blown it. True, Ecuador was a much better team than in years past, but there is nothing worse than losing a match because of lack of spirit. It's one thing to leave it all on the field and lose. It's quite another to go after it half-heartedly and get pounded. To quote Paolo Cesar, "We have played in three World Cups and, yes, this has been our worst."

We left the stadium, stopping outside to watch the Ecuadorans party it up. One huge group had a huge flag, fluttering brightly in the breeze as they lifted and lowered it as a group, chanting, "E-cua-dor, E-cua-dor." But in victory, they weren't too magnanimous. Some who saw me in my *Tico* get-up would sneer, or make an unflattering remark to a friend. I heard one guy on his cell phone say, "Yeah, we beat those sons-of-bitches." It's an odd response. I don't know what the *Ticos* had done in his eyes to provoke it.

Hannia received no calls from Costa Rica. When she called, no one answered. I had a vision in my head of everyone in Costa Rica paralyzed in front of a TV set, staring blankly at the screen, mouth open, unable to move to pick up an endlessly ringing phone. This was a day of national tragedy.

We made our way back by bus and train, commiserating with dejected Costa Ricans on the way. I overheard one Spanish guy on the train say, "Well, they don't have too much there in CONCACAF." I was disappointed with Costa Rica's performance myself, but this comment irked me. I'd say most Europeans have never watched a CONCACAF qualifier and probably couldn't name ten players from the region. And Spain, of course, from the most successful region, was a perennial failure. They had just trounced the Ukraine 4-0, so I supposed he was a bit pumped up from that. Spain was still scheduled to play Tunisia and Saudi Arabia, two of the lowest-ranked in the tournament. And, of course, even Sweden, a European team with some history, couldn't beat Trinidad and Tobago, CONCACAF's fourth-place team. But, hey, that's how you feel when you win: Suddenly, you're the supreme critic. And that's how you feel when you lose: Everything's a slight, and so unfair. We hid out in our hotel room, after having run the gauntlet of yellow jerseys in the lobby.

We watched Paraguay vs. Sweden and England vs. Trinidad in our room, exhausted from the loss and oppressed by the sounds of celebration that wafted in from the streets.

England vs. Trinidad was a bit surprising. England had most of the ball, but couldn't score in the first half. Trinidad's defense managed to frustrate the Brits for most of the game. It wasn't until minute 83 that tall, gangly Peter Crouch got on the end of a David Beckham cross and headed it past Shaka Hislop. In injury time, Frank Gerrard scored another. It was a big relief for England, who hadn't scored a second-half goal since 1998. Trinidad was a bit disappointed after holding the English for so long, but it wasn't an unexpected result. It showed that the English are less than dominant, which I think pretty much everyone but the British knew anyway.

Sweden vs. Paraguay was an uninspiring affair, which was almost a repeat of the Scandinavians' scoreless draw against Trinidad. Sweden dominated play until very late in the game, when Manchester United's Freddy Ljundberg finally ended their scoring drought. The Swedish fans (remember, Sweden is Germany's neighbor to the north) went crazy in minute 89, when the Swedes finally broke down the Paraguayan defense. It was their first goal of this World Cup, and their first win in 2006. Sweden was then poised to take second place in the group, depending on their outcome against England in their final first-round game.

Historic Mainz.

The view from our room in Mainz.

Everything for the discerning soccer fan. Aren't you glad that Europeans don't get too crassly commercial?

L: Some old Hamburger statuary.
C: Hannia at the bell tower.
R: The view of Hamburg from the tower.

Canine hijinks at ground level.

L: "Gimme some a dat rice and beans," *Tico* festivities never stop.
R: The tunnel to the stadium: CRC v. ECU.

234

The Battle of the Banana Republics.

Mark sits on a Giant Foot

Hamburg's stadium with rigging.

Ticos' pre-game celebration.

The *Tico* section.

Decked out in the colors.

Honorary Costa Rican.

The saddest *Tico*.

The lucky wig didn't work this time.

Exultant Ecuadorans.

JUNE 16TH - TRAVEL

We awoke bright and early. We were bushed. The noise from the Ecuadorans celebrating in and around our hotel had continued unabated throughout the night. We ate our breakfast among hungover Andeans, checked out, and headed to the train station.

While waiting for our train to arrive, we started chatting with some *Ticos*. They were understandably bummed out. They had tickets to the final Costa Rican match against Poland, but were low on enthusiasm or hope. But our Costa Rican friends were quick to admit that four years from now, everyone will have forgotten the disappointment, and if they can qualify, a ton of *Ticos* will be headed to South Africa, hopes held high once again.

We piled onto the train to Mainz and collapsed in our seats. At one spot, in the heart of the Rhineland, the train came to a stop for no apparent reason. It stayed put for more than an hour, due to some sort of problem down the track. It was frustrating and oppressive, sitting in a vehicle designed to transport us at high speeds. The lack of movement grated on my nerves. At one point, the public-address system crackled to life. From a stream of German, we made out, "Argentina 6-Serbia 0." Everyone in the train reacted: 6-0? Ouch. The Netherlands had only squeaked out a 1-0 result against Serbia and Montenegro. Was this the year for Argentina to reassert itself? Of course, if you asked an Argentinean, the answer was always yes, whatever year you asked. And if Argentina lost, it was always because of politics--they had brought the wrong players, or the coach favored this guy or that guy. In my experience, Argentines never will say the have a weak team.

When we got back to the hotel in Mainz, we retired to our room to watch Netherlands vs. Ivory Coast. The Ivorians had been touted from the beginning as a team with the potential to upset the big powers, but had been drawn into the "Group of Death." They had done well against Argentina (yes, the same team that beat Serbia, 6-0), and now they could try their hand against the Netherlands, the best team never to win a World

Cup. It was a mostly partisan Dutch crowd at Stuttgart's Gottlieb Daimler Stadium. They started out in control of the match. Both teams played aggressively and with lots of flair. Holland got up by two goals, van Nistelrooy redeeming himself after a lackluster first game. The Dutch dropped back in a defensive posture after the second goal, and then looked very uninspiring. The Ivorians got a goal back, and it looked like there might still be a chance they could equalize, but the Dutch successfully killed off the match. The Dutch fans were ecstatic, chanting, "*Hup, Holland, Hup,*" toward the end, conscious of the fact that they were all but through to the second round. For my money, though, Holland looked less than convincing. Certainly Arjen Robben was flashy and exciting, involved in both goals, and van Nistlerooy had scored flamboyantly, but the overall performance lacked conviction. The Ivory Coast is a talented team, but inexperienced in World Cup play, and this could have been exploited. You can't argue with a win, but I felt I had seen the seeds of defeat in the Dutch squad.

We then migrated to the hotel's sports bar for the Mexico vs. Angola match.

Watching Mexico play is always a love/hate experience. They are the USA's bitterest rival, and yet Mexico also provides hope for CONCACAF. Part of me hates to see them prevail, because I can hear Mexican fans crow about how wonderful they are, yet another part of me hates to see them fail, because I can hear the Europhiles bleating out their criticisms of our region.

After dispensing with Iran (a team we didn't manage to beat in France '98), Mexico was in position to confirm passage to the second round by beating Angola. The African team, on the other hand, had suffered a defeat at the hands of Portugal (1-0), and needed points to stay alive. What ensued was a feisty match that resulted in a 0-0 draw. The man of the match was Ricardo, the Angolan keeper, who played brilliantly to frustrate the Mexicans, who were heavily favored to win. Mexico was without star striker Jared Borgetti, who had been injured in the first match. Mexican fans were out in force in Hamburg, and it was basically home-field advantage for the boys in green. In minute 79, Angolan Andre was ejected for a second yellow card (an intentional handball), and the remaining men had to fall back in a defensive posture. So the result suited my purposes well. Mexico didn't flame out, but still couldn't beat a lower-rated team that was down to ten men for the last eleven minutes.

The few spectators wearing Mexican jerseys in the hotel's bar had to pray for a result versus Portugal in their final group match.

JUNE 17 - GAME DAY #3, ITA VS. USA

We got up early to accomplish a few things before the fun and games began. We did our laundry, Hannia bought some sign-making materials, we checked our e-mail, and bought some phone cards. We wandered around a street fair for a while along the waterfront. I found some old World Cup '94 pins, which I bought and affixed to my hat. It was a festive affair, a flea-market, yard-sale atmosphere located in a picturesque spot on the cobblestones along the Rhine. It was fun to see the sort of silly odds and ends that people had accumulated, and were now trying to unload.

At three p.m., we hopped aboard an *S-Bahn* train to the Frankfurt *Flughof.* We were seated next to a cop, and conversed with him a bit to confirm that we were headed in the right direction. A middle-aged guy with a bushy mustache, he was very pleasant and happy to help out the silly tourists. He told us we had to go to the *"Fern,"* or long-distance terminal, which involved crossing over the tracks on a long walkway to the other side of the station. He was headed to the Portugal vs. Iran game, assigned to crowd-control duty. He was relaxed and very much in his element, smiling and chatting with people on the train. With him, however, were some young cops, obviously without much experience, who were all keyed up and way too serious. I remembered the over-zealous kid who got all worked up about my video camera at the game in Hamburg. These clean-cut youths were sitting bolt upright in their ridiculously well-pressed (by *seine Mutti?*) new uniforms, riot helmets tucked under their arms. They had large batons, to which they clung like security blankets. You hoped that if the proverbial *scheist* hit the fan, that they'd listen to the middle-aged guy and not do anything rash. He was kidding a couple of them, which they obviously didn't get, answering his questions seriously as if they expected they'd have their wrists slapped with a ruler if they responded incorrectly.

We arrived at the *Flughof,* and followed the cop's instructions, climbing the escalator and walking to the far side.

We found the proper track, found our reserved seats and arrived in comfort at Mannheim, where we were to change trains. When the Kaiserslautern-bound train arrived, we searched for the proper car. There were no markings on the outside of the train to tell which car was which, and there was such a huge press of people boarding that we couldn't get inside to see the car number until the train was about to leave. Once inside, we realized we were about three cars off, and asked which way our car was. A couple of passengers told us to go to the right, as the train started moving. We pushed and shoved our way through the throngs of people in the aisles (not everyone could reserve a seat). When we made it to the next car, we realized we had wrongly advised, and that in fact we had fought our way to get farther from our seats. We turned around to head in the other direction. However, so many more people had piled in that we no longer could move down the aisle, and since it was an express train, so couldn't get off at the next stop and change cars. Though we had paid for reserved seats, the train was so tightly packed that we were forced to stand for the entire trip.

With cramping legs, we arrived at the Kaiserslautern *Hauptbahnhof*. It was the proverbial zoo. There were soccer fans everywhere. When we exited, we came face to face with a giant dinosaur. A twenty-five-foot-long plastic replica of a Tyrannosaurus Rex was mounted on a trailer, with large banner proclaiming, "*Grosste Dinosaurier-- Ausstellung Europas, Gartenshau Kaiserslautern, April–Oktober.*" As best I could figure, this said, "Big Dinosaurs, European Exhibit, Kaiserslautern Garden Show, April through October. Before finding the soccer game we sought, we'd discovered Jurassic Park.

As our first task, we found the shuttle bus stop. Once we had that established, we backtracked to the center of town, where a huge celebration was under way on the main street. We cruised up and down the boulevard, surrounded by a press of USA and Italy supporters, all chanting, singing, celebrating, and trying the local brews and brats offered at the myriad booths and stands that had been set up in the street for the occasion. Everyone's faces and/or bodies were painted, and everyone from babes in arms to elderly grandparents was decked out in team colors, many with the #10 Totti jersey. We stopped a number of groups from both sides, and they screamed into camera while we snapped photos. We bumped into the Harlem Globetrotters again, and a bunch of Italian semi-Elvises, with artificial sideburns. We even bumped into the Soccer Head Guy, whom we had seen in Korea and later in the L.A. Galaxy's stadium. After making the rounds of the street festival, and filling up on beer and junk food, we started for the stadium. We asked a cop how far it was, and he told us it was a short walk, pointing and telling us where to turn. Just up the hill a bit, he assured us. We decided it was probably faster to hoof it than to take the shuttle bus. Crossing through a park on our way, every conceivable type of human being was on display, reclining on every available patch of open grass.

As we started up the "little hill" to the stadium, the incline turned out to be steeper than it had been advertised. It was a very pleasant tree-lined street, and a nice, sunny day, but after standing on the train for hours and bumping our way through the crowds at the street festival, we could feel the burn of the climb. There were stands every hundred yards of so, each bearing signs proclaiming, "Last cold water before stadium." When we reached the top, it was much easier to get through security than at the previous two games we'd attended. Either they were getting better at it as time went on, or Kaiserslautern was particularly adept at patting down the great unwashed. I had left my video camera at the hotel to avoid the experience I'd had in Hamburg. And on the way in, we saw Frankie Hedjuk again. Despite his knee trouble, he was definitely making his presence felt at World Cup 2006.

It struck everyone as we entered the stadium: There were TONS of U.S. fans. Not just the usual hardcore couple of thousand. We were EVERYWHERE. There had been a hint of that in the downtown area of Kaiserslautern, but suddenly, concentrated within the stadium walls, this pulsing, writhing, screaming leviathan of USA supporters was overwhelming. Everyone was looking around at the crowd in awe and wonder. The chants of "USA, USA!" were not just strong, they were powerful and dominating. It may have just been my position in the stadium (we were high in the rafters in the northeast corner), but it seemed like a U.S. crowd. As I've described ad nauseum, this was a unique circumstance—being part of a U.S. presence even bigger than at the game against the Czech Republic. After years of being outnumbered by Mexican fans, or Costa Rican fans, or Honduran fans, this was something to write home about. Which is what I'm doing, of course.

I looked a couple of rows above me, and there was Justin, the blonde American kid I'd met in Gelsenkirchen. We smiled and greeted each other, but it was too loud to carry on a conversation. We were fine with that. This was an atmosphere to be savored.

A guy directly behind me shouted at odd intervals, "I believe! I believe!" It turned out he was from Texas, though I'd never have guessed it from his accent. His name was Matt, and he was just as gung ho as I was. I knew that I was in the right section.

Kasey Keller took the field and the crowd erupted. Keller, no stranger to intense European crowds, looked up and smiled his smirky, gum-chewing grin. The man whom I'd seen prevail against Brazil in front of a paltry 12,000 fans, most of whom were Brazil partisans, was enjoying a long-deserved hero's welcome.

More players came on the field, and, as with the Czech game, they stared up at the vast U.S. contingent with pleasure and awe.

Farther into the southeast corner and a little higher up was a large banner proclaiming the presence of the "Minnesota Volunteers." The late afternoon sun was poking in through the beams and roof, giving the Minnesotans a spiritual glow not to be believed. They were on their feet screaming and yelling, waving arms, banners, and anything else to show their enthusiasm.

As the game started, the noise level rose to an impenetrable wave of sound. At about the seven-minute mark, the U.S. found a rhythm. They started passing the ball around quickly, moving into space, finding the open man. The U.S. dominated play. It was an odd thing to see. Prior to the 2002 World Cup, Italy had played a tune-up game against the U.S., and the Italians had been lucky to come away with a 1-0 win. Somehow, stylistically, I think the U.S. was starting to get Italy's number. You could see that the Italians knew they were in for a challenge. Much of their play was tentative. They looked a little desperate as the U.S. beat them to most balls, frequently picked them, or ran circles around them. We were moving the ball well and frustrating the *Azurri*. But Italy, who has by far the craftiest team in the world, managed an early goal: Gilardino got on the end of an Andrea Pirlo free kick and headed the ball into the back of Keller's net. Eddie Pope had held up for an offside trap while his teammates tracked back, keeping Gilardino onside.

It felt awful to concede a goal in minute 22, and I couldn't help but wonder if we were in for another long evening. But the U.S. team came back strong, still dominating play. It seemed, however, that the calls were all going against us. It's always dangerous as a partisan fan to make a statement like that, because frequently your emotions color your perceptions. Still, it seemed rather obvious to me that the referee, Larrionda, a Uruguayan, was bending over backwards to protect the beloved Italian stars, and to keep the upstarts in their place. If you examine the rosters of Serie A, you'll discover tons of Uruguayans, which at the very least would make a Uruguayan much more aware of the Italian personalities on the field. At the very worst, you have to wonder about the World Cup team from a country in which the biggest soccer headlines of the year revolved around match-fixing. Time after time, corner kicks weren't given to the U.S., fouls were called on us, but not on them.

After a while, the U.S. tied it up with an Italian own goal, the product of a Bobby Convey free kick that Cristian Zaccardo knocked into the net as he tried to keep it from reaching Brian McBride. Then Daniele di Rossi threw a vicious elbow at the head of McBride. The Minnesota Volunteers went nuts. McBride had played for the Minnesota Thunder in the A League, and he was their homeboy. A gash on his cheek was dripping blood. It seemed the Italians were scared to death of McBride. Di Rosso saw red and was gone.

In minute 45, Pablo Mastroeni slid in late against Andrea Pirlo and hit his ankles. Pirlo writhed on the ground. Out came a straight red card for Pablo. It seemed harsh. The tackle was a bit reckless, but I felt it was more deserving of a yellow. Considering how heavily the Italians had been fouling and the way the calls had been going, I felt that the ref was going out of his way to even things up at ten men per side. No one will be ostracized for jobbing the Americans, but sticking it to the Italians might result in recriminations. As soon as he was taken to the sidelines, Pirlo miraculously recovered and reentered the game.

Two minutes into the second half, Eddie Pope made a tackle on Gilardino. He got the ball, but his momentum carried him though Gilardino's legs. I wouldn't even consider this a foul, but Larrionda gave Eddie his second yellow card, and our veteran central defender was ejected. Again, I didn't feel the card was deserved, and I had company. The U.S. crowd was chanting, "Bullshit! Bullshit!" unrelentingly. We were now down to nine men, against one of the giants of world soccer.

Bruce Arena took out Clint Dempsey and inserted DaMarcus Beasley. Though I'm a big DaMarcus fan, I wondered about this. Dempsey was really blossoming and had done some great things. Still, Beasely defends very well and has the speed and stamina to go both ways. It made sense, but I had misgivings.

My misgivings were erased when DaMarcus put a ball into the back of the Italian goal in minute 70. Unfortunately, the goal was also erased. Brian McBride was called for being in an offside position. From the stands, this didn't look like the right call. It seemed that McBride might have been in an offside position, but didn't have anything to do with the play. Once again, emotion colors perception. I have since watched a recording of the game, and McBride was in an offside position blocking the keeper's view, and jumping out of the way as the ball passed. I will say, however, that in watching the game back through the modern miracle of the DVR, most of the other bad calls still seemed like bad calls.

The crowd was yelling, "Bullshit! Bullshit!" Keller whipped up the crowd by lifting his arms repeatedly, as if to say, "Louder!"

For the last twenty minutes, the U.S. was alternately back on its heels and attacking judiciously. The Italians were doing everything in their power to kill off the game. They were diving, falling at the slightest contact, rolling around on the ground as though deathly injured. Keller made some beautiful saves, most notably on two shots by the plucky Alessandro del Piero.

In minute 49, Cannavaro went down--seemingly for nothing. The Italians kicked the ball out of bounds to accommodate the "injury." The player stayed on the ground, waiting to be carted off on a stretcher, obviously employing this very Italian time-wasting tactic. The crowd howled its disapproval. Keller took the goal kick, just as the stretcher cleared the sidelines. He showed great marksmanship and gamesmanship by striking the officials who were carrying the Italian player some seventy yards away. The crowd went bananas, chanting, "Kasey Keller, Kasey Keller," over and over, in recognition of the feat.

The Americans were clearly exhausted, having to cover the extra ground that the two red cards had opened up, but they held tough to the very end. The Italians threw three forwards at the goal, and the Red, White, and Blue closed them down. It was unbelievable that Arena hadn't subbed Johnson in. McBride was still working his butt off, but he was obviously out of gas. With a fresh Johnson and Beasley in, there would have been more hope of scoring the go-ahead goal against the tired and depleted Italian back line. Someday, I hope I can ask Arena why he didn't bring Johnson in.

I turned to Matt behind me, and he kept on chanting, "I believe, I believe."

When the final whistle blew, the U.S. team collapsed to the ground, thoroughly spent. They'd held the three-time world champions to a tie, playing a man down for the last twenty minutes. They'd stopped the likes of Del Piero, Luca Toni, and Francesco Totti cold, in spite of questionable refereeing, and some nasty, cynical elbow-throwing and physical play.

The team came out to the corner we occupied and applauded the fans. We applauded them right back. It was a supremely ballsy performance, and we all felt that it gave the U.S. enormous credibility. Oddly, it was the first point the U.S. had earned in World Cup play in Europe.

Matt and I assessed the situation. The tie was also enough to keep our hopes of progressing to the second round alive, but only barely. Earlier that day, Ghana had beaten the Czech Republic 2-0. We would need a win in our last game, against Ghana, and we'd need the Italians to beat the Czechs. Those two results seemed possible. I felt that it was more likely that the U.S. would beat Ghana. I didn't think the Czechs would have trouble with Italy. As we danced and chanted our way out of the stadium, I saw Thomas Rongen, who had followed Arena as DCU's coach, and was at that time coach of the U20 men's national team, standing to the side of the crowd. I went over to him and extended my hand.

"Hey, coach," I said as he shook my hand, "If anyone had any doubts about U.S. soccer, they should be gone after that display." He smiled and agreed. I melted away into the crowd, with the Elvises and the Globetrotters and the thousands and thousands of U.S. fans who were proud and optimistic.

I passed a group of Italians, and one was philosophically analyzing the game, "*E come la panna...*" he started ("It's like cream..."). I couldn't hear the rest, but thought it was quite appropriate that an Italian would pick an analogy that involved food.

The bottom line of the game was this: the U.S. hadn't won, had only barely stayed alive, and now had to win against Ghana. They would be playing, however, without Pablo Mastroeni and Eddie Pope, both veterans, both critical to the "spine" of the team.

We took the *S-Bahn* to Mannheim, and then the ICE toward Mainz. The train was virtually empty, except for another U.S.-color-wearing couple. The train arrived in Mainz at around three a.m.

I quizzed our cab driver a bit in my mangled German between the train station and the hotel. We discussed the Italian tendency to dive, and to manipulate referees. *"Ist wie sind die italianisches Spieler,"* he said philosophically ("That's what the Italian players are like"). He said he had watched the game and had been impressed with the play of the U.S. team. I took the compliment with a grain of salt. I seriously doubted that a cab driver would tell a paying customer that his team sucked. Still, he was very affable and magnanimous, and very pleased that I was attempting to communicate in his native tongue. We stumbled out of the cab, into the hotel, and fell asleep as though drugged.

Welcome to Kaiserslautern.

Americans out in force.

The Italian response to the Elvises.

Dueling hair.

Globetrotters 'r' US.

Takin' it to the street.

Yankee occupation zone.

Gringos on parade.

The yanks are coming.

Ready to rumble.

It warms my heart to see this many USA fans out in force.

A partisan crowd.

A voice of dissent. I happen to agree.

This score held up. The USA was the only team to get a point out of Italy.

Bathed in the afternoon light.

The happy couple.

JUNE 18TH - RECUPERATION

We came to consciousness around nine in the morning, and dragged our pathetic selves to the breakfast buffet. Thus refreshed, we marched back to our room, and with the resolve of the mighty travelers that we are, we went back to sleep until about one p.m. We went out briefly to run a couple of errands. It was Sunday, and virtually everything was closed--most disappointingly, the photo-processing place. It's easy to forget, living in Los Angeles, or some other major metropolis, that in many parts of the world things actually do pretty much come to a halt on Sunday. The obsession with commerce in the U.S. has far overshadowed the obsession with the Sabbath.

We watched the day's games in our room and the bar. Croatia tied Japan 0-0 in a colorless match featuring good goalkeeping and bad finishing--including a Croatian PK that the Japanese keeper Yoshikatsu Kawaguchi snuffed. Both teams looked fated to be eliminated in the first round. The other game in Group E was Brazil vs. Australia. Brazil was heavily favored, of course, but did not shine. Adriano scored the opener, doing a "baby dance" in celebration--his child had been born in Brazil on Friday. Fred came off the bench to score the second goal, and Brazil won handily. The Brazilians failed to impress as World Champions, however. The seemed complacent and slow and not at all sharp. This was their second game in a row that they managed to win, as expected, but without magic.

The nightcap was a bit of a surprise. Heavily favored France scored early, not surprisingly on a strike by Thierry Henry. South Korea, however, never gave up, and ran the very talented and technically superior French around with their athleticism and persistence. In minute 81, South Korea's Park Ji-sung poked a ball over French keeper Fabian Barthez and equalized. It ended in a tie. Surprisingly, South Korea was now atop the group and France was second to last. Zidane had picked up a yellow card, and wouldn't be able to play in their final first-round game against Togo. It looked possible France might be ejected in the first round for the second World Cup in a row. This might well have been Zidane's final appearance.

June 19 – Make Mine Mainz

We got up a little late and hit the buffet. We went to the photo-developing shop and picked up our pictures. As we were leaving the shop, it started to rain. It wasn't torrential, and it felt like it would let up, but Hannia insisted on finding an umbrella to buy. We hit a couple of nearby shops, but came up empty-handed. The rain subsided.

Our touristic visitations in Mainz started with the *Mainzer Dom*, a beautiful old cathedral with ancient roots. The *platz* out front has a pillar with an inscription that reads, "On the 1000 year celebration of the Cathedral this market column was set up." The Guttenberg museum was closed that day (Monday), so we pressed on to the *Schillerplatz*, and went in search of *St. Stephan Kirche*, which reputedly had stained glass windows by Chagall. I'd love to say that the windows were spectacular, but if I hadn't had advance notice that they were Chagalls, I'd have noticed nothing all that special. We backtracked, had some ice cream, and retreated to our room to rest.

We took a bus to the *Mainz Hauptbahnhof*, where I got reservations for our next trip on June 22, and then we took a train for the *Frankfurt Hauptbahnhof*, where we boarded a tram for the *Römerberg*. This was the old historical portion of Frankfurt, literally the Roman hill, whose history dates back to the time when it was a Roman encampment. On one side of the town square was a row of picturesque old half-timbered buildings, known as the *Ostzeile*. Opposite the gingerbread houses was the iconic *Rathaus*, instantly recognizable by its three-stepped Gothic rooftops. It the center of the square was the Fountain of Justice, famous for having run with red and white wine for the coronations. The rest of the time that we'd been in Frankfurt I hadn't felt this kind of old-world ambience, but this section oozed Teutonic history. Sadly, I've seen prewar aerial photographs of Frankfurt, taken when the entire city was filled with structures like this.

We visited the *Kaiserdom*, the cathedral, saw the ruins of the foundation of the original Roman outpost, and made our way to the Goethe museum.

The museum was next to a re-creation of the Goethe family's residence, which was bombed out during World War II. It was a large, but fairly mundane building in the middle of the downtown area. where *Faust*'s proprietor put pen to paper more than two hundred years ago. As a former student of German, the place held interest for me, and it was fun to get a window on the world from Goethe's time period. As we entered the building, there was a large plywood cutout of the poet, a cartoon-like rendering of the Weimar Classicist holding a soccer ball, in honor of the *Weltmeisterschaft*. It was pleasing to see that the museum staff didn't take themselves too seriously. They were less stodgy than the bar managers at the hotel in Berlin who didn't want their establishment to be seen as a lowly "sports bar."

It was interesting to discover that Goethe was from a political family, which I normally would consider a disqualification for creative work. Considering the economic conditions of Europe in the eighteenth century, you'd have to be from a well-to-do family in order to be educated and idle enough to write. Goethe was also an influential scientist, and I couldn't help but compare him to his contemporary, Benjamin Franklin, also a "renaissance man" though not one from patrician roots. It's an interesting contrast between old world and the new, though Jefferson and Washington were from upper-class circumstances as well.

Visiting old houses like that makes me think of all their practical differences from modern life. From bathing to sanitation to food preparation to lighting, the daily slog was much more challenging. It was a four-story house, so just carting things up and down must have taken some athleticism. Certainly the Goethe family—the daughter of the mayor, married to a lawyer—employed servants to handle most of the physical exigencies of household management.

Once out of the Goethe museum, I sought out an Internet café to take care of some business. The deadline was looming for the Emmy voting, and I had to put in my two cents' worth. I was able to view the candidate list online, and fill out my paper ballot. Hannia was feeling a bit sick, so we made our way back to the *Hauptbanhof*, found a post office, mailed my ballot, changed some money, and took the train and bus back to the hotel.

Spain was playing Tunisia in the automotive capital, Stuttgart. We watched the first half in the hotel room. Spain started the same lineup they had used in their 4-0 thrashing of Ukraine. In the eighth minute of play, Jawhar Menari scored off his own rebound, as Spain keeper Iker Casillas couldn't hold onto the ball.

We moved to the hotel bar for the rest of the game. We made friends with a referee from San Jose, who was wearing a Sharks jersey. He and his wife were in Germany for the cup, though they didn't have any tickets. They were enjoying themselves immensely, going to the Fan Zones for some of the games, and watching the rest in the hotel or at local bars. They told us about a wonderful *Biergarten* nearby that they felt was the best in town. The ambience in Germany made the trip worthwhile. He told us a little about his refereeing career, mostly at the college level, the highlight of which was a friendly match featuring the San Jose Clash (who later became the Earthquakes, then moved to Houston and became the Dynamo). He remembered fondly giving Eric Wynalda a yellow card.

Spain brought in three subs in the second half: Fabregas and Raúl came right after the break, and Joaquin Sanchez came in at minute 56. With the increased offensive clout, Raúl got the equalizer for Spain at minute 71.

Fabregas made a nice pass to Torres for the go-ahead goal. The substitutions were paying dividends. Spain topped off the scoring in minute 90 with a penalty kick, which the Tunisian keeper nearly stopped.

Spain, the perennial underachiever, had booked itself a ticket to the second round. Theirs was a weak group. In a way, I wish the U.S. had been in that group, but it was still an accomplishment, and the team looked pretty sharp.

JUNE 20 – MORE MAINZ MEANDERING

We got up early, but Hannia still wasn't feeling well. She decided to stay in the room and rest, while I visited a few local sights I'd missed. I headed downstairs, saw our New Hampshire friend in the lobby, and overheard an interesting conversation between a couple of Brits and Swedes. Their two teams were squaring off that day, and the Swedish guy was unloading a couple of tickets to the Brit, who was clad in his national team colors. "You can't be in the Swedish section with that England shirt." "Oh, I'll change."

This exchange highlighted a fundamental difference between sports in the U.S. and in the rest of the world. At most soccer games in Europe, the supporters are kept segregated to avoid conflict. I can't imagine going to a Dodger game, knowing that Giants fans would be told they'd have to sit on the opposite side of the stadium. In fact, many fans love to nettle the opposition in a jokey way. It would never dawn on most Americans that this could be dangerous.

Not so in Europe, where it is expected that rivalries will get out of hand. There is a strict separation of supporters. Of course, in most instances it has less to do with the game than other things. Many of the rowdies are merely seeking out a venue in which they can cause trouble. Big groups of people present a fertile opportunity. Also, many of the cities have deadly rivalries that go back centuries. I remember going to a Fiorentina vs. Lazio game in Italy. There were some violent incidents at the train station between rival fans that owed much more to the fact that these two former city-states have a long history of rivalry and war. Michaelango's David, very much the icon of Florence, is symbolic of the mighty underdog prevailing over the brutal giant. See any parallels?

When I was in Pisa, I asked a few people at souvenir stands if they were Fiorentina fans. Florence was the closest city with a Serie A team, and they were fellow Tuscans, after all. I might well have been insulting their mothers. Florence had gone out of its way the build a bigger cathedral than Pisa, overtook them as the regional power, and occupied them for ninety years--from 1406 to 1496. The people I spoke to were A.C. Milan fans. The enemy of your enemy is your friend, right? The funny thing was that behind these people, Batistuta jerseys fluttered in the breeze. They were selling the violet number 10 shirt of their hated rival: Fiorentina. Commerce, as well as politics, makes for strange bedfellows.

I went to take a few photos of the *Mainzdom*. There was a street fair in the plaza, where farmers from the surrounding regions were selling their wares. I ended up buying some *Rhein Wein* from a local vintner. I went to the Guttenberg Museum, to see the presses. As a former journalism student, I was fascinated to see the old technology, and they've got an impressive array of it. As I stood outside, next to a bust of Guttenberg, a fellow tourist remarked on a certain resemblance between myself and the master of movable type. Beyond the beard, I saw little resemblance, but did snap a couple of pictures of myself with the bust in the background, just to humor my fellow vagabond.

Germany was playing Ecuador that morning at the *Olimpiastadion* in Berlin, and the press accounts (no longer using movable type), announced that more than 700,000 people had shown up at the Fan Fest to watch the game.

Germany prevailed over the South Americans 3-0. Two goals were scored by Klose, and one by Podolski. Germany was on a roll. It was a bit disappointing after Ecuador had so soundly defeated Costa Rica. I had hoped that Ecuador would give the Germans some trouble, but, especially at home, Germany rolled over them with ease. They scored early and often. Klose only waited four minutes in to find the back of the net. Ecuador was resting strikers Tenorio and Delgado, and didn't have the finishing skills to respond, though they created a few credible chances. Klose found the net again forty minutes after his first. In the second half, little changed. Just forty seconds in, Schweinsteiger made a powerful shot on goal. In minute 57, Schneider made a nice cross, which Lukas Podolski hammered home. The rout was complete. *Una goleada.* Still, both teams knew they were going to the second round, so it was just a matter of whom their opponent might be. It looked like England for Ecuador and Sweden for Germany, but that, of course, would depend on the next match.

Sweden played England, and the Limeys were the favorites. Particularly after tying Trinidad, Sweden was vulnerable. England, looking forward to the return of speedster Michael Owen up front, was immediately dealt a blow. In minute four, laying off an easy ball, Owen twisted his knee and went down on the grass, writhing in agony. He had to be stretchered off and replaced by Peter Crouch.

England was unsettled, but came back to get goals from Joe Cole in minute 34. Marcus Allback scored for Sweden in minute 51, but Steven Gerrard's goal in minute 85 looked like it sealed the deal. Henrik Larsson, however, had other ideas. This was to be his final World Cup. I'd seen him play for Celtic in the Scottish League and had always been impressed. He's fast, skilled, and he hustles. He's a true goal scorer, always looking for some way to get it into the net. He's the kind of guy who may get a funky, funny, offbeat goal, but is more than likely to come through in a pinch. In minute 90, Larsson leveled it at two goals each, and that's the score that would stand.

We were frustrated that there were no telecasts of the Costa Rica vs. Poland game. The other match that was being ignored by the broadcasting brain trust was Paraguay vs. Trinidad and Tobago. All four teams had been mathematically eliminated at this point, but they were certainly still playing for pride.

That night we watched the newscasts for highlights. They showed clips of Paraguay scoring twice to beat Trinidad, but there were no CRC vs. POL highlights. They gave the score line quickly before moving on to the next newsworthy bit. Unfortunately for us, the Costa Ricans hadn't really played hard enough for pride. The Poles beat them 2-1.

I grabbed the newspaper reports of the game, which were generally complimentary toward the *Ticos*. In front of 43,000 fans in Hanover, Ronald *"la Bala"* Gomez scored first at minute 25. Things looked good for our boys in white, blue, and red. Bartosz Bosacki brought Poland level at minute 33, and then at minute 36 the same guy notched his second goal in the game. The *Ticos* had managed to emerge from the tournament with no points, despite scoring three goals. The memories of their upsets of Scotland and Sweden in 1990 were becoming distant and dim. They had an obviously talented squad, but there was something missing. The focus, urgency, and organization that coach Bora Milutinovic had instilled in 1990, and which had informed the 2002 squad, had now faded.

Of course, back in Costa Rica, they were calling for the head of the coach, Alexandre Guimaraes. *"Guima,"* as they call him, was deemed to have screwed everything up, despite the fact that he was brought on in the middle of the qualifying process. After the 2002 World Cup, he had been shunted aside in favor of two different coaches, Colombian Jorge Luís Pinto and, after they fired him, the dreaded Steve Sampson. The team was in shambles when he took the reins, and he still managed to get them qualified.

I have to agree that the faults of the *Tico* team must have had something to do with the coaching, but it was odd how short the collective Costa Rican memory was. Everyone suddenly forgot that *Guima* had presided over the famous victory against Mexico in Azteca stadium, affectionately referred to as the "*Aztecazo.*" The sports world certainly abides by the adage, "What have you done for me lately?"

With Wanchope retiring from international play after the cup, and a few other stalwarts hanging up their cleats, it was difficult to envision just where Costa Rica was headed. A small country with a small population, it might be quite some time before the planets aligned correctly to provide them with sufficient talent and depth to again become a David in a world of Goliaths.

Panama was moving up the rankings (this was where Guima would land his next job), and Honduras was always in contention. Heck, at any time Guatemala and El Salvador could wake up and turn their programs around. And then Jamaica, Trinidad, or Haiti could rise up out of the Caribbean, brush off the Sargasso seaweed, and steal the third CONCACAF slot at a moment's notice. Canada, with many players in England, and now with an MLS team to develop more homegrown talent, could again become a contender.

JUNE 21 – FRANKFURTERS AND ORANGE CRUSH

We got up early and ventured into downtown Mainz. I got Hannia settled in at the Laundromat before disappearing into the Internet café down the street to book us a room at Augsburg, our next stop. I managed to garner an Ethernet hookup for my laptop, and found a hotel right by the train station. Since we wanted to travel into Munich and elsewhere from there, the location would be convenient.

I took great care to hide my credit card number from those around me as I typed it in to seal the deal. Suddenly, out of nowhere, an older gentleman appeared and tapped me on my shoulder. He was asking me, in a strangely accented German, how much my laptop had cost. I replied that I had bought it a few years ago and told him what I had paid. I said that something comparable was probably cheaper now. He told me that his daughter needed one, and he was thinking about buying one. I got the sense that this gentleman was Turkish or from the Middle East. In a way, he reminded me of my old soccer coach, Nubar Nalbandian, an Armenian immigrant who, like so many of his countrymen, had found refuge in Fresno, California, where I'd lived during junior high and high school.

If this gentleman was, in fact, Turkish, it would be a little tactless to liken him to my Armenian mentor, as the Turkish persecution and slaughter of Armenians prompted so many to emigrate to the United States. But this guy genuinely reminded me of Nubar, short, stocky, grey-haired with bushy eyebrows, and he reeked of cigars. I finished chatting with him about the computer, and he went on his way after very politely excusing himself. It then dawned on me that I was holding the credit card in my hand all through the conversation, and I wasn't sure I'd kept the number obscured. I felt a bit odd, and tried to replay the encounter in my head to see if it seemed like the gentleman had been fishing for something, or had gotten a glimpse of the card. I knew I was being ridiculously paranoid, but... you never know. I was such an obvious tourist and potential target. It was odd that the guy had approached right when I was typing in the card number. Had I held the card face down on my leg when I was speaking to him? I though I had. Had there been anyone else looking over my shoulder while I was distracted? I didn't think so. The storytelling impulse got the better of me for a few moments, and I concocted several scenarios in my mind by which the kindly old man--in cahoots with any number of different people in the Internet café, or working alone--could have been tricking me to get personal information. I suddenly had visions of thousands of dollars being charged on my account, and the old man living it up in Vegas with a long-legged bimbo on his arm. I shook off the paranoid fugue and went about my business. However, I did check my account online for the next few days, to make sure no strange charges appeared.

We decided to go into Frankfurt to the Fan Zone for one of the games I most wanted to watch, Argentina vs. the Netherlands. These two teams had tremendous international reputations and a history of rivalry. In 1978, when the World Cup was held in Argentina, the home team ended up playing the Netherlands in the final, beating them 3-1 on two dazzling goals and an assist by the irrepressible Mario Kempes.

It was Argentina's first world championship, and the second time in a row that the Dutch had lost in the final to the host. Since then, the Netherlands has beaten Argentina twice on European soil, so it seemed both teams had a lot at stake. As for this World Cup, however, they both had already qualified for the second round. It was really only a question of which team would face Portugal, and which would face Mexico.

The Mainz train station had a few groups of Dutch fans, clad in orange, of course, singing and waving banners. As we piled into the train, more and more Orange fans appeared. At each stop, more and more Dutch fans crammed into the train. Soon it was standing room only, and, as Holland is right next door to Germany, and especially close to Frankfurt, we were surrounded by a beer-guzzling, orange-wearing, singing and chanting and shouting miasma of Dutchness.

The train picked up speed along a large curve in the track and banked its way toward the station nearest the Fan Zone. Without warning, the train cut power and coasted to a stop. Everyone looked at one another, expecting that shortly we'd start moving again. We didn't. It was getting very warm in the train, so windows opened and people hung their heads out the window to see what was happening. Nothing was happening as far as we could tell. We were frustratingly close to our target station, it was maybe a mile ahead. Soon a police helicopter was buzzing overhead. Jokes started flying back and forth that they were coming to get us. Large numbers of Dutch were waving out the window to the 'copter, which continued to circle overhead. Rumors started that there was some sort of incident at the station. After letting our imaginations run wild for a while, the conductor got on the P.A. system and told us that there was a student demonstration disrupting travel. If we just waited a bit, everything would get back to normal shortly. People were starting to wonder if we should get out of the train and walk. After fifteen minutes or so, people started prying the doors open for ventilation. Another few minutes passed, and some brave souls started jumping off the train and making their way on foot. The conductor got back on the P.A. and told us to remain on the train. Some police in our car were yelling at people to stay on the train. After a while, however, some of the police got off as well and started walking.

Hannia and I decided to take the plunge. Considering the German obsession for order, I was loathe to improvise and risk being put under authoritarian scrutiny. But plenty of Germans were following suit, and so many people were breaking ranks and flowing out along the tracks that it hardly seemed likely that they'd detain the entire bunch of us. We hopped down, and followed the crowd to a utility walkway along side the tracks. Ahead of us was a huge, motley column of orange-garbed pedestrians, arrayed like an advancing army, though in a more disorderly, festive way.

It was refreshing to get out of the hot, cramped train car and stretch our legs. It took us fifteen minutes or so, but we arrived at the *Frankfurter Hauptbahnhof* without incident. The station was absolutely crammed with people. Lines of police restricted entrance and exit, and the station was clogged with hot, frantic humanity.

We shuffled through the crowd and made our way to the exit, where we were told to wait by a line of cops. They were only letting small groups of people through at a time, but we managed to get into a group that was released quickly. As we made our way across the small plaza in front off the station toward the trams, we saw the student protest. We had imagined that it was some sort of anti-globalization thing, or an anti-commercialism-at-the-World Cup thing, but it turned out to be a protest against rising tuition rates. One of the protest signs I saw read, "¡*Basta Ya!*" ("Enough already!"), which was an unusual sight in Germany. Perhaps the protesters from the Spanish department were out in full force. The vast majority of the placards and signs complained of rising tuition rates, how education was being held hostage, and so forth. The students certainly picked the very best (or worst, depending on your perspective) time to disrupt the subway, perfectly coordinated to inconvenience the hordes traveling to the stadium and the fan zone. We hopped on a tram, the same number that we had gotten on before to go to *Romerberg*. This time, the route was screwy, the line having been redirected in order to avoid the protesters, who at that moment were marching toward us in waves. The route switch was clever, but it caused further confusion. Many regular commuters, noticing the difference in route, were panicking, hopping off, then hopping back on, and vacillating, unsure whether they should stick to their usual trams. They were all quizzing the driver at once, trying to figure out if the improvised route would get them close enough to their respective objectives.

We made it to *Romerberg*, the tram having found its way back to its the normal path after skirting the chaos of the student march. The doors opened, and the crowd spilled out into the historic center of Frankfurt. We had been there only two days before, but it could not have been a more different scene today.

It was now a festival of orange. Or, rather, a sea of orange. It was filled wall to wall with human beings, all but a few clad and painted in bright, Dutch colors. It reminded me of the square in Rome that they used to fill with water to let children wade. But here it was filled with an Orange Crush, flowing in waves and bubbling with flotsam and jetsam. There were brass bands, leading the crowds in supporters' songs, wearing orange wigs, big orange hats, giant orange foam-rubber fingers (we're number one!), orange wooden shoes... There was barely room to walk through the plaza. Even the Fountain of Justice had gotten into the act. Rather than spouting the red and white wines used during coronations, there were fizzing tablets of orange dye had been added to the water shooting out of the fountain's jets and whirling in her pool. The figure of Justice wore an orange dunce cap of sorts, had an orange banner draped around her shoulders, and had her fingernails painted a bright orange. Her scales of justice were likewise draped.

Instead of a Roman encampment, central Frankfurt was now an outpost of *Niederlandische* occupation. But the invading forces were friendly. I spotted a few Argentinean jerseys in the crowd and wondered how their wearers might be treated. Invariably, they were being hugged and photographed en masse by insanely happy Dutch fanatics. There was scarcely a person without a smile, or a face full of wonderment. We made the rounds, danced with the brass bands, enjoyed a group of drummers whom we thought might have come from Suriname, and encountered a large orange Cadillac, a 1970s model, with a few middle-aged, very serious guys standing around it. These were the only Dutch I saw who weren't smiling. They obviously took their status as the proprietors of the Orange-Mobile very seriously, pompously enjoying the attention, and documenting their journey with a camcorder.

We plowed through the crowd and down to the waterfront, where the Fan Zone was set up along the Main River (remember, it's Frankfurt *am Main*). It seemed to take forever to get into the Fan Zone. We were packed in with all manner of Dutch and Germans and Argentines and Lord-knows-who-else. The cobblestone promenade along the water was the perfect place for a Fan Zone, and as we passed through the checkpoint (where they only barely patted me down), we could see the long line of orange ahead of us, leading up to grandstands that had been erected high on the banks to our left to accommodate fans. We stopped at one of the numerous beer stands and I picked up some Dutch suds, which I sipped as we made the rounds. As we came out from behind some stands and trees, I could suddenly see why the grandstands were facing out toward the river.

In the middle of the waterway, which is probably about 150 meters wide at this point, two giant-screen TVs were mounted on pilings back to back. Both banks of the river were covered in orange, and the spectators could watch the game from either side. The river dwarfed the screens, and it was hard to tell how big they really were until a riverboat passed by. It was a double-decker, probably three stories high and forty feet wide, and it barely reached the bottom of the screen. These are known in professional parlance as big-assed jumboTrons. The Mexico vs. Portugal match was playing itself out on the TVs. Portugal ended up beating our CONCACAF rivals 2-1. Hannia was pleased by this result, and, as Mexican fans streamed past, she made sure to yell out, "POR-TU-GAL! POR-TU-GAL!" as loudly and obnoxiously as possible. Mexico had played pretty well, from what I saw in the last twenty minutes or so of the match. It did look as though Portugal was the stronger and more talented team. Despite the loss, the Mexicans were headed to the second round. Both of these teams had beaten Iran. Mexico had tied Angola and Portugal had beaten them. Angola and Iran had tied each other, and were thus eliminated at one point apiece. This game basically determined who would be first in the group. The winner got the loser of the next match, and vice versa.

We had figured that by arriving early, we'd be able to get a decent vantage point, but we were wrong. The stands were absolutely packed, and mostly with supporters from the upcoming match, so they wouldn't be budging any time soon. We had enjoyed enough wild and crazy crowd life for one day, so we decided to return to our hotel. We had planned an early departure the next morning, so it didn't make sense to wait until these thousands of people, as well as those at the stadium, all decided to jump on the subway at the same time at eleven p.m., or shortly thereafter. After our experience of sitting on the tracks for what felt like forever in an immobile train on the way over, we could only imagine a repeat performance at midnight.

We hopped on the S8 to head back to Mainz, but for one reason or another, this train--which was brand, spanking-new, and a different model than we'd seen before--stopped halfway, and the P.A. announced that we'd have to disembark. We grabbed another S8, which was bound for Castel, just across the river from our hotel. We figured we could catch a bus across the bridge. It would be another twenty minutes until a Mainz-bound train came along, and we knew from experience that it would be packed.

The train deposited us at the Castel, and we went prospecting for buses. We managed to find a 55 bus, which was one of the lines that ran past the hotel, but we (meaning I) failed to notice that it was a 55a bus. The addition of the "a" meant that it was a truncated route, and it deposited us near the bus yard, a substantial distance from our objective. So much for our little shortcut through Castel. There were no return buses from that point, according to our driver, who was retiring for the night. We found a location a few blocks away from which we could catch a bus to the *Mainzer Dom*. We eagerly jumped aboard, and were dumped off very close to our erstwhile home. We were starving by this point, but nearly everything was closed as we walked through the center of town. We managed to find a *Dönner Kebap* place that was open, and bought a couple of pita wraps to go. For a native Californian, the name "Donner" on an eating establishment conjures up disturbing thoughts--one begins to wonder if the chef's name might be Sweeney Todd. The kebabs were tasty, but I had ordered chicken, just in case.

We made it back to the room in time to see part of the Netherlands vs. Argentina match in progress. After watching for a few minutes, I was quite glad we hadn't stayed at the Fan Zone. Despite the two teams' exciting histories, the match was dull as dirt. Already qualified for the next round, both teams weren't going out of their way to win this one. It was really about the opponent in the next round, and that didn't seem a major issue to either team. Argentina took the bigger risks, and poured on more offense, but the Dutch very comfortably neutralized them in the defensive third of the field. The Dutch were resting winger

Arjen Robben, one of their main offensive threats, and both teams coasted to a 0-0 tie. It made sense, but it was disappointing. I could imagine the Dutch and Argentines on the banks of the Main River feeling spent and unfulfilled after traveling, braving the crowds, and downing all that beer only to witness a lackluster, flaccid display of competent, but uninspired soccer. A hard-fought defeat is more invigorating. Additionally, whenever a team plays for a tie like that, it is frequently difficult to get their intensity back for the next game. Ideally, a team builds in cohesion and strength as the tournament progresses. This game was a drain. I couldn't see either squad winning this World Cup, though most observers considered them both top contenders, at least up until this performance.

Back in Mainz at an open-air market in the main square.

A church in Mainz.   This kid has his priorities straight.

Römerplatz, Frankfurt. Compare this to the later photos of this same square filled with Dutch fans.

L: Note the soccer players' faces towering over the historical section of the city.
R: Roman ruins, Frankfurt.

Hannia contemplates the Goethe museum.

L: And you thought Goethe was a stodgy guy.
R: Goethe's family home.

The Dutch on the march.   Stalled train? No problem.

Niederländische invasion, *Römerplatz*, Frankfurt.

Tulips, wooden shoes and brass bands.

Orange music and automobiles.

Orange-dyed fountain. An extreme close-up would show orange polish on the statue's fingernails.

Hannia frolics with Dutch wildlife.

The Main River as our communal living room. Note the big screen.

JUNE 22ND – GAME DAY #4, GHANA V. USA

Game day for the USA We got up early, did the breakfast buffet, and made it to the train station lickety-split. I double-checked that we had a reservation for first class, and we got aboard. In the train, we sat near a few fellow U.S. fans, from Chicago, Los Angeles, Stanford, and New York. They were young guys who'd been engaged in what they referred to as "extreme partying" throughout the tournament. They had been to a bunch of games and Fan Zone viewings in addition to the U.S. matches. I noticed as we talked that all our voices were still shot from the Italy game. We discussed the U.S. performance at length. We concurred that the game against Italy had been a victory in a draw's clothing. After that, we could chalk up the lousy showing against the Czechs to first-night jitters if--and this was a big "if"--the U.S. played with the same intensity in this game as we had against the *Azzuri*. We would be without the services of Pablo Mastroeni and Eddie Pope, both having been red-carded in the last game. This was no small loss. Pope was by far our most experienced and talented defender, perhaps in the history of U.S. soccer, and Mastroeni was a pit bull in the middle. In 2002, he was the guy who had harassed Cuatemoc Blanco out of the game against Mexico, and had kept the Germans honest in the quarterfinals.

Still, the fill-ins were also solid guys. We expected Jimmy Conrad to replace Pope, and maybe Arena would drop Reyna back to the defensive midfield spot for Pablo. We knew that a large part of it had to do with spirit. The Ghanaian team was fired up. They had succumbed 2-0 to the crafty Italians, but had shocked the Czechs 2-0. They were the one true hope from Africa, and had a few top players from big European squads on their roster, most notably Michael Essien from Chelsea and Stephen Appiah, a product of Italian Serie A who had moved to Turkey's Fenerbahçe a year before. They were a very skilled, fast, and tremendously athletic outfit. Additionally, they had the chance to go farther than any African team in history. They boasted a Serbian coach, Ratomir Dujkovic, who had instilled a lot of structure and discipline into the squad, which was, after all, an inexperienced team at the World Cup.

We rambled on with our little discussion of the day's match through the Bavarian countryside as we drew closer to Nuremberg. It was beautiful agricultural land, greener than the hills of the Rhineland. It was all bucolic and tranquil and salt of the earth. In Germany's tumultuous twentieth century, it made some sense that the inhabitants of this simple countryside were whipped up into a frenzy against the "foreign-influenced" city dwellers. They were told they were the "real Germans," and they were a bit too ready to believe it.

We arrived on time in Nuremberg and sought out the local *S-Bahn* route to the stadium. It was packed, but the hordes flowed efficiently, with an *S-Bahn* train leaving every six minutes. We made like sardines yet again and packed into the train. We were closely quartered with a couple from San Jose and New Hampshire. They were with a pharmacological group that was attending a business seminar in Germany, and this provided a great springboard for them to enjoy the festivities. We arrived at our destination, the *Frankenstadion*, which naturally invites puns about mad scientists and Boris Karloff. As we came out of the train station and headed toward the stadium, I saw some vaguely familiar structures to my right. There was a large field, headed by massive concrete grandstands. Surrounding it were concrete towers (thirty-four of them, the website says) spaced at even intervals. The grandstands were being used as a bus staging area, with hordes of spectators were piling out of buses as they pulled up to the field.

Suddenly, I had a film-school flashback. I was seeing a panorama from the camera of Leni Riefenstahl, but this time, in person and in color. My background as a documentarian summoned images of a rally held nearly seventy years earlier. This was the site of the rally featured in "Triumph of the Will," the notorious Nazi propaganda film. This was the infamous Zeppelin Field. I remembered sitting in a darkened room in Fullerton, California, watching a scratchy 35mm image of Hitler himself addressing adoring throngs from this same field. I remembered the giant swastika-emblazoned banners, and the bright lights. I remembered the mustachioed fanatic fuming and frothing at the mouth as he espoused his hateful exhortation to the thousands of Bavarians before him.

I snapped back to the present long enough to listen in on a group of Americans who were discussing the same thing as they marched past the infamous site. "Oh, yeah, this was the Nazi power base," said one guy in his fifties, with a U.S. soccer hat and a dark beard. He looked a bit academic. If he had worn a tweed jacket with elbow patches, you'd have taken him immediately for a professor. "Because of that, Nuremberg was bombed mercilessly by the Allies, more than the population or strategic value would have indicated. They wanted to demoralize his partisans."

It was amazing to me that this field, with its very Albert Speer, Nazi public-works look to it, was still intact. I would have thought it would have been bulldozed during the postwar occupation. But then, its symbolic value may well have been amplified in my mind by my studies and my profession. The utilitarian value of the site may have outweighed its iconic value for most. Actually, it turns out that the Allies did make a show of blowing up the giant swastika atop the grandstands as a display of regime change. Later, for structural reasons, the municipality demolished the columns along the top of the stands. So it was not completely intact. And since the field had existed before Hitler's rise to power, it was not as Nazi-specific as I initially thought. The name derives from the arrival of one of Count Zeppelin's dirigibles in 1909. Still, for me it was a striking reminder of the Second World War, and the huge shadow it cast on the rest of the century and beyond.

It was odd to return to the festivities of the moment, following the festive crowds toward the stadium, where there were the usual tourist-trappist monks of commerce hawking commemorative garbage to the celebrants. There was a band playing, and people dancing and the now-normal blissful cacophony. It was a juxtaposition I will never forget.

Suddenly, I was reintroduced rather forcefully into silliness, surrounded by U.S. fans costumed as Superman, Captain America, Flash Gordon, Batman and Robin, faces painted, flags unfurled, beers in hand, and hearts on sleeves. There was a small stage erected at the end of the row of commercial booths, where fans of all stripes could climb up and dance and cheer and take pictures of one another. The stage was adorned with Coca-Cola logos and paintings of a hand lifting the World Cup trophy. There was a video camera mounted above the stage, and a large-screen TV to the right of it so the participants could see what a spectacle they were making of themselves. Across the top of the stage was a giant slogan, "It's your *Heimspiel*!" ("home game").

We drank in the ambience, and sauntered toward the entrance. As we were walking, we came across a crowd of Ghanaians who were also strolling toward the stadium. They looked at us in our red, white, and blue clothing, Hannia wearing a wig of those colors and draped in a big flag. We regarded one another awkwardly, until I broke the ice by saying, "Hey, let's hope for a good game today!" Smiles immediately lit up everyone's faces. One or two chimed in, "Yes, a good game!"

Hannia couldn't leave well enough alone, and became the emissary of divisiveness by chiming in, "Yes, a good game where the USA wins!" One of the Ghana supporters, without missing a beat, shot back, "Sorry, this is not basketball." They all took it fairly good-naturedly and in stride, but you could sense how seriously they regarded their soccer. I flashed Hannia a stern look for ruining my wonderful moment of international solidarity and good-sportsmanship. She just grinned back with an unrepentant partisan swagger. She was having fun, just like when she taunted her brother about their ongoing Saprissa vs. Alajuela feud.

The *Frankenstadion* had a very different vibe from the other stadiums we had visited. It was an older, more time-worn structure, comfortable, but far from new and slick. Everything about it was more rural and rundown. It was full to the brim with 41,000 fans. Our seats were again in different spots, and I sent Hannia to what I thought was the better seat. We were both in the end zone with Sam's Army, but I was in the very last row of the bottom level (Row 20), while Hannia was in the fourth row of the opposite corner of the section. We actually both had a pretty good view of the field, though mine was obscured a bit by the cement bottom of the balcony, which had a couple of speakers affixed to it, very strategically, to prevent me from seeing some of the most important action. As this was not a "soccer-specific" stadium, we were separated from the field by a track, so the goal was a bit of a distance from our section. An older German gentleman settled into the seat next to me and took out an America flag, which he very proudly waved. I spoke to him in my limited German, and he said he was hoping to see the Americans go through. He spoke no English. I wondered if he was a child of the occupation who might remember the liberating forces. He seemed to be roughly my father's age, which would have put him in the proper window of opportunity. Sam's Army started up its chants, drowning out any possibility of conversation.

In addition to the stadium being a bit shabby and in need of fresh paint, I noticed a difference in the ushers. They were all kind of dumpy old men, who rather than uniforms, wore an official vest over their rural-style German slacks and sweaters and shirts. They had all brought sack lunches with them, which they cached behind the back row for later. They appeared to all be old friends, calling out greetings to one another across the packed rows. Occasionally, one or two would show up to greet the guy in my section, and they'd disappear around the corner for a smoke, obviously a time-tested social rite.

The game kicked off. The U.S. played well right out of the gate. They were moving the ball around snappily and keeping possession. I wondered what Arena had devised as the tactics of the day. The lineup made sense, though I would love to have seen Eddie Johnson up front. In minute 17, Clint Dempsey made a nice header on goal, but didn't score. It looked like we were making things happen.

Then at minute 22, Claudio Reyna got the ball at the top of our box, right in front of my section. He paused a moment to look up at the field, and instantly Ghana's striker Haminu Draman went after him and stripped him of the ball. Reyna went down hard, and it looked to us in the stands like a bad foul. To our amazement, there was no whistle. Draman, who plays for Red Star Belgrade, charged toward Keller's goal and chipped it past him. The U.S. had given up three early goals in three matches. This is not how you win at the World Cup.

Our section was dead silent and downcast as Claudio Reyna stayed on the ground for a long time. He was either badly hurt, or trying to mitigate his defensive error by feigning injury. I later watched a recording of the game, and it looked like Reyna stepped off balance when he saw the striker coming toward him, twisting his leg badly and injuring his knee. Bad timing, both for him and for the U.S. Reyna was stretchered off, but returned to the match, which now became a desperate affair. Reyna made a bad pass that Essien picked off and crossed in. It almost became the second Ghana goal. Luckily for us, Razak Pimpong shot wide right. Reyna was subbed out in minute 40. As he went limping off, I realized this was probably the last time we'd see "Captain America" in a U.S. uniform. A fixture since the '90 World Cup was now gone. Ben Olsen replaced Reyna. An Arena protégé, Olsen had been a phenomenally promising player until he went to England, where he was severely injured. A spirited and smart midfielder, Olsen made an impressive comeback in MLS, but was never quite the same. Many U.S. fans felt he had no place on the World Cup squad.

The U.S. turned up the heat. Beasely intercepted a pass chipped it in to Dempsey in minute 40. Clint put it away. It was a competitive game again. There was joy in Mudville.

We all felt heartened. The U.S. hadn't played well for the entire forty-five minutes, but they seemed in control at the end. If they could build on that, most in the crowd felt we could prevail.

Then disaster struck. A cross came into the U.S. box. Oguchi Onyewu, our six-foot-three-inch center back, took a bead on the ball. He planted and headed it out of trouble, but as he did so, Pimpong flung himself backwards into the mammoth Gooch. He bounced off the far larger defender and fell down in a heap. Markus Merk, the German referee blew his whistle pointed to the penalty spot. We were thunderstruck. It was so clearly not a foul. It was Gooch's ball all the way, and he had played the ball all the way. Pimpong was guilty of playing the man, if anything. It struck me as a familiar scenario. I'm about Gooch's size, and I've played a lot of central defense. I can't count how many times I've been called for a foul when a small player has bounced off me. I'm convinced it's because I look imposing, and if the little guy is being flung through the air, the ref is afraid I'm manhandling the smaller player, regardless of the reality of the situation.

You would hope that the refs in the World Cup would be a little more sophisticated that the refs in the metro league in L.A, but, in this case, your hopes would be dashed.

Our entire section began screaming epithets at the officials. After the questionable officiating at the Italy match, this was just too much. The shrieking chants of "BULLSHIT! BULLSHIT!" had a very ragged vehemence to them. As I watched the players line up for the PK, I thought about Brad Friedel stopping the PK against Korea in 2002. In Friedel's case, I had been prescient. I had somehow known he'd come up big. His body language and intense glare had tipped me off. As a longtime follower of the U.S. national team, I had seen Keller pull off amazing feats of goalkeeping, but this time, with the goal straight ahead of me, I didn't feel the same rush of confidence.

Keller assumed the position, and flapped his arms to try to make himself look really big in the goalmouth. Appiah struck the ball, and Keller guessed the wrong way. We were down by a goal just before the half. Lousy timing, a lousy call, and a lousy feeling.

At the half the entire U.S. section was up in arms. Angry conversations rippled through the crowd. Still, there was a grim determination to right the wrongs. If the U.S. could come out like they had against Italy, there was hope. Plenty of hope.

The ushers retrieved their bag lunches from their hiding places and munched away.

In the second half, the ugly USA reappeared. Suddenly, they were hesitant and sloppy. They were being beaten to every ball, making bad passes, backing off at key moments. Again, it looked like the game against the Czechs. Donovan disappeared. Everyone was off just that little bit that gave the opposition a chance. To Ghana's credit, they came out strong and held up.

As the clock ticked away, the Ghanaians started to dive, roll around on the ground, and kill off the clock. Eddie Johnson came in for Steve Cherundolo, and immediately ignited the offense. Bobby Convey came in for Eddie Lewis. Still, everything was just a little off. Gooch headed a corner just over the crossbar. McBride knocked one off the post. There were a few more near misses. Donovan skied one. Then, in a clear opportunity, he just inexplicably didn't shoot. The crowd was livid.

I saw one Donovan moment, and I don't really recall at what stage during the game, that soured me on our very talented little star. Someone made a long, errant pass toward the Ghanaian goal that was obviously headed to a defender. Donovan ran at the defender as the latter drew a bead on the ball. My reaction was, hey, this is good. Donovan's small, but he knows that he can distract or mess with the defender and possibly cause an error. Once again, as a large defender, I know that a little guy can give you lots of grief if he's scrappy and hits you strategically. Look at what Pimpong did against the towering Gooch in the first half. The defender sensed that Donovan was coming, and just before heading the ball, he dropped his shoulder readying himself for the hit. When Donovan saw this, he veered off and avoided impact. I was livid. The slightest opposition, and our big star backs off! That symbolized Donovan's effort throughout the tournament. As long as it was easy, he was working away, running, dodging, and passing. But as soon as the going got tough, he just stopped. This was the World Cup, fer chrissakes. This is where you leave it all on the field, remember? Especially in this game, which was as "do or die" as it gets. There's no shame in losing, as long as you've given it your all. But what if you don't even try?

The ref added five minutes of stoppage time, but after watching the U.S. play, I didn't feel it would help. Sure, I kept cheering and hoping, but I did not have the effervescence of possibility coursing through my veins. I could see the writing on the wall.

The final whistle blew, and the Ghanaians were ecstatic. The U.S. team looked like the girl who hadn't been asked to the prom. Shell-shocked, they came over to the rooting section and applauded us. Then came the *coup de grace*. Up on the big screen, the other score flashed: Italy 2 – 0 Czech Republic. The Italians had come through for us. All we had to do was win our match and we were home free. The table was set for us, and we didn't show up to dinner. Sam's Army and the others of us in the section stood, long-faced, holding up our USA banners so the players on the field could see them. I'm not sure who was more disappointed, us or them. We finally paraded out, a slow, dirge-like plodding of dejected feet thudding on asphalt.

Hannia and I were totally drained by the experience. The travel, the tense game, the screaming and yelling, the bad calls, and the uninspired play managed to sap our strength. Additionally, we had to make it back to Mainz on the train, so we bolted to the station. We succeeded in getting on an *S-Bahn* train before the vast multitudes, arriving quickly at the *Hauptbahnhof*.

The train back to Mainz, however, was packed to the gills. We had first-class reservations, and it was tough to make it through the crowd to our seats. There were people sitting and standing in the aisles everywhere. We settled in for the long ride home.

This was the part of the itinerary that bugged me the most. The day trip to Nuremberg was aggravating at best. If I'd been more economically carefree, I'd have booked a room in Nuremberg and then pressed on to Augsburg or Munich the next day. For that matter, there were interesting things to see and do in Nuremberg that could have occupied us for a couple of days, and we could have used the town as a base of operations to the rest of Bavaria. But it didn't make sense to have to pay for a duplicate night, then run the risk of the U.S. qualifying for the second round, then having to scramble northward again to either Dortmund or Hamburg, where the second-round games were being held. We had no way of knowing that there was little chance of this. In retrospect, staying in Bavaria would have been much more efficient, but it also would have meant moving on game day, which could have been a royal pain as well. It still gnawed at me that the package hadn't moved us to Nuremberg immediately after the second game. So much for the best laid plans of mice, men, and soccer fans.

Somewhere in our journey, it was announced that Japan was leading Brazil, 1-0. Murmurs bounced around the car. It was very surprising for one and all.

Tired and dejected, we resolved that we would now become tourists, cast away the cares of following a team, get off the roller-coaster ride of fandom (though this roller coaster had a one-way trajectory), and get to know Germany a bit. We knew we'd still watch as many games as possible and participate in celebrations as much as possible, but now as disinterested observers, not as participants on pins and needles.

The public address system on the train crackled to life. "Brazil has now scored a goal to equalize against Japan, 1-1," a German-accented voice said in English. Heads around the train nodded in recognition that the world was back on balance.

We dozed and watched people and scenery, and the train ride passed quickly. We made it to the Mainz *Hbf*, bussed it to our riverside accommodations and headed up to the sports bar. The last few minutes of the Japan vs. Brazil game were playing themselves out, and the score was 1-4 in favor of Brazil. It was disappointing that the underdogs hadn't pulled off an upset, or at least a tie, but it made perfect sense. Probably the early goal had only nettled Brazil into producing the lopsided score. Had they felt less pressured, they probably would have been content to cruise to a 1-0 victory. Still, Japan--and especially goal scorer Keiji Tomada--will always have that memory of being ahead of Brazil, if only for twelve golden minutes.

We bumped into our referee buddy from San Jose. He and his wife had made a trip to Wiesbaden to watch the U.S. game in a military bar. It was the only place that he could find the game, which was being played at the same time as Italy vs. Czech Republic. Eurocentrism? Perish the thought.

"I wanted to ask you, since we didn't get to see the replay--" I began. The ref read my face perfectly, and cut me off.

"We saw the replay. There was no PK on Gooch."

I shared with him my theory about large players getting called when other people foul them. He concurred, saying that it was hard as a ref not to side with the small guy, even if he's in the wrong.

We wandered up to our room and watched the final minutes of the "other match," Australia vs. Croatia. The Aussies, whose play against Brazil and Japan had been so stellar and determined, tied the Croats 2-2.

That put them through to the next round, where they were scheduled to take on the evil, dreaded Italians. As part of the broadcast, they replayed the controversial play in which Gooch got the PK called against him. It was clearly not a foul. In a way, it was vindication, but then again, we wouldn't have progressed even with the tie, though you could argue that the momentum might not have shifted in the game. No matter how you slice it, I felt we had dug our own grave through lackadaisical play. Good teams find a way to win even when the refs screw thing up. Giving away an early goal leaves you vulnerable to the vicissitudes of the game. Had we been up 2-0 when the bad call happened, it would have been a different story.

We packed our bags and got to bed at 12:30 a.m.

Superheroes arrive in Nuremberg.

Frankenstadion, Ghana vs. USA

The stalwarts

L: Painful elimination.
R: Commiserating with Elvis.

Zeppelin field in the background, of Leni Riefenstahl fame (or infamy).

June 23rd – The Road to Augsburg

We were up at 6:30 a.m., and quickly breakfasted, checked out, and caught a cab to the train station. The driver was a middle-aged blonde woman. I asked her if she was following the World Cup. She said yes, not as crazily as most of the men were, but she was paying attention. She commented favorably on Germany's chance in their first match in the second round, the following day against Sweden in Munich. She said the Germans had the advantage because it was an *Eigenfeld spiel* ("home game"). This was a term I'd heard bandied about a lot, and filed it away in my cluttered brain for future use. Though the sign in Nuremberg said "*Heimspiel*", "*Eigenfeld spiel*" seemed to be the preferred term. I made sure to insert another buzzphrase into the conversation. In reference to an upset, I said, "*Das war eine Überraschung.*" ("That was a surprise"). Every time I used the phrase, Germans would light up, and you could see in their expression an unspoken, "This guy really speaks German!" I had fooled them—for about fifteen seconds.

The lady cab driver dropped us off at the train station, and I hurried to the DHL office nearby. We had packed a box with memorabilia and excess clothing to send home, lightening our load for the rest of the trip. It took some doing, but I managed to figure out the cheapest shipping method, the five-kilo rate of 32 Euros. An older woman behind the counter was kind enough to bear with me as I haltingly asked all my questions and figured out the options. As I packed off our goodies, I realized that I had conducted the entire transaction entirely *auf Deutsch*. This was one of those tiny victories that make any language student proud. It was a fairly complex affair, and I had pulled it off, if not perfectly, at least without disaster.

I met Hannia by our track, waiting for the arrival of our train. We struck up a little conversation with a couple next to us, likewise U.S. fans who now had become tourists. They were a bit older than us, professors at a community college near Denver, and they talked about making trips with their grandchildren, perhaps to South Africa in 2010. They liked to travel extensively, and had discovered all sorts of ways of making it affordable.

We got onto the train and sought out our seats. We were in the non-smoking half of the car, but since there was no partition, we might as well have been in the smoking section. The cigarettes spewed forth grayish-yellow smoke without regard for seat designations. Once again we appreciated California's strict anti-smoking regulations. It's funny that we're more exacting than the Germans on this score.

The train chugged through Nuremberg and familiar Bavarian sights until we hit Augsburg. When we disembarked, we learned that our hotel was literally just outside the train station, part of a chain that specializes in travel-convenient sites. It was a modern, very clean glass-and-chrome affair, but like many things in Germany, it was designed to resemble a transparent Thermos bottle. Certainly in the winter this would be a great advantage, but in the summer, it was oppressive. The Germans didn't seem to think so. When we went to the lunchroom, every window on the front of the building was closed. It was hot, muggy as a sauna, and way too bright. When we went to our room, we opened all the windows, then propped open the door at the end of the hallway so that some fresh air could make its way in and provide us with some much-needed cross ventilation. Outside it wasn't really hot, but cloudy and humid. It was the heat-trapping structure that made it unbearable.

We rested a bit and settled into our new digs, but soon wanderlust gripped us, so we went out. I asked the cute little blonde attendant at the desk for a map of town, *auf Deutsch*, which she provided with a coquettish smile. Hannia glowered darkly at the young flirt. I'm sure the young *fraulein* would have little interest in an aging coot like myself. Still, old habits die hard.

We strolled out and walked the *Bürgermeister Fischer Strasse* through the heart of the city. Augsburg is a smallish Bavarian burg established under the regime of Augustus Caesar. The tourist guides will inform you that it was the birthplace of Mozart—not of Wolfgang Amadeus, but of Leopold Mozart, Wolfy's *Vater*, and the inspiration for the famous "Requiem." We reviewed all the businesses on the street as we walked along, noting what would prove useful—as always, coffeehouses, restaurants, and post offices. We stumbled upon the town's main street, *Maximilian Strasse*, a stretch of intact, *echt* Bavaria. We visited yet another *Rathaus*, this one with a "Gold Room" that was a gilded meeting hall. Outside, a beautiful fountain displayed a statue of old Augustus himself, presiding regally over the conquered Goth tribes. He is so celebrated that you would think that the Bavarians were on the verge of inviting Roman occupation again. Maybe this could become *Citta* Berlusconi, with a statue of Roberto Begnini, leaping to replace Augustus.

We strolled down the ornate old *Maximilian Strasse,* noticing the flurry of activity that precedes a street festival. Tents and stages and bandstands were being set up, each with some sort of entrepreneurial tie-in: a beer company or a radio station, or a local eatery (like the incongruously located Zac's California Bar and Restaurant) as a sponsor. Technicians were running cables everywhere they could think of, and lighting grids were going up like some new form of political protest. We had stumbled into MaxFest 2006, an annual summer festival of heaven-knows-what. We had arrived completely unaware of the festivities, and out of pure luck, had arrived on the proper day to enjoy them.

At the end of *Maximilian Strasse* was Saint Ulrich's--two churches in one. Two structures clung together: one Protestant, one Catholic. We entered the Catholic side of Saint Ulrich's and discovered a youth orchestra performing a pleasant program of classical music. They were practicing for a concert that evening as part of the MaxFest. The musicians all appeared to be of high-school age, and they were damned good. One thing you have to say about the Germans, they take their classical music seriously. We wandered around the church a bit, looking at the ornate architecture and artwork, and listening to the strains of Strauss' "Emperor's Waltz" as the conductor put his squad through their paces. He started and stopped them, and prattled away in an imperious tone after each musical phrase. The kids were focused and professional, but bubbling with mirth and mischief as befitted their age, and we resolved to return that evening to see the real thing. I asked the longhaired lighting technician, who was focusing Fresnel lenses on the young violinists, oboists, and tympanists, what time the performance was to be. He replied, between tweaks of light, that it would start at eight that evening. We had a target—back by eight.

We backtracked through the streets, which had now begun to fill up with revelers, though the party had not really started yet. The preparations were nearing completion.

We used the passes that the hotel had given us for local transit to ride a tram back to our hotel. The tram system was well-designed and comfortable. We stopped at a *Nord See* restaurant for good, greasy fish 'n' chips, German-style, and we ate our fill. Back at the hotel, we flung open the windows to air out the tightly enclosed space. We watched some of the games that were on that afternoon, but it was hard to get really excited. Saudi Arabia was getting beaten by Spain, as expected, and the Ukraine was playing Tunisia. The Ukraine attracted my attention because I wanted to see A.C. Milan's Andriy Schevchenko in action, but the team itself was less than inspiring. Now that my teams were out of the competition, I realized it would take a few days to rekindle my interest. I figured that when the final round of sixteen began, my enthusiasm would surge again. None of the games on this final day of the group stages were "make or break," but I felt compelled to pay attention.

We then plotted out our next day's trip. Hannia had expressed interest in visiting a concentration camp. I felt that this was a necessary part of our trip to Germany, as it is definitely one of those things that you feel compelled to remember. The nearest camp was Dachau. That would be or first stop the next day. I figured out the *U-Bahn* and *S-Bahn* routes we'd need to take, and we got everything arranged as the sun began to set over the train station.

Back on the street again, we boarded a tram and headed for *Maximilian Strasse*. The tram wound its way through the commercial downtown area and then took a hard left. *Max Strasse* had been blocked off, and, in contrast to the open spaces we had seen earlier, it was now an absolute beehive of activity. We hopped off the tram and made our way through the crowd. It was difficult to proceed through the densely packed humanity. Large sections of the street had been cordoned off as impromptu beer gardens, which were packed with folding tables, surrounded by beer-swilling Bavarians in full party mode. It was obvious that this was the big event of the year for this town. The entire population of Augsburg, but especially the teens and twentysomethings were taking full advantage of the long, warm summer day as liberty to cut loose. I looked at my watch and wondered whether we'd be able to cross the few hundred yards separating us from the church in time for the concert. It was more of a wrestling match than a stroll to made headway through the crowd. All of the stands and tents and bandstands were now fully deployed, and loud music hammered us from all sides as we elbowed our way through the scrum.

Finally we reached the church. As we approached, the crowd thinned out--fewer people were concerned with classical music than with getting into their preferred *Biergarten* or restaurant. We swung through the doors of the church and grabbed some pew space. The orchestra was in place, now all suited up in formal wear, and their conductor introduced their first piece. They launched into something by Sibelius, then Bach, then Strauss' *Kaiserswaltz*, which we had heard them practicing. They were damn good. This was a highly polished, near-professional performance. Some members of the audience were obviously friends and family of the orchestra, but many were not. The crowd was enraptured. This was apparently a local all-star team sort of orchestra, and you could see regional pride glowing on everyone's faces as the young musicians negotiated the tight musical turns and straightaways that the masters had composed for the ages. This stuff was both challenging and very well-known. The audience appeared familiar with these pieces, as well as possessing the critical chops to judge just how well each composition had been performed. They were appeared quite pleased with the young orchestra, and their pride showed.

The conductor then announced that a medley of tunes by John Williams would follow. The orchestra launched into the theme from "Star Wars," followed by snippets from "E.T.," "Jaws," and "Raiders of the Lost Ark." It was quite a juxtaposition to have traveled thousands of miles from Los Angeles to hear the work of the quintessential American film composer, performed in the heart of Germany, but we enjoyed it. The conductor then introduced the orchestra's tribute to Louis Armstrong, a medley of Satchmo's best-known stuff. Though precisely rendered, classical players are going to have a little trouble making American jazz really swing—especially when they're painfully young, white, and German. I'm sure that the crowd was impressed with this section of the program as well, but it struck me as a bit labored. Still, you have to give the musicians points for stretching themselves a bit, and trying something outside their comfort zone.

For us, it had been an excellent choice to kick off our Augsburg visit, sitting in a beautiful, cool church, and listening to a gifted young orchestra play some of the best-known German favorites. We contributed enthusiastically to the collection funding the youth orchestra, and left the church into what was now a fully dark town, crammed with festival-goers, all of whom seemed to be carrying glasses of beer. Now that the sun had completely disappeared from the sky, the noise and activity had reached a new height. One of the big tents had huge disco lights that were flailing away, sending brightly colored beams and strobey pulses out into the throng. Now that we didn't have to be anywhere in particular, the press of people didn't seem so oppressive. We just floated with the flow of bodies, grabbed a beer or two or three, and soaked up the madness. We arrived at the tent sponsored by a popular energy drink. They had one of the loudest set-ups, with a DJ, full light show and--I'm not kidding—go-go dancers. We watched in awe for a while as the crowd tried their best to act like they were the hippest, coolest people in the world shuckin' and jivin' at this retro-lame-o display. We pressed on and found a street booth from an Argentine restaurant. We got some *churrasco*, which we ate standing at some bar-style tables. Did I mention beer? We drank beer.

We made the rounds to all the booths and tents and it was all very festive and loud and nutty, and the funny thing was that it wasn't exclusively World Cup-related, although there were plenty of World Cup-themed booths, and items for sale. The Germans had a lot of steam to let off after thawing out from a long, cold winter.

Hopping back on the tram, we returned to the hotel. We had missed the telecasts of the last two games, but managed to catch the highlight shows. No surprises: France beat Togo 2-0, and Switzerland beat South Korea by the same margin. In a way, I could have seen the Koreans prevail, but Switzerland had shown a lot of gumption and organization, and were practically playing at home.

The first round complete, I checked my scorecard to figure out who would comprise the round of sixteen match-ups. Germany vs. Sweden looked intriguing, as did Argentina vs. Mexico, Portugal sv. Netherlands, and Spain vs. France. My interest was already perking back up.

JUNE 24 - DACHAU

I'm tempted to leave the trip to the Dachau concentration camp out of this book. The subject is such a downer, and it is such an "on the nose" topic in relation to Germany. Part of me feels that the subject has been covered so often and so well by other, more talented writers, that I might as well stick to soccer and light summer festivities, and leave it at that. But I can't. While Germany was doing an excellent job of hosting the World Cup, and probably most of the country's current inhabitants had little or nothing to do directly with the Second World War, one simple fact remains: When a nation decides to take on the whole world, and wantonly exterminates millions of innocents, it casts a long shadow, it's a shadow in which we all grew up.

In my mind, Dachau's name has but one association, but the first thing you discover is that it's just another, smallish Bavarian town, north of Munich. There's an *S-Bahn* stop marked, "Dachau." The train station and its environs seem perfectly normal and pleasant. A short bus ride from the station, however, is a former gunpowder factory that was put to a much more nefarious use in 1933.

When you enter the grounds, past the famous gates reading, "*Arbeit Macht Frei*"—these gates are duplicates of the originals, liberated by the liberating Allied forces--you can't help but be overwhelmed by the somber mood that envelopes the place. This deep sense of tragedy still lingers, and I would image it will remain as long as humanity remains. All of the most potent clichés apply, and cannot be improved upon. There's a giant commemorative statue in the middle of the main yard, and a museum that includes some of the original barracks. As we wound our way through the museum exhibits, Hannia was truly aghast. Her exposure in Costa Rica to history about the camps was a bit less extensive than mine. There is a sprinkling of Polish Jewish refugees, and their descendants, in Costa Rica, often referred to as "*polacos*," but it's a small community, many of whom arrived before the war. I've known a few sons and daughters of survivors and since the U.S. was much more directly active in the war, it resonates more with us than with the *Ticos*.

Our tour was led by an excellent guide, a local resident who volunteered after developing an interest in the local history. He told us that he had known very little about that part of German history until he was transferred to the area and discovered that he lived near the Dachau camp. His knowledge was encyclopedic, and he gave us the basic information. Dachau had not been a "death camp," i.e., a place specifically for putting prisoners to death. The most infamous of these were Treblinka and Auschwitz, in Nazi-occupied Poland. Since the Nazis wanted the extermination camps to be on foreign soil, Dachau was a "work camp," from which prisoners were farmed out to local industry as slave labor. Of the 200,000 prisoners housed as Dachau, some two-thirds were political prisoners, and one-third were Jews, with a total of 25,613 prisoners said to have died in the camp, mostly from disease, malnutrition, and suicide.

Shuffling through the crematorium and gas chamber (apparently not used) provokes all sorts of powerful emotions, and of course, is a reminder of how easily humankind can slip into madness.

Our guide told us that his father worked on airplanes, specifically the pressurized cabins of planes that Hitler used. As a boy, he said, he had confronted his father, asking him why he didn't sabotage the cabins to try and kill Hitler. His father said that anything he had done would have been easily traced back to him, and that he had to worry about the well-being of his own family as well. Since we all, sadly, have personal factors that limit our heroics, the Nazis, of course, counted on this.

On the bus out of the camp, we passed a large truck emblazoned with a McDonald's logo, and a giant Fiberglas figure of Ronald McDonald on the roof. Big, bold letters beneath the smiling clown read, "Dachau." I reached quickly for my camera, but, in a way, I'm glad I didn't get it out in time to snap a picture as it flashed by. Too dark and surreal even for me.

The trip to the camp, though only lasting a few hours, had been exhausting, due to the emotional weight of what we had come to witness. We felt totally drained, and the heat and humidity were particularly oppressive. We thought about what to do the rest of the day, but couldn't really muster much enthusiasm for any other activity.

It dawned on me that we had a few legs of our rail pass that we wouldn't use, so what if we just headed up into the Alps until it got cool. It would have to, eventually, wouldn't it? Surely as the altitude increased, the temperature and the humidity would decline. It seemed worth a try, and we had no desire or energy left to do anything else anyway.

From the Munich central station, we figured which train ran toward hills that just might be alive with the Sound of Music. First it was just rolling farmland, beautiful and picturesque. Soon, however, it turned into mountainous gorges, forests, rivers, and rock formations. It was still humid, but the big fluffy clouds looked more and more like rain as we climbed higher. We passed mountain towns and wound our way past Garmische-Partenkirchen toward the end of the line: the Austrian border. We decided that as it was getting a little late, the frequency of trains might strand us at the end of the line for too long, so we got off in one of the smaller towns to reverse direction. We figured that we could get a meal in Garmische-Partenkirchen, relax for a while, and head on home.

As we got off the train, the skies opened up. Huge black clouds pounded us with cold rain infused with hail. It was bracing, and precisely what we needed to shake off the effects of the heat and humidity of Augsburg. We scrambled, laughing, for cover and found it under the roof of the waiting area.

We hopped on the train to Garmisch-Partenkirchen, where the first restaurant we stumbled into was called, of all things, *Sausalitos*. For two Californians, it was a godsend: Mexican food! It was also close to the train tracks, and it was raining. As we entered, we were approached by our host, a young man whose dark complexion made him look like he belonged to the eatery, at least thinking in stereotypical terms. Hannia asked him in Spanish, "Are you from Mexico?" He laughed, looked around furtively, then pointed at the mix of flags printed on my cell-phone lanyard.

"I'm from there," he said, indicating the Tunisian flag. We winked and nodded. Obviously, most patrons would accept him unquestioningly as Mexican, but he was honest when asked. He guided us to a table, and we had a passable, if not wonderful, Mexican meal. It was certainly as good as much of the commercial Mexican food back home, and *Sausalitos* served that nectar of the gods, Margaritas. (Another advantage of train travel: I didn't have to drive home.) We pounded a few down, finished our dinner, and returned to the train station.

The train trip had precisely the desired result. We broke the oppressive heat, if only for a few hours, and enjoyed a diverting ride through some beautiful country. The Margaritas were a side benefit, but an important one. We proceeded down the slope of the Alps to our Augsburgian home.

Old Gus.   Augsburg girds its loins for the MaxFest.

Maximilianstrasse by night.

Just another town in Bavaria.   Words are insufficient.

Up into the Alps to escape the heat and humidity.

Munich.

It means *jewelry*. No, not that kind of jewelry.

JUNE 25TH – A TALE OF TWO MATCHES

Amidst visiting various points around Munich and Augsburg, the important issues of the day were two matches from the round of 16. The first promised to be a magical match, Portugal vs. the Netherlands. It was Christiano Ronaldo, Luís Figo and Deco's technically gifted and creative side versus a Holland squad that boasted stars from the top clubs of Europe: Sneijder, Van Bommel, Van Persie, Robben, Cocu, Kuyt, amd Van Nistelrooij. On paper, it had all the earmarks of a classic display of skill, flair, and beautiful, improvisatory soccer. In reality, it turned out to be one of the most brutal, thuggish affairs I've ever seen, featuring sixteen yellow cards and four red cards. This set a record for most cards shown at any FIFA-administered international tournament--quite a distinction. Especially when you consider that many of these players have been teammates at the club level. Giovanni Van Bronkhorst, Deco and Mark Van Bommel played for Barcelona in 2006. Goalkeeper Van der Saar, Ruud Van Nistelrooij, and Christiano Ronaldo were teammates at Manchester United. Chelsea players included Ricardo Carvalho and Arjen Robben. Go figure.

If anyone's interested, there are some pretty good video compilations of the mayhem on YouTube, most notably:

http://www.youtube.com/watch?v=zSOW0CRcmKU

This video had more than 1.7 million hits when last I checked. Remembering Portugal's shameless display against South Korea in the previous World Cup, I'd have expected the aggressors to be Iberian. Oddly, the worst of the offenders were Dutch. Boulahrouz's cleat into Ronaldo's thigh was probably the most egregious act of mindless hostility, but there were plenty to choose from. After this bizarre exhibition, it was hard to remember that a Maniche goal had won it for the Portuguese in the minute 23.

The other game of the day was England vs. Ecuador. This was of particular interest for us, having seen our beloved *Ticos* dispatched by the opposing Banana republicans. Additionally, England is always kind of an underdog to go all the way, and a sentimental favorite as the inventor of the game. It was by all accounts tremendously hot in Stuttgart, which did not favor the Brits.

Carlos Tenorio nearly put the South Americans ahead in minute 11. John Terry headed a ball up in the air instead of clearing it, and it fell to Tenorio in behind the British defense. He controlled it, squared up, and shot, but Ashley Cole came sliding in from behind and tipped the ball enough to make it glance off the crossbar. There were a number of near-misses from both sides, and Ecuador looked very much the equal of England.

It was be a trademark David Beckham free kick that decided matters at minute 60. From thirty yards out, Beckham took his time sizing up the wall before him. He curled the ball over the wall and down, just grazing the post, bending it like… like Ronaldihno. He became the only British player to score in three World Cups.

June 26 – Border Town

After seeing the sights in Munich, we headed back to Berlin for a last bit of foreign travel. It was odd how familiar the city felt, considering that we had only been there for a few days at the beginning of our trip. We knew our way around, at least the train stations and the hotels, and we decided that we'd spend a day traveling to the eastern border to visit Poland. The short train ride took us to the German border town of Frankfurt am Oder. This is a smallish, formerly East German town, very orderly and pretty, and we traipsed around its environs for a bit, contemplating the crossing of the Oder River into Poland. We found the bridge that served as a border crossing, and passports in hand, we made our way out of *Deutschland* and into *Polska*. Our first stop was Polish immigration. I handed my U.S. passport to the very military-looking official at the desk. He contemplated the document, sniffed, raised an eyebrow, and examined my photo. He looked up and examined me. "Baldwin?" he asked sententiously.

"Yes," I responded, wondering what interest my last name could hold for him.

"Alec Baldwin's brother?" he asked. He was serious.

"No," I responded. "Not related." Even in Eastern Europe, the grip of Hollywood is strong. The official smiled, knowing he had been silly, and passed the document back to me. We plodded across the bridge into the land of Copernicus, Karol Józef Wojty, Chopin, Lech Walesa, and Bobby Vinton.

Upon crossing the river, the character of our surroundings changed. Slubice was notably poorer. The buildings weren't as ornate, well maintained, or orderly. The odd thing is that Slubice was part of Frankfurt am Oder until 1945, but borders are capricious. Border towns are always a little strange, too, and there was definitely a difference in character and style between these two border towns. We passed a *Wechselstube*, and I noticed that Poland was still not on the Euro. It was a *Zloty* economy. The exchange rate was 3:1 on the dollar and 4:1 on the Euro.

There was an overabundance of *Tabac* shops around the bridge, with big, bold cigarette prices posted in their windows. I imagine many Germans skip over the border regularly to load up on cheap cancer sticks.

We went into a shoe store, and the prices were very, very low. Unfortunately, there was nothing in my ridiculously large size, so I was unable to take advantage of the bargain prices.

Two businesses of interest on the main drag were a beauty salon called "Ania" (a variation of my wife's name) and a dress shop named "Natalia" (our daughter's name), so we felt a little more at home. In Costa Rica, we were told that "Hannia" was a name popularized by the Jewish community. Most Jewish families in Costa Rica have their roots in Poland, so this made some sense. We visited the shops, tooled around, and finally had some lunch at the sidewalk tables of a restaurant. Of course, I ordered the requisite *pivo* and downed it with gusto. It was a warm afternoon. I asked the waitress to pronounce the name of the beer, *Zywiec*, in Polish for me. With my Anglo-Hispano-Italo-Germanic linguistic sensibilities, I had no hope of coming close to pronouncing it correctly, but tried again and again as she patiently repeated and corrected me.

I told her, in my halting German, that my wife's name was Hannia, and that we had heard that this was a Polish name. She lit up and smiled, saying, yes, it was a very familiar name. I asked her how to say, "thank you" in Polish. It's *Dziekuje*, which, when pronounced, sounded to my ears something like "Chin-kyu-ya." She and a busboy very politely contained their laughter at my incompetence as I thanked her. The waitress went about her business and a German tourist, obviously feeling a little disoriented, came up to us and started blathering away *auf Deutsch*. He seemed relieved, thinking that he'd found a countryman. I could tell he was asking about the location of some store or other, so I told him I didn't know my way around the town. He realized I was not a native speaker, and suddenly looked very embarrassed.

We continued walking around town, through some residential areas to get a sense of how the locals lived. What we saw were Soviet-style apartment buildings, despite the fact that there seemed to be ample space for single-family dwellings. The buildings were nice enough, and were surrounded by grown trees and strips of grass, but the overall effect was a little bleak. Once again, I don't know whether to attribute this to the fact that it was a border town, or a former Soviet bloc country, or just Poland, but it was very different from the East German burg across the water.

We crossed back into *Deutschland.*

JUNE 27 - THE KNOCKOUT ROUND

We awoke with a steely determination to spend the day as lazily as possible. We had breakfast out, getting our last little walk in Berlin, albeit a short one to the *Nollendorfplatz*. We returned to our hotel, mostly packed and ready to hightail it home the following day. We settled in for a day of soccer viewing.

The first game was Brazil vs. Ghana in Dortmund. Of course, Ghana had beaten us and proceeded to the knockout stage, but the old adage, "Be careful what you with for," seemed an appropriate warning here. Playing Brazil on the world stage was a double-edged, *verdeamarilho* sword. Any competitive athlete wants to test himself or herself against the best. But the prospect of being pummeled by the masters of the game had to cause a little bit of consternation even amongst the plucky Ghanaians.

Ronaldo immediately sparkled. In the first minute, he received a ball on his chest and was about to shoot when he was whistled offside. In minute 5, Ronaldo was again through, and this time he was definitely onside. He put the ball in the back of the net and became the World Cup's all-time scoring leader with fifteen goals. The Ghanaians' faces all wore the same expressions, as if to say, "It had to be Brazil, didn't it?" But they turned on the heat and created a few really choice opportunities in the first half. They could have easily equalized or gone ahead with better finishing. Brazil looked lackluster, or even sloppy, but that's frequently the case. They do what's necessary, and little else. Against the run of play, they got another goal in injury time when Adriano poked one in with his thigh.

In the second half, Brazil improved its organization, but still played without flair. Asamoah Gyan, who put together several attacks for Ghana, finally sealed his country's fate. He got a second yellow card for diving in the box. Ghana was down to ten men, down by two goals, and had just ten minutes left to redeem themselves. At minute 84, Ze Roberto broke through and put the final nail in the coffin. The 3-0 score made Brazil look like champions, but their overall play in the game did not. I couldn't help but feel they were more vulnerable than one usually expects of the five-time World Cup winners.

The second game of the evening was Spain vs. France, held in Hannover. This seemed like the year for Spain to finally vanquish their historical jinx. Their roster was a marvelous agglomeration of high-priced talent from Real Madrid, Barcelona, Atlético Madrid, and Arsenal. Of course, across the field from them were the 1998 champs, led by the inimitable Zinedine Zidane.

The Spanish got on the boards first at minute 28, a penalty kick well called and well taken. Lilian Thuram had stepped on Ibañez Pablo's ankle in the box. David Villa deftly slotted the spot kick past Fabien Barthez. The French equalized at minute 41, as a Patrick Vieira pass found Frank Ribery, who had already established himself as a maniacally spirited attacking player, and confirmed the assessment here. The French turned up the heat in the second half, and at minute 83 Patrick Vieira got on the boards himself, heading home a deflected Zidane free kick. Zizou himself rippled the net at the death, with a dazzling display of dribbling and misdirection in the box. This ended Spain's ten-game unbeaten streak in the World Cup, and its twenty-six-game winning streak in international competition. France had progressed to the semifinals, where they were to meet their nemesis from 1998, Brazil.

JUNE 28 – OUR RETURN

The flight back was suitably uneventful. We backtracked through Berlin to the airport, via taxi. The city was now less of a confusing jumble and seemed more comprehensible after our brief acquaintance, much like Seoul had felt in 2002. We were tired and ready to go home. The long haul across the western half of Europe, the Atlantic Ocean, and the American continent was exhausting, but we were happy to be home at long last. Oddly enough, we discovered that it was substantially cooler in our little corner of Los Angeles than it had been in the soccer capitols of Germany. This pleased us, too.

THE QUARTERFINALS: JUNE 30 – JULY 1

For the quarterfinals, we found ourselves comfortably ensconced in our happy home, able to roll out of bed (which took some doing at first, due to the rigors of jet lag), scamper down a flight of stairs, and install ourselves in front of our very own television set, still in our pajamas.

The first game was Germany vs. Argentina in Berlin. I assumed that the *Che* team would put Germany away handily, but that was not the case. They fought out a 1-1 draw through regulation and overtime. Oliver Kahn shook Jens Lehman's hand as the latter made his way to the lonely space between the pipes to defend his nation from Argentine PKs. Germany prevailed. The Germans, who initially had received so little support and respect from their countrymen had proven themselves more than worthy. Jürgen Klinsmann, a novice coach who had been pilloried in the media, took them far beyond what anyone expected. They were headed to the semifinals. On the other hand, the players for Argentina, a team always assumed to be in contention, were on their way home.

The second game of the day, Italy vs. Ukraine, played out predictably in Hamburg. Zambrotta got on the boards early, at minute 6, putting the Italians firmly in control. Seldom in need of more than a goal to win, the Italians managed two more, both from Luca Toni in minutes 59 and 69. The Ukraine had started attacking after the second goal, but it was too little, too late. Schevchenko's band of merry men had done well to get that far, but they were out.

England played Portugal in Gelsenkirchen. It was again a game that pitted teammate against teammate. This time, that would have implications. Beckham and Luís Figo had played together for Real Madrid the year prior, while Wayne Rooney and Cristiano Ronaldo plied their trade together at Manchester United.

The game was well played, but lacked the abandon necessary to make a breakthrough. There were a few opportunities created on both sides, but the killer instinct was lacking. The most notable event in the game came at minute 62. At midfield, Wayne Rooney was trying to dribble through a couple of Portuguese players, who were tangling him up badly. He slipped and tripped and almost held onto the ball, but Ricardo Carvalho was frustrating him to no end. Rooney ducked and kept a low center of gravity, bumping Carvalho, who also got tangled up and tumbled to the ground. A petulant Rooney tried to free himself and, seemingly in a fit of pique, stomped on Carvalho's groin. The referee was standing literally a yard from the play. Players converged to protest, most notably Cristiano Ronaldo. Ronaldo got in the ref's face, so Rooney grabbed him, pulled him away, and then shoved him. The ref calmed things down a bit, then pulled out a red card. Rooney was headed for the showers. In the pause that ensued, players headed to the sidelines for water. TV cameras were trained on Ronaldo, as he was such a part of the fracas. As if things couldn't have been more contentious, Ronaldo, whose face filled the TV screen in a huge close-up, winked at someone on the sidelines as he walked. The British, of course, interpreted this as self-congratulatory, that he had known how to set off his volatile teammate. Personally, I think that stomping on a guy's groin right in front of the referee was more than enough to get Rooney sent off.

The rest of the game, with England down a man, was less than eventful. All they could do was maintain the 0-0 tie through overtime and pray for penalty kicks. They managed a few offensive plays, but mostly succeeded in killing off the game.

The British, who have never won a PK shootout in the World Cup, were without Beckham and Rooney, their most reliable spot kick specialists. Portuguese goalkeeper Ricardo was on fire, and saved three PKs. He also got a hand to Owen Hargreaves' shot, nearly stopping it. Remarkably, the Portuguese also missed one and had one saved by British keeper Paul Robinson. Christiano Ronaldo, who had figured in Rooney's sending off, was the anchorman for Portugal. He stepped up to the spot and scored the winner.

The wholesale fury directed by the British toward Cristiano Ronaldo continues to this day.

The most interesting match of the quarterfinals was, perhaps, the last one. It was a rematch of the 1998 Final: Brazil vs. France. It was a chance for the Brazilians to redeem themselves and prove how things should have gone eight years before. For the French, it was a chance to show that 1998 wasn't a fluke, that it wasn't merely some failing of the

Brazilians or home field advantage that had handed the trophy to the Gauls. It was also a chance for the French to prove that they weren't all that far over the hill. The aging Zidane, Makékélé, and Thuram were the subject of much speculation. Of course, young guns like Frank Ribery brought some energy and intensity to the mix, but Brazil was an opponent that could reveal any flaws in the French lineup.

The stands were sprinkled with soccer elite like Franz Beckenbauer, Michel Platini, Joao Havelange, and plain old everyday elite like Jacques Chirac. From the kickoff, the pace of play was a notch above previous matches. Zidane looked very sharp. The Brazilians earned a few free kicks in dangerous areas, well within Ronaldinho's formidable range. The number of early offside calls is testimony to the aggressiveness of play. The Brazilians threatened early, but France controlled most of the first half. Ronaldo got a yellow card for handling the ball, just outside his own penalty area. Zidane was constantly "out-Braziling" Brazil. He might have lost a step, but the touch, vision, and control were still stellar. He moved at will between *verde-amarilho* defenders, clinically crossing them up with shifts in direction and speed and slicing pinpoint passes through the *Carioca* ranks to his French compatriots.

In the second half, France immediately threatened, with a free kick that Vieira headed wide. Henry headed one in, but it was called back for offside. Then at minute 57, Zidane curled a long free kick to the back post, where a totally unmarked Thierry Henry slapped it in with the side of his foot.

The French held tough and showed an admirable organization and intelligence in their defensive line. At the end of ninety minutes, Zinedine Zidane and his troops in Frankfurt had successfully defended their 1998 victory. Brazil was out of the World Cup.

THE SEMI-FINALS: JULY 4 AND 5

The Germans could finally say, *"Zum Finale!"* with some confidence. They had looked vulnerable against Costa Rica and Poland, but had won both games and thumped Ecuador pretty soundly, and then had taken out Sweden by a two-goal margin. Their game had improved steadily, which is how you want the momentum to flow. They managed a penalty kick shootout victory over Argentina, and were now ready to claim a ticket to the finals. Three-time champions Italy were, however, thinking differently. The game was a clash of the titans: Germany's potent and aggressive offense against Italy's clever, stifling defense. There was one wrinkle in the usual script for Italy, however. The Germans were damn good at penalty shootouts. And their goalkeeper, Jens Lehman, was one of the best in the world. Their backup keeper, Oliver Kahn, was a living legend, if a little past his prime. Italy might be wise to concentrate on scoring during the match. They did.

Despite attacking with gusto, both sides were unable to score through regulation. The introduction of Gilardino at minute 74, Iaquinta at minute 90, and Del Piero at minute 104 showed that the Italians were bent on scoring a goal. Gilardino bounced one off a post, and Zambrotta knocked one off the crossbar. David Odonkor put in a cross that Podolski missed, but that required a brilliant save from Buffon. At minute 119, everyone dead tired but pressing on, Del Piero's corner kick was headed down to Andrea Pirlo at the top of the box. He made a nifty move to his right to spread the defenders in front of him, did a stutter step, but instead of shooting, slotted the ball to Fabio Grosso on the right side of the six-yard box. Grosso one-timed it with his left foot, curling the ball around Lehman's fully extended hand to the far post and into the net. The Italians went insane. TV cameras at the *Circo Massimo* in Rome showed a sea of Italian celebrants bathed in the red light of blazing flares.

Much to their credit, the Germans shook off the late-minute goal and attacked with determination. As often happens, this left them vulnerable in the back. Cannavaro scooped a ball out of his defensive third, carried it forward and dished it off to Gilardino. Dribbling to the left corner of the box, Gilardino engaged a defender one on one, pushing him inside, and then slotted the ball to an overlapping Del Piero, who popped it to the right corner. After a drought of 119 minutes, it was a two-minute deluge of goals--more than enough to float Italy to the World Cup final.

The Germans, both team and public, were crushed. They had started out with virtually no hope, and gradually come to believe in their young and dynamic team and its young and dynamic coach. They seem to have gone the distance with Italy, but had succumbed only at the very last moment. It was traumatic for our hosts.

The next day, France took the field against Portugal. It was Zidane vs. Figo, the old guard from Real Madrid facing off. British fans, who apparently had shown up in droves to the Allianz Arena in Munich, booed Cristiano Ronaldo every time he got the ball, in response to his involvement with Wayne Rooney's red card. Ronaldo was in good form, and made some dangerous runs, much to their dismay. The Portuguese looked to be the more dangerous squad at the outset, but soon the French got their rhythm and started to dominate play. Henry in particular seemed on fire. He was bobbing and weaving: using his speed and long legs to dribble around and cross up defenders. Pauleta made a nice attempt, but missed. At minute 33 Henry made a run past a Carvalho, who in the process of kicking at the ball, fell down, stuck his feet out, and tripped Henry in the box. Zidane walked up to the penalty spot and calmly put the ball past Ricardo, despite the fact that the keeper guessed correctly. Ricardo, who had been so stellar against England, had exhausted his magic.

The rest of the game was interesting and well played, but the one goal score stood. France was again headed to the final.

JUNE 9, 2006 - THE FINAL

The stage was set. It was to be a classic confrontation between good and evil. The free flowing, exciting, attacking, French, led by ball wizard Zinedine Zidane, versus the negative and defense-minded Italians, led by the likes of the enforcer Gennaro Gattuso. Certainly, I'm overstating things. It was more complex than that. After all the Italians have the very skilled and creative Del Piero and Totti on the attack and defensive-minded Claude Makelele and Patrick Viera and a very organized back four had gotten the French past Brazil, but in general it would be hard to argue with the above characterization. I have a great affection for Italy, but the Italian style of soccer, particularly in their international game, leaves much to be desired. Though I feel compelled to acknowledge the Italian mastery of the game, the signature *catenaccio* of the Italians has affected modern soccer quite negatively, and I'm not alone in that assessment.

And the French had just beaten Brazil and Portugal, matching the legendary *jogo bonito* and "Golden Generation" step for step.

The issue with the French was age. Zidane had announced he'd hang up the boots after this World Cup. He was certainly past his prime at 34, but still capable of magic. He was presented with the tournament's "Golden Boot" before the final. Zidane and Claude Makélélé had both come out of international retirement for the 2006 campaign. The Italians were aging, too, but it suited their defensive style more: age and guile go hand in hand.

Hannia and I had invited a few friends over to watch the final, and most were rooting for the French. One of our friends, José Fernandez and his son Esteban however, expressed a preference for the Italians. José proclaimed that the Italians had figured out the game tactically better than any team on earth, and would prevail. This was a quite reasonable assessment and the difference of allegiance is what makes for a horse race, after all. For the rest of us, the thought of watching Zidane go out on a high note was irresistible. It's always a bit odd to me that José is interested in soccer. He moved to the U.S. from Cuba at around age 12. Cubans generally are baseball fans, and not drawn to soccer. Living in the U.S. certainly doesn't nurture an interest in the game. José, however, is a man of broad interests, and has a refined appreciation of soccer that transcends nationality. He's married to a Costa Rican, Mari, who was also part of the throng.

Christopher Dill was there with his wife, Heidi, and daughter, Kendall, as was Ywain Cheney a Metro League teammate of ours from South Africa. John Toman and his wife-to-be Jen showed up as well. John was a friend of my daughter's, but had also played with our Metro League Team.   Natalia, who had just moved into her own apartment, dropped by as well. My Brother-in-Law, Luís was still with us, after taking care of our house and dog, Keiko during our absence. Hannia and I put out the requisite snacks and refreshments, and everyone chattered away about the game to be. The game happened to fall on Luís' birthday, so we had a cake for him, and he was particularly festive.

Chris and I, soccer compatriots for many years, had a similar view of things.

"So whattaya think?" Chris ventured. It was how many of our conversations about soccer begin, a chance to sound out the other guy. "I think Gattuso'll break Zidane's leg at about minute 5, " I responded, only half-joking.

"Then Gilardino dives in the box to get a PK?"

"A very likely scenario," I nodded. It turned out that the Italians wouldn't need to go after Zizou's legs.

The game was immediately action filled. Both teams were playing with admirable intensity. It didn't really look like the defense vs. offense duel that I had anticipated.

At minute 7, France was awarded a penalty kick – Marco Materazzi clipped Malouda's foot in the penalty box. Zidane, France's PK specialist, chipped it off the crossbar and into the net. He became the fourth man to score in two World Cup Finals. France was in the driver's seat. Italy couldn't sit back, grind out a 0-0 tie and pray for a win on penalties. It was a much more wide-open and offensive affair than anyone would have predicted. Italy poured on the attack.

In minute 19, Andrea Pirlo executed a marvelous corner kick, and again Materazzi was in the thick of things, heading it home past a frustrated Fabien Barthez. The Italians were turning up the heat. Materazzi had another header cleared off the line by a defender and Luca Toni headed a ball into the crossbar, both off Pirlo corners.

It was a spirited battle and the tension was mounting.

At one point Heidi got up to use the bathroom. Chris leaned over to me and said, "Watch this. During the semis she missed a big goal during a bathroom break." He waited 'til she'd disappeared behind a closed door and had a chance to settle in. He used his hands to create a makeshift megaphone and shouted "Goooooooooooooal!" Keiko barked in response, she knew the word. In a minute, Heidi came running out of the bathroom, eyes wide, flustered, anxious and adjusting her clothes.

"Who scored? Who scored?"

She looked at the on-screen score line and realized she'd been had. She landed a pretty good shot on Chris' bicep.

"Very funny."

In the second half, Arsenal striker Thierry Henry started giving the Italian defense fits with his speed and cleverness. Toni headed in a second goal for Italy.

We all reacted with screams and cheers and applause, then reacted again when it was annulled by an offside call.

At the end of 90 minutes, it was still 1-1. It was looking like it might end up in a penalty shoot out after all. The French had some good PK men, most notably Zidane, so it was not necessarily an advantage for the Italians. The French took control of the overtime periods, but were unable to score.

Then, with 10 minutes remaining Marco Materazzi again played a prominent role in the game. He tumbled to the ground off the ball, and there was general confusion on the field.

"What the heck was that?" I asked. "Anybody see what happened?" The whole room was nonplussed.

The television commentators were also at a loss.

Considering the Italians' penchant for diving, my initial impression was that this was so much play-acting. I was wrong. The referee ran over to his assistant and conferred. He ran back to the middle of the field, approached Zinedine Zidane and proffered a red card. Zidane had been sent off.

José and his son stood up and exchanged high fives.

Chris, Heidi, Ywain, Jen, John, Natalia, Luís, Hannia, and I just stared in disbelief.

This was a confirmation of the supremacy of Italian gamesmanship. The French number 10, aging, battered, exhausted and harassed, had snapped. Replays showed that Materazzi had been grabbing Zizou's jersey, the two had exchanged words, and Zidane had started to walk away, but, after a couple of paces, turned back toward his adversary and head-butted the Italian. My suspicion is that Materazzi knew just how to nettle the old Frenchman. There was, of course, much speculation about the specifics of the conflict. Materazzi's account kind of stuck as the definitive account. He had grabbed Zizou's jersey, not an uncommon practice among defenders, and Zidane had gotten a little miffed, saying, "Hey, if you want my jersey so badly, I'll give it to you after the game." Materazzi responded reflexively with typical Mediterranean charm, "I'd rather have your whore of a sister." As Zidane is a Muslim, this couldn't help but push some buttons. Materazzi claimed he didn't really know if Zidane even had a sister, but had just come out with a convenient stock insult. Something tells me it may have been a little more pre-meditated and strategic than that, but of course we'll never know.

Zidane left the field, head bowed. On his walk he passed a large pedestal where the World Cup Trophy sat, awaiting a victor. He looked up at the Cup as he walked. The wistful expression on his face spoke volumes. Here was the grand prize, the most coveted thing in all the world, which he may well have just lost for himself, his team and his country. He was at the end of his career, out of the game, out of contention. The golden trophy gleamed in the German sunshine.

Chris and I exchanged glances. It was high drama and destined to draw endless press coverage, even in the Soccer-deficient U.S.A., but we couldn't help but feel it was a blemish on both the tournament and the final professional moments of one of the game's all-time greats.

The rest of the contest played out as expected. The Italians killed off the game and went happily to the PK Lottery, knowing that the best French penalty man was no longer on the field.

The Italians put their PKs into the back of the net with characteristic confidence. The French missed one. That's all it took. Italy hoisted its fourth World Cup.

Our party died slowly. Most of us had been disappointed, though José and his son were pumped. Still, it had been an exciting match, dramatic to the end and the controversy of Zidane's ejection had added some spice to the mix. We had been able to enjoy the final with some good friends and family as the curtain drew closed on a month of the best soccer you could imagine.

THE AFTERGLOW

As with any big journey or experience, there's something of a letdown afterwards. Let's call it akin to postpartum depression. In addition to the exhaustion of a big trip, the U.S. had done poorly, and the team I'd backed in the final had lost. I felt the weight of the past month. But I'd been tremendously fortunate to have been able to travel across the Atlantic to witness some exciting stuff, gotten to know a country, practice a language long-dormant in my brain, and spend some quality time with my lovely wife. And as always, hope springs eternal. I started thinking about 2010 in South Africa. There would be a changing of the guard on the U.S. team. Perennial stars like Claudio Reyna, Eddie Lewis, Kasey Keller, and Brian McBride would inevitably fade away, and some of the promising youngsters, Freddy Adu, Jozy Altidore, Kenny Cooper, Eddie Johnson, Ricardo Clark, and some surprises would appear on the scene and establish themselves. Bruce Arena would give way to another coach, and another style and approach would take hold. And the U.S. team can't help but get better, if not over the next four years, then over the long haul. Our domestic league has given players a place to ply their trade and develop. Players who in years past would have become insurance agents or accountants after college were now professional soccer players, and many were finding success in Europe as well. Soccer is by far the most competitive sport in the world, so while U.S. ascent into the ranks of the big powers would be slow, I can't help but feel that it is inevitable.

2010 - THE ROADBLOCK TO AFRICA

I'll keep this brief, but it warrants some discussion. As you might imagine, I was eager to book my trip to South Africa for the 2010 World Cup. I dutifully submitted my application to FIFA within minutes of the lottery being opened. I didn't get tickets. There were a record number of applications from the U.S., and I didn't prevail. I looked into a commercial travel service that is U.S. soccer's official travel partner, and put a deposit down on a package. I asked what the price of the package would be, including tickets and hotels. Before the draw, the travel service had no way of knowing where the U.S. team would play, so they couldn't say for certain how much it would cost. I asked for a ballpark figure, and they replied that it would be somewhere in the neighborhood of $2,000 to $3,000. I felt that price was higher than I could wrangle in my own, but since it was the only way I could obtain tickets, I'd bite the bullet and once again visit the Biggest Party on the Planet.

Once the draw occurred, it was established that the U.S. would play in and near Johannesburg. Good. This made it easy to have a centrally located base of operations, at least for round one. The travel service announced the price of the ticket packages—approximately $8,000 apiece, not including airfare. No thanks.

In January, I submitted an application for tickets in one of the subsequent rounds of ticketing. U.S. Soccer controls a block of tickets that they distribute. Considering the volume of U.S. interest, I figured I didn't have much chance of getting tickets, but I applied anyway. I prevailed. I was ecstatic. I had the "follow the USA package," for as far as they went in the tournament. I jumped on the Internet to book accommodations and airfare. I figured I'd have to pay something of a premium since it was a little later in the game than I'd anticipated. I did a search for hotels and bed-and-breakfasts in South Africa. The rates I found were surprisingly reasonable. Many very nice places listed for around 350 Rand (around $65) per night. Premium places could be had for $150 a night. Great. When I made inquiries about reservations during the World Cup, I discovered that the 350-Rand rooms now cost 1,300 or 2,300 Rand. I figured I had happened on the more "touristy" sites, which must have been gouging. After investigating hundreds of other sites, I learned that the price jump during the World Cup was universal.

Then I looked into airfare. The least expensive flight to South Africa typically costs about $1,100, but during the World Cup, the fare jumped to $2,800 at the low end, with most flights costing around $3,500.

My wife said, "Maybe you should just go by yourself, it'd be cheaper." My initial impulse was to start calculating the lowest-priced package for just one person, searching for fares on the Internet. I couldn't bring myself to pursue the matter further. While I might expect to pay "high-season rates" of, say, ten to fifteen percent more than usual, I couldn't countenance paying thousands of dollars extra simply because someone knew they had me over a barrel. I'd rather take those few thousand dollars and spend them on a vacation in a country that actually values my patronage, and doesn't view me as a sap. Having lived in a developing country, I know that the arrival of Europeans and Americans can provoke irrational flights of fancy as to just how much the market will bear. But the World Cup is a celebration that should transcend business as usual. Certainly the Cup will stimulate tourism and commerce, but the most important aspect of it--especially for a country as remote as South Africa--is to lay the groundwork for future investment by cultivating international good will.

Faced with the opportunity to host the World Cup, the South Africans have shot themselves in the foot, I suspect. If travel to the World Cup is curtailed by such astronomic prices, there most likely will be a last-minute rate reduction, followed by the chaos whipped up by the feeding frenzy of crazed fans. For me, however, this wouldn't help. I've got to plan in advance, and let the people I work with know whether they can count on me during June and July of 2010. I can't simply drop everything at the last minute and leave. I think it's safe to assume that there are many people in similar circumstances.

But of course Hannia and I will be holding down the homefront, watching with rapt attention from our native shores, and thankful we had the opportunity to experience the two previous World Cups. Maybe we'll be fortunate enough to go to Brazil in 2014.

Party On!